The
Capable
Cruiser

By the same authors

Cruising in *Seraffyn*
Seraffyn's European Adventure
The Care and Feeding of the Offshore Crew
Seraffyn's Mediterranean Adventure
The Self-Sufficient Sailor
Seraffyn's Oriental Adventure

The
Capable Cruiser

Lin and Larry Pardey

W.W. NORTON & COMPANY
NEW YORK LONDON

Published simultaneously in Canada by Penguin Books Canada Ltd., 2801 John Street,
Markham, Ontario L3R 1B4.
Printed in the United States of America.

The text of this book is composed in Electra, with
display type set in Palatino. Composition by ComCom
Manufacturing by Haddon Craftsmen
Book design by Roy Tedoff

FIRST EDITION

Library of Congress Cataloging in Publication Data

Pardey, Lin.
    The capable cruiser.

    Includes index.
    1. Sailing. 2. Seamanship. I. Pardey, Larry.
II. Title.
GV811.P29 1987   797.1'24   87-21988
ISBN 0-393-03321-X

W. W. Norton & Company, Inc., 500 Fifth Avenue, New York, N. Y. 10110
W. W. Norton & Company Ltd., 37 Great Russell Street, London WC1B 3NU

1 2 3 4 5 6 7 8 9 0

To Monk Farnham, Patience Wales
and Murray Davis
with thanks—because you cared
and encouraged two neophytes

Contents

   15   Taking the Emergency Out of Steering Failures
        186
   16   Cruising Canvas Care   195
   17   Bare Wood—The Salty Scrubbed Look   203
   18   Nuts, Bolts, and Screws   218

SECTION IV   *Taking Care of Yourself and Your Crew as You
        Cruise   225*

   19   Safety Aloft   226
   20   Cut the Shouting Out of Sailing   235
   21   Writing and Cruising—Does It Pay?   242
   22   Getting the Photos that Sell Cruising Articles   256

SECTION V   *Seamanship as You Cruise   259*

   23   Coral Reef Cruising: The Sailors' Venus's-Flytrap
        261
   24   "No Oceans to Cross"   275
   25   Murder in Turtle Bay   288
   26   The Jinx   291

SECTION VI   *At Anchor   299*

   27   What Happened at Cabo San Lucas?   300
   28   Voyagers Lament   317
   29   Technical Report from Cabo San Lucas   322
   30   A Ground Tackle System List   342
   31   Selecting Chain   347
   32   Stern Anchor Systems   359
   33   Your Anchor Light—A Friendly Beacon for Other
        Sailors   371

        Appendix   381
        Index   391

Foreword

The wind blew, the rain came down, the insects made their presence known, and it was a fine party. The crews from eleven long-distance voyaging boats sat together under canvasses strung between trees on a quiet beach and devoured two whole lambs that had been slowly barbecued over an open fire, sheltered from the rain by an upside down Avon dinghy suspended between two uprights. We ate dozens of raw and cooked oysters, shared casks of wine, sang, joked and talked of other holidays in other lands. The highlight of the afternoon came when "Silent Night" was sung first in English then in each of the languages spoken by the sailors from seven different nations: French, Italian, German, Dutch. The next day we sailed *Taleisin* away from our cruising friends, across beautiful Whangaroa Bay which hides behind a sheltering point on the northern end of New Zealand to rendevous with Faye and Richard Stephens, two New Zealanders we'd met only a week before, during our stop on the Keri Keri River thirty miles south. We anchored near their handsome 36-foot sloop, *Young Nick,* and planned the next day's scallop hunt. Sometime during that evening we began discussing the people who were out voyaging across oceans. "How many are successful?" Richard asked.

I thought about the group we'd been with the evening before. All of them were eager to sail onward. The talk had been heavy with "after New Zealand." Each of the women were as eager to go on, as enthusiastic to be out cruising as their mates. Three couples had children who were bright and well educated to our eyes. All of these people had been able to sail away from the threats of hurricanes in Fiji or Tonga, across a thousand miles of sometimes tempestuous ocean, yet keep their boats in cruising condition so that they were willing to sail from Opua, their port of entry, only a week or two after making the passage, and come to rendezvous in this beautiful out-of-the-way spot.

From our twenty-one years around the cruising world, our fourteen years of actual passagemaking and voyaging, we knew this was an unusually satisfied group.

If success in cruising is finding satisfaction or enjoyment from what you are doing, having a sense of harmony on board, feeling glad you had the experience, eager to continue or to go off again, we'd say that the success rate among people who set sail for a defined limit cruise of six months to a year and a half is about 35 to 40 percent. Among people who say, "I'm going off forever," or "I'm going around the world," the rate drops to less than 20 percent. Other people who are interested in cruising statistics have said this figure might be as low as 10 percent. There are probably dozens of reasons for these disappointments, so we find it far easier (and more enjoyable) to look for reasons certain people are successful at meeting the challenges of cruising and voyaging.

When we compiled our first *Self-Sufficient Sailor* volume, we wrote that the careful choice of boat and equipment, skills gained through practice and self-sufficiency, were what could make you a successful voyager. Now as we rewrite and update several of the articles we've written during the past five years and add new ones for this book, we realize two other qualities are found among that group of successful long-term voyagers, voyagers like the ones we shared Christmas day with: self-confidence tempered with prudence and a willingness to leave their shoreside values behind when they set off to sea.

Self-confidence makes this group willing to go ahead with cruising dreams inspite of friends saying, "You'd be crazy to give up such a good job, great house, a permanent slip in the marina, just to go off wandering." Self-confidence lets these people make their own cruising plans and decisions independent of other cruisers who might say, "Forget inspecting your rigging, let's go skin diving." Or, "This roadstead is safe enough, let's climb over that hill to the pub before it gets dark." Finally, self-confidence lets you relax, knowing that you have done your best, you have considered the problems, done your preparations well, kept your gear in shape and know enough to make the decisions that will keep your crew, your boat and yourself safe. In other words, now you can lie back and relax, knowing things are under control.

Leaving landsmen's values behind can be very difficult for people who take up sailing and voyaging late in their life. These people have been conditioned to schedules, to seeking physical conveniences, to knowing when they were succeeding. Living to a schedule ordained by the weather, heaving-to until dawn, laying offshore for two days while you wait for clear weather to thread your way past reefs and shoals or, waiting in an isolated lagoon for seven days until a front passes, can frustrate the person who takes his landsman's values with him, tempting him to take unwarranted risks just to keep a self-imposed schedule. Insisting on conveniences such as you'd easily have on shore, instead of simplifying your desires so your gear is within your budget and maintenance ability can frustrate your attempts at successful breakdown-free cruising. And finally, expecting the rewards, the pleasures and satisfactions of cruising to be the same as those you had on shore can ruin your cruise. This is a completely new environment, you have to put aside your onshore survival skills and learn new priorities that will help you be safe at sea. As we look through the final typed pages of this volume, it seems the emphasis is much more on seamanship than it was in *The Self-Sufficient Sailor*. And maybe that is as it should be because once you've learned to be self-sufficient, it will become almost second nature. But seamanship is such a multifaceted skill, conditions you'll meet as you cruise are so ever-changing, that danger lies in thinking your knowledge is complete. In other words, everytime we think we have got it all figured out, Neptune gives us a kick behind the knees.

Our egos are bruised, our boat scraped, our cruising kitty dented. Only in the most extreme cases, like those we write about toward the end of the book, are these moments of over-confidence totally destructive. What we learn from our own lapses and those of other people, reminds us that constant vigilance will swing the balance of fortune in our favor. We learn once again that the real basis of seamanship is being able to recognize when we are safe and when we are not.

These attributes we talk of, self-sufficiency, self-confidence, seamanship, can be gained by the simplest of people. You don't need a higher education, you don't need to be particularly clever, quick thinking or physically strong to practice them. We've seen eighteen year olds who were skilled seaman and seventy-eight year olds still out there doing it. Cruising is still a wonderfully personal, attainable goal and we hope this book will make you feel like getting out for a trial cruise, be it your first overnighter, your first voyage away from land. We hope it gives you ideas to outfit or upgrade your boat. We hope it shows you some of the lessons we and other people learned the hard way. Then maybe someday you'll be among that group of successful, well prepared, positive thinking voyagers who rendezvous for a holiday barbecue far from home.

Lin and Larry Pardey
Arkles Bay, New Zealand
June 1986

Acknowledgments

Several of the articles included in this book have been published by *Cruising World, Sail, Yachting, Practical Boat Owner, Cruising Helmsman, Cruising Skipper* and *Nautical News*. We'd like to thank their editors. We often used their grammatical, spelling and context changes to improve our finished product. To Keith Taylor, editor of *Sail* we wish to give special thanks for encouragement and assistance. Because of this we were able to fly to Cabo San Lucas to interview the unfortunate people involved in the story and later to make long-distance phone calls to confirm information we were given there. We'd like to thank the people we met at Cabo for their candid answers to our questions, their willingness to share what they learned from this devastating event. Thanks go also to those people who were at Pacific Marine Supply Store in San Diego, California, when the Cabo incident occurred; Ces Bailey, Chris Frost, Linda Stanley, all helped us at that time and became willing sources of information for later articles on other subjects.

Our thanks to Lyle C. Hess for providing us drawings and plans of *Taleisin, Nautical News* editor Bruce Laybourne for the use of his photos, Jim Townsing at the *Coaster Newspaper* here in New Zealand for his help with our photographs and conversions, and Stephen Davis for his fine illustration of *Taleisin,* and Mike Davidson, editor of *Australias Cruising Skipper* for the use of his photos. There are dozens of people who answered our questions and gave us their ideas as we wrote the articles in this book. We have tried to include their names in the text wherever possible. If your name was not included, please excuse and accept this impersonal thank you. We did appreciate your help and hope our articles are more precise because of the information you provided.

Wayne Dillon has loaned us his beautiful beach front bach, as summer cottages are called in New Zealand, so that we would have room to finish this project. John Maurice has helped us have a safe, well watched mooring for *Taleisin* at Salthouse Boatyards near Auckland. Thank you, knowing our real home is well protected has made this project more fun. Cecilia Turnbull has used her school holidays to get our typing load under control. Her smiling face added to our days, and also A.B. and Adrienne Atkinson contributed their time to this project, reading the whole manuscript and showing us some helpful improvements.

A separate and heart felt thank you goes to Patience Wales, circumnavigator and managing editor at *Sail*. She has been the sounding board for many of our articles and ideas the past fourteen years. She has pointed out where we appear cranky and said again and again, say it in a positive way. We've tried.

A final acknowledgement is due to the people who we meet as we continue to cruise. The knowledge each of them seems so willing to share, gives us an almost unending list of ideas to research then write about.

Lin and Larry Pardey
Arkles Bay, New Zealand
June 1986

The
Capable
Cruiser

Section I

Preparing to Go

The decisions you'll have to make when offshore cruising becomes your dream, will be the first test of the self-confidence you'll need to succeed in this new life. Scores of books, dozens of magazine articles, hundreds of advertisers and friends will tell you what is the perfect cruising boat. Most of the people in your community; your family, employers, friends, will tell you you shouldn't go at all. Others will say you can't afford to go. To keep your dream on track, you'll have to ignore the negative and soak up the positive, get out sailing every chance you can and gain knowledge to sort out fact from opinion, practical information from advertising, then have the self-confidence to say, "This is *my* learn-to-sail, prepare-to-cruise plan, this is the boat *I* can afford, the one I'll be able to safely handle, both physically and financially." Then you'll need the confidence to stick to your plans in spite of the hundreds of distractions that will be piled in your way as you save and scheme to get free.

1

Parameters for Choosing a Cruising Boat

Someone once said that even the most perfect marriage is an exquisite compromise. The same can be said about cruising boats. Just as with any long-term partnership, there is no such thing as perfection. The boat that fits like a glove as you cruise to sunny tropical lands, may shrink to discomforting proportions when you head north to winter in a wet or snowy clime. The luxurious 45-footer that is a dream to handle as you romp downwind with four friends on board, can become a nightmare when there are only two of you working to sail it to windward for two or three thousand miles, on that long passage back home. Some people dream of a life of full-time cruising, others dream of a one year intermission in a life they enjoy on shore. Some people put aesthetics ahead of comfort, others say function is beauty and choose their boat from that point of view. So when we are asked to give a simple answer, to say one brand of boat or another is the perfect cruising home, we can't. If we could we'd never have had to build two of the boats we cruised on, boats that looked similar but were different in their final concepts, just as our plans for them and our list of requirements were different as our lives and fortunes changed over the fifteen years between their construction dates.

To begin the process of choosing a cruising boat, you have to define your exact cruising goals. If your plan is to make a trial cruise of four or six months, trying to build or buy the ultimate cargo-carrying, full time live-a-board passagemaker would be a bit like getting a D8 Caterpillar to dig a flower garden. For those who dream of taking a year or eighteen months to voyage to Tahiti or the Azores, it might pay to use a less than optimum boat, maybe the well-built cruiser-racer you already own. If you like voyaging, you can then return and use your acquired knowledge and skills to help choose the next, more perfectly evolved cruising yacht. It is only when you know for sure that you want to cruise for three or four years, when you see your life as a nomadic one with your home being that complicated mini-island called a boat, that it will pay to invest years and dollars to search out, build or refine a "perfect cruising boat."

Through the years we've noted that people who plan to return home after four or six months, can afford a larger boat than those who voyage long term. The short termer usually has a steady income, a job to come back to. He can cut the costs and problems of maintenance by taking the boat back to its home port before haulout time rolls around. There he can get the best prices and do the more expensive repairs in his own workshop. Short termers often take friends along, so handling a bigger boat isn't a problem. It is easy to find and schedule half a dozen sailing friends who want to meet you along the way when the farthest destination of your cruise is only $200 away by air. With these extra guests it will pay to have the spaciousness of a 40-footer, but you won't need the cargo carrying capacity a long-term nomadic voyager needs. From our delivery work, we have found that on boats ranging from 36 to 53 feet we needed two extra crew, and for two month voyages found that an allowance of 400 to 600 pounds of extra cargo per person was sufficient. This included the weight of extra stores, water, paper goods, linens, personal gear, the spare dinghy you probably want to carry.

If these short-term jaunts were my personal goal, I would look for a strongly built racer-cruiser with an active class association in my area. That way your resale value would be assured if and when you decided your cruising goals were more ambitious.

Unless you are sure you plan to keep this short-term voyager for several years and take off again and again, avoid over-customizing it. It is rare to get back even half of the costs of outfitting when you sell.

It is difficult to decide where the break-even point is on customizing a yacht for offshore cruising. We think it lies somewhere between a planned nine- to fifteen-month cruise. Then the cost of a fitted self-steering vane, an efficient ice chest or reefer, the perfect bunk or stove arrangements, etc., will pay off. We've found that people who stay away six months or more find it harder to guarantee they will have crew to help them steer and reef as they travel beyond the $200 air fare limit. So steering assistance systems and easy sail handling arrangements must be set up to be handled by the permanent crew of two. Storage becomes more of a problem as you now need to allow for about 1,200 pounds per crewperson. This extra weight includes the short-term cruise list plus extra ground tackle because you will be encountering more varied anchoring conditions, spare parts for all boat equipment, repair tools, more entertainment gear like stereos, books, and skin diving equipment. You'll also need personalized storage areas so you feel, "at home." Once again we think the cruiser-racer you now own could be the best bet for this type of dream. Instead of investing in a costly D8 tractor type boat, it might be better to spend your money fitting out a good secondhand cruiser-racer that you will be able to sell relatively easy if you decide cruising is not for you.

When we meet would-be long-term voyagers who have not yet owned boats capable of taking them on two- or three-month voyages, we suggest they look at older, CCA-type racer-cruisers with rudders attached to the keel or with a long fin and skeg underbody configuration. We have seen boats like these successfully and inexpensively strengthened and converted to serve as safe, weatherly medium-term voyaging homes. Careful buying in the secondhand market, plus some elbow grease could improve this interim cruiser so it becomes an investment that helps in part to pay for a full-time passagemaker.

Only when cruising gets in your blood, when you know home is the place you are, not the place you started from, when you find you can earn as you go and need to carry your life's possessions with you do you need to look for the highly specialized tool, the long-term cargo carrying passagemaker. This paragon must be capable of carrying 2,000 pounds per crew to include everything short-term voyagers need plus all your tools, more books, more spares, clothes for warm and cold climates, some special clothes for dressing up, your favorite pair of ski boots and shell collection. It needs to be easily handled by its permanent crew, affordable, easy to maintain and have the sailing qualities to make it able should its engine fail.

Every voyager who has been out there for a few years will point at a different boat as he reads this, but I think all will agree with at least ninety percent of the general specifications we discuss in the next pages.

The basis of safe, enjoyable cruising is sailing. This may sound obvious, but in our opinion many cruises have been ruined because people choose boats with other parameters placed ahead of sailing ability. All cruising boats need to have a reasonable turn of speed, need windward ability, should be maneuverable in relatively small harbors under sail alone with its minimum crew on board. We met a family in Tahiti who were going home, selling the boat and getting out of sailing because they'd chosen a romantic looking, but poor sailing older 44-foot Hanna ketch design. Not only did they find they took fifty percent longer to complete passages than other boats the same length, they felt nervous because when their engine quit, they didn't have enough confidence in their under-rigged, slow-tacking ketch to sail out of Papeete harbor. "What if it quit and a current was setting us onto a reef?" the owner asked.

Six American boats were towed into Opua, New Zealand during the first two weeks of December 1985, inward bound from Fiji and Tonga. The five-mile-long estuary leading into Opua is well lit and at least a quarter-mile wide. You can anchor safely anywhere along the estuary. Yet these six cruisers lost the use of their engines and felt so insecure about their boats' ability to beat to windward in enclosed water that they called for outside assistance. One of them lost a bowsprit during the tow, another, on an undercanvassed 32-footer, felt he couldn't cover the last twenty miles in eight hours with the eight- to ten-knot breeze radio reports predicted.

This sailing performance problem extends to passagemaking. We met one owner who said, "My 29-footer is too small for cruising because everyone else makes port sooner than I do. Twenty-nine footers are just too slow." When we compared notes with him we agreed—*his* 29-footer was too slow. His passages were fifty percent slower than those we made on 29-foot 6-inch *Taleisin*, fifty percent slower than those made by acquaintances on *Eleu* a 31-foot Cape George Cutter. But one look at his boat showed the reason. He'd bought a light displacement boat then tried to carry everything he owned. The boat was down eight inches on its lines and vastly undercanvassed for its loaded-to-cruise displacement.

This is the second most important point to remember when you are choosing a passagemaker. It is a fallacy to say that all heavy displacement boats are slow and unweatherly, just as it is a fallacy that light displacement means speed. Speed is a design problem, a sailing problem, not a type problem. Cruising speed depends on the ability of your boat to carry extra cargo, its ability to pack its canvas, your ability to keep it cleaned out so it doesn't become overloaded, your desire to keep it properly canvassed in light and heavy winds, to keep its bottom clean and smooth and finally on the type of propellor you choose to carry. Allan Warwick, a respected designer of both light and heavy displacement boats here in New Zealand, told us, "If I wanted to carry everything I owned for years of cruising, I'd go to a fuller keeled displacement hull for any boat under 40 feet. It could carry more weight yet retain a good average turn of speed on all points of the wind because its underbody would change its shape less as it sank into the water." Likewise, we feel lighter displacement underbodies on hulls over 45 feet can work well for cruising because they can carry the 2,000 pounds of cargo per crew they need without sinking below their proper sailing lines and picking up the extreme wetted surface that slows them down. The smaller your cruising boat choice becomes, the more important it is to look towards a heavier displacement, cargo-carrying type hull.

Length alone will not give you a great increase in voyaging speed. To drive a longer boat to its maximum takes more crew strength and work than keeping a shorter one going well. You also need a tremendous increase in length to gain worthwhile speed increases. The 28-foot Bristol Channel Cutter with its 26-foot 3-inch waterline, designed by Lyle Hess, regularly turns in 145-mile-a-day passages. At least one of these boats, *Zipthias*, sailed by Roger Olsen, a non-racer, made an average of 140 miles a day on passage from California to the Marquesas. Steve Dashew, a hard-driving, ex-racing sailor on his Columbia 50 with a 42-foot waterline, turned in a 177-day average for his passage from Mexico to the Marquesas and said he often had 160-mile-a-day passages. To get a 20 percent gain in boat speed he had to own, maintain and sail a boat with a load waterline one and a half times longer and easily three times the replacement cost of *Zipthias*.

Quality boats cost by the pound, just like New York steak. Don't be lured into buying hamburger; don't choose a boat that has the lowest price for overall length. To get the quality of workmanship and materials you need for long-term voyaging, you will most likely have to pay five-to-seven dollars per pound of finished displacement for a new series-built (production) boat of moderate displacement in sailaway condition with an interior and very few options. This price per pound will go up for larger, light displacement boats because they require more scientific construction to be as strong as needed. Look for a price per pound in the seven-to-ten dollar range for boats that are in the light weight, above forty foot range. If any builder offers you lower prices than these, be skeptical. They may be cutting corners on either materials or finished work. You might never discover how they saved costs until you have to repair problems far from home. Even by going to an overseas builder you cannot safely pay less than 75 percent of these figures. At Cabo San Lucas we saw the wreck of one 12-month-old 44-footer from overseas that was sold to an unwary potential voyager for less than four dollars a pound and were stunned to find there were no bolts holding the deck to the hull, there was no flange, it was held at the stern only by screws going into the end grain of the plywood transom stiffner. Consequently the deck had separated from the hull like a rip-along-the-dotted-line cardboard box. Everywhere we looked inside the hull, what couldn't be seen either hadn't been done or had been done poorly with the cheapest possible materials.

The only bargains in cruising boats are occasionally found in the secondhand market. Even here it pays to find what the original price per pound was for this brand of boat, then add inflation to it and see if it falls within the brackets above. When you are looking for the boat you'll depend on for your total safety, you must think quality, not quantity.

I guess there is a bit of the Ralph Nader in us—we don't want to see people out there in poorly assembled or structurally unsound boats. We know that, unlike the automobile, aircraft, motorcycle or bicycle industry, there are no government ordained or supervised construction standards that yacht builders must comply with. We personally prefer it this unregulated way and know that if we as yachtsmen don't learn about and demand good construction, if there are too many boat failures, some government agency will step in and try to regulate all of us.

Once you have decided on the broader parameters of the boat you can afford and need, you have to look at each aspect of hull, rig, deck layout, interior design and construction methods separately and form a rating system that will help you make the compromises that are inevitable. There are several suggestions we can offer.

Don't choose any extreme fin-and-skeg designs for offshore work. The short thin upper connection areas of the fin keel on many high-tech hulls cause constant problems. Lin happened to be at the haulout yard in Auckland two months ago when a Farr 55, designed for offshore cruising, was hurriedly lifted from the water. Once its narrow, vertical fronted fin keel was dropped onto a pallet, the boat builders began estimating the extent of the damage. This boat had hit a rock at about six knots. A boat with an angled forefoot and keel such as in figure 1.1 would probably have slid up onto the rock, absorbing most of the shock. The straight fin on the Farr 55, which is similar to figure 1.2, brought it to a teeth-jarring, instant stop. A longer underbody with wineglass sections would have absorbed and spread some of the shockloads so probably the damage would have been confined to the front of the lead keel. Instead the narrow, tapered, after end of the keel tilted upwards into the keel timber like a hatchet, splitting the wood laminations of the backbone, breaking bulkheads, cabinetry and framing. The final repair bill was over $30,000 in U.S. funds.

Look for well-rounded garboards on any fin keel type boat. If this area is too narrow, the keel connection cannot be as strong as it should be

FIGURE 1.1

FIGURE 1.2

FIGURE 1.3 This is an example of the problem you have if you bolt a lead keel onto a flat-bottom boat. Notice the water dripping from the keel-to-hull connection.

to reduce racking and movement. Each of the Maxi racers in the Whitbread Round the World race in 1985 was hauled at McMullen and Wings yard in Auckland. We were shocked to see that each showed signs of cracking in this area. UBS Switzerland, Lion, Cote D'Or, each had bondo optimistically applied before repainting to fill the cracks that showed the narrow keel-to-hull connection was working.

Look at the underbody of any boat you wish to buy as if you had to block it and haul it out of the water yourself. Remember that extra

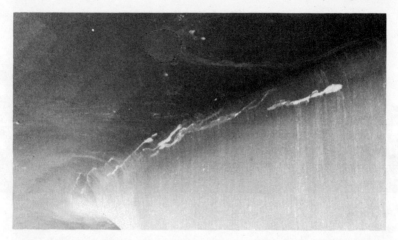

FIGURE 1.4   This is the hull-to-keel connection on New Zealand *Enterprise*. Every Maxi in the Round-the-World race fleet had cracks similar to these.

blocking fore and aft cost $30 an hour this year in Papeete, Tahiti, above and beyond the regular haulout charges. In other places it is much the same. This means boats with underbodies, like the Swan line, are harder and more expensive to pull out for the yearly repainting. In places like New Zealand, England or Australia where a good tidal range lets most people scrub and paint their boats on a tidal grid for two or three dollars, cruisers with fin and skeg boats that either settle down onto their bow, or cannot be conveniently set on their keel, will be stuck with expensive haul out charges.

Boats with flat sectioned, U-shape hulls instead of wineglass shaped sections have no sump area. That means even a small amount of water from a leaking stern gland, a spilled bottle, will slop into lockers or onto the cabin sole as you sail. The owners of *Cezzane*, a handsome Townsend-designed modern type boat had this complaint after an enjoyable four-year circumnavigation. Mona told us, "We took a bit of water inside during a storm and it traveled up into the clothes lockers and made a major clean-up problem." So avoid any boats with sumps so shallow that five or ten gallons of water mean the floor boards are awash.

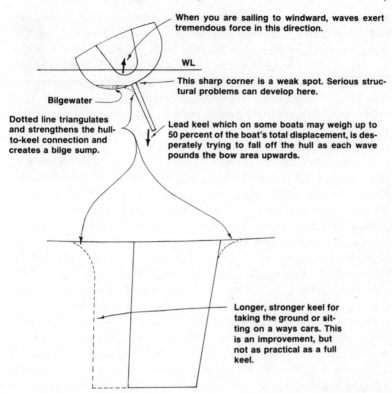

When you are sailing to windward, waves exert tremendous force in this direction.

WL

This sharp corner is a weak spot. Serious structural problems can develop here.

Bilgewater

Dotted line triangulates and strengthens the hull-to-keel connection and creates a bilge sump.

Lead keel which on some boats may weigh up to 50 percent of the boat's total displacement, is desperately trying to fall off the hull as each wave pounds the bow area upwards.

Longer, stronger keel for taking the ground or sitting on a ways cars. This is an improvement, but not as practical as a full keel.

FIGURE 1.5

Look for a beamy hull. Beam pays amazing dividends in interior space. Boat volume increases far faster with beam than with length. More beam gives you better choices with interior layouts, it lets you have wider, safer side decks and if the boat is carefully designed, it can cut down rolling tendencies. But to carry beam well, the boat has to be carefully designed and its ends nicely balanced or it can become hard to steer in heavier winds.

Look for the longest waterline possible on a boat within your size budget. Excessive overhangs look handsome, but don't add much room or convenient cargo-carrying capacity.

The final hull design aspect to consider carefully is the rudder. It must be strongly connected and either protected from danger by a full-length keel, or the skeg it hangs on must be super strong. If your anchor drags and you smash a coral head or stone quay, it will be enough work to repair the rudder without the insult of having to rebuild the skeg too. Unsupported spade rudders are not a wise choice because relatively minor mishaps can bend the shaft and jam the rudder against the hull. A serious grounding could pound the rudder right through the hull. Your rudder should be relatively easy to remove and repair. If it has a long, through-the-hull shaft, you might have to dig a very deep hole to drop it in the shipyard.

Rigs are often chosen because of personal or aesthetic preferences. But some general parameters apply whether you prefer a ketch, sloop, cutter or schooner. *Do not, no matter what your instincts are, cut down the size or height of your rig to go voyaging.* Cruising boats need power to keep them moving since they are almost always heavily laden. We feel 85 square feet of working sail area per 2,000 pound ton (main and one hundred percent jib for a sloop, main, jib and staysail for a cutter) at the fully loaded-for-cruising displacement, will give you a boat that is enjoyable to sail in the 7- to 10-knot wind range without immediately resorting to genoas or extras like drifters and spinnakers. From our experience delivering boats, on *Seraffyn* and now *Taleisin,* 65 percent of all voyaging is done in winds of 12 knots or less. Eric Hiscock told us the tradewinds he has used for three and a half circumnavigations averaged force 4 or 11 to 15 knots. South Pacific voyagers coming to New Zealand in December of 1985 all reported winds of less than ten knots once they sailed below latitude 23 south.

Although we feel you need a good sized rig for cruising, we agree completely with those who say 350 to 400 feet of mainsail area is enough for a crew of two to handle. On the other hand, Lin says she finds a 600-square-foot nylon drifter easy to set, easy to stuff in its bag. So get big headsails by looking for a masthead rig with as long a J measurement as possible.

The staysail rig is a great advantage for cruising offshore, especially if the staysail is large enough for the helm of your boat to be balanced with the staysail and a single reef in the main. This will let you move your sail plan inboard as the wind increases. It provides a multipurpose, quickly shortened sail arrangement with only three working sails. (For more on staysails, see Section II, Chapter 9.)

Don't look at any overly specialized rig for a cruising boat. Only first-time voyagers, dreamers, or an occasional lucky circumnavigator who goes around the world in two years on the direct tradewind route, will find a rig designed just for downwind work pays off. Voyaging where you want to go, not just along the tradewinds, means you need a boat that will go to windward acceptably. I've had the privilege of sailing on some fine racing machines, half tonners, Olson 30s, Cal 40s and 39s plus many types of long keel boats, and I can say with certainty, no boat goes to windward well enough—it is a matter of relativity. But do look for one that can make good, 90-degree tacks on the compass (comparing pointing ability with the compass is more accurate than using apparent wind instruments). Don't consider any boat that makes more than 100-degree tacks, don't expect closer than 85 degrees tack to tack, only high-tech racing machines do this and they have to ease sheets and fall off to 45 degrees from the wind to keep driving when the sea becomes lumpy. Reaching or downwind is a cinch; almost all boats move well in these conditions.

Do avoid fractional rigs or any rigs that are heavily dependent on running back stays. They are basically labor intensive racing rigs. I think jibing a fractional rig at night is scary as hell. A masthead rig with a permanent backstay is a better choice. The spar can be lower and more securely supported than the fractional rig with the same sail area.

Finally, avoid rod rigging like the plague—it has absolutely no place on an offshore passagemaker. We have seen it fail more often than any other type of rigging. No matter how carefully you inspect it, it can still fail with no warning signs. The crew on *Atlantic Privateer,* the Maxi that was originally slotted for line honors in the 1986 Whitbread race, lost her mast and had to drop out of the leg to South Africa when a brand new piece of rod rigging failed two hours after the crew had gone aloft to check the rig. When *Atlantic Privateer* was in Auckland, Lin and I spoke with Marko the sailmaker and watch captain who had looked at each piece of the rig and run his hand over the area of the shroud that failed. He saw no cracks, no discoloration. The shroud had been x-rayed when it was new, three months before its failure. It was of the highest quality available in England; the end had a cold forged head on it and all the correct toggels and flexible connections aloft and below. Wire of any type, stainless, or galvanized, will almost always give you some warning before it fails. Individual strands break off or show signs of rust pitting before the whole wire fails. Wire, because it is flexible, is less prone to work hardening and metal fatigue than single strand rod rigging. It is also cheaper and easier to replace anywhere in the world.

A well-thought-out deck and cockpit plan should be high on your priority list as you look at passagemaking boats. Look for ease of movement in and out of the cockpit, then fore and aft along the side deck. You will have to get from the cockpit to the foredeck in a hurry at times. Make sure the step out of the cockpit is easy for all members of the crew. There must be handholds and a clear area to step onto since this is one of the most vulnerable moves you make on a boat. Too often winches, sheets, track and high coamings make this move from cockpit to deck dangerous and difficult.

Wide side decks are the next essential. We feel 18 inches is the minimum, uncluttered width you need for safe boat handling. If you have inboard shrouds or sail track on the deck, you need more width again. Your foredeck should also be clear enough so you can flake out a sail or clean a pile of dirty chain without running out of working space.

You'll want to carry a hard tender or keep your inflatable blown up and stored on deck while you gunkhole in good cruising areas, yet still need a clear deck. Dinghies that must be stored on the foredeck not only make handling sails and ground tackle more difficult, they block the forehatch which could be an important escape route for someone who is caught below during a fire or other emergency. They are also hard to secure. We were beating out of the lagoon at Tahaa, French Polynesia, during a casual race with another 31-foot cutter when both boats took some heavy seas over the foredeck. The 31-footer's tender was lashed on the foredeck. Seas got under it and pushed it aft onto the side deck. Had there been storage room on the cutters cabin top there would have been no problem since the sea didn't go past the mast area.

Look for easy access to mast halyards and winches. We prefer a one-level deck area near the mast so we don't have to climb up onto the cabin top to reach halyards or reefing pennants. But this means we have a short cabin and have to duck to go into the forward area of the boat. Most production boats have longer cabins with the mast going through the cabin top. To make this arrangement safe, look for inverted U-shape guard rails either side of the mast which you can grab to help you climb up onto the cabin top then lean against as you work the halyards and reefing pennants.

If you must have some items stored on deck, make sure they have permanent lockers, clear of the side decks. Clear side decks are a vital safety factor when you are working sails in rough weather.

We've become addicted to eight-inch-high bulwarks. They keep us and other things from immediately going overboard. They also form a strong base for lifeline stations.

Although easy access to your interior is nice, it is far more important to be sure that the water that inevitably gets into the cockpit is not funneled into the boat. Remember that if a large following sea boards your boat and fills the cockpit, it could fill it to the top of the coamings, so you must have a high companion way sill or strong dropboard arrangement to stop this heavy mass of water until it has time to get out the cockpit drains. Even if you have a low volume cockpit area, look for dropboard arrangements that make it possible to raise the level of the companionway sill to the level of the top of the cockpit coamings, yet still allow you easy access to the interior.

Interior accommodations are never perfect. The space constraints of hull shapes always limit designers. That is why most cruising boats are amazingly similar below decks. For full-time cruising, look first and foremost for layouts that give the cook safety in the galley. The galley is in use three or more times a day, in port or at sea. So make it a top priority as you plan. This will pay dividends because your mate will know she is a partner in this big adventure with you.

Try to find a layout that gives you an area near the companionway that can get wet with salt water. One of the best interior improvements we have on *Taleisin* is the watch seat area near the companionway. It has a wet gear locker on one side, a toilet under the other. Each are topped by bare teak. The settees are far enough forward of the companionway area that I can come below in soaking foul weather gear and sit down for a few minutes on the watch seats without worrying about getting salt water on our synthetic velvet settees.

Look for adequate area in the main cabin so that all members of the crew can stretch out after meals and be comfortable. If at all possible try to have in-port sleeping areas separate from the main cabin. This will provide a private area so if one member of the crew wants to hide for a while they can. When Lin was suffering from a pulled back in Pago Pago, she had privacy in the forward stateroom, yet I could still have friends on board amidships.

Storage should be high priority on your list. It is well worth sacrificing the spaciousness of an interior with wide floor areas for the huge storage lockers you can get when you move settees and bunks closer to the centerline of the hull. The storage lockers under these amidships pilot berths and settees are the best in the boat, large, easy to get to at sea, well shaped to handle large containers. Unfortunately they are also perfect for watertanks. Designers love tankage here, it is out of the ends and adds stability and helps eliminate hobby-horsing. Builders love to put tanks amidships, where they are easy to shape, to install and plumb. On race boats this is exactly where they belong. But as a voyager you need this prime, convenient space for food and stores so either look for a boat with the tanks in the bilge, fore or aft, or plan to change the tankage when you acquire the boat.

I've been on boats where half of the extra cruising gear was stored in bunks or lashed under tables. For short-term voyagers this is just an inconvenience. But for long-term cruising everything must have a storage space that is out of the way.

Although I know the following statement will not be popular among my male sailing friends, I feel the navigation station should be on the lower end of any interior priority list. Although it would be nice to have an organized chart table, sat-nav consol, seat and a line of dials to watch, I have successfully plotted our courses on *Seraffyn*'s galley table for eleven years. *Taleisin*'s ice chest top works fine during the forty to sixty days a year we are at sea. Even during those days I am rarely working at charts for more than a total of forty minutes. Compare this twenty to thirty hours a year with the time spent in the galley or lounging on the settees. If after the other interior priorities are covered, you have space for a nav-station, make sure it is clear of the spray zone near the companionway to protect moisture-sensitive electronic gear.

Hull material choices seem to take up ninety percent of the conversation when people talk about the next cruising boat. Each type of hull material has advantages and disadvantages. Each is only as good as the integrity of the builder. To get a fine cruising home costs a lot of money or a lot of personal labor no matter what material you choose for the hull. Wood hulls are often prettier than other types of hulls, especially inside. They are naturally insulated, and have a more personal feeling, and if you enjoy working wood as we do, they're more fun to build. On a one-off basis wood hulls are similar costwise to one-off glass or aluminum hulls of the same yacht quality. They can be restored to like-new condition with relatively little material outlay costs, i.e. in two or three days you can sand, putty, and repaint the hull to shiny newness for the cost of two dozen sheets of sandpaper, a quart of enamel and some thinners. Because you plan to recoat the wood hull frequently, minor dings and scratches like those you may get when people come alongside in unfendered boats and launches, are not quite so frustrating. On the other hand, unless you build your own, it is often very hard to find a well built, well maintained sound wooden yacht. They don't often appear on the market. Instead they are asked for before the owner is ready to sell. In fact they become so personal they are almost adopted out. I feel that wood, steel or glass boats maintained to a high standard require about the same amount of labor during a six or seven year period, but you cannot delay wood or steel maintenance until a better time; you must do the work on a regular schedule or you will have two or three times the labor six months down the line. Wood or steel boats that are ignored, deteriorate cosmetically more quickly than glass hulls that are left to sit. But the material and labor costs to restore any type of hull that is ignored for long, wood, steel or glass, can be just as high.

Glass hulls can be exceptionally strong and shock resistant since they are one-piece structures. Repairs are relatively easy. Prices are reasonable if they are built in series. Unfortunately they are hard to survey. Even the most knowledgeable buyer can only guess at how carefully the resin to mat and roving content was monitered, how precisely the catalyst was measured. Osmosis has become an almost endemic and increasingly expensive problem to cure. Friends voyaging in a Swan 43 are having to give up cruising for at least a year, just to pay for osmosis repairs to their 20-year-old boat. Another couple, owners of a high quality, Canadian-built small cruiser, had a $3,000 osmosis repair bill after only three years afloat. Materials to recoat a faded, scratched or damaged gel-coat can cost $1,000 just for the topside coatings. The charges to rent a sprayer or the labor for professional spraying can make long-term glass hull maintenance costly. A professional spray coating only, not the sanding and preparation, cost $3,500 for a 35-footer here in New Zealand this year.

Steel is often touted as the perfect cruising hull material. "You can hit a reef and get off again with only a few dents to show for it," I heard one yacht salesman tell a prospective client. Don't believe this. The rescue rate for any type of hull that is sailed onto a reef is very low. Steel will be driven up the windward side of a reef just as badly as any other. Its spars will be destroyed, its interior shattered, its engine ruined, leaving only a battered hull that you may or may not be able to drag off the reef. No boat belongs on reefs, no one should feel their hull material will give them leeway from constant vigilance. Any well-constructed hull can take a few bumps on the leeward side of a reef, away from pounding surf. A wood boat, just like *Seraffyn*, spent three days on the reef in the pass into New Caledonia and was restored to like-new condition for less than a thousand dollars; five glass hulls survived the pounding 14-foot surf at Cabo San Lucas. Two steel hulls were total losses at Cabo during that same storm. Bernard Moitessier sold the remains of *Joshua*, which consisted of only a deeply dented steel shell, for five dollars. A fifty-foot steel motor yacht was hauled out to sea and sunk since all that was left after a night in the surf was its hull, and this sprang leaks as it was being towed away. The real advantages of steel lie in its lower initial construction costs if you stick to simple chine construction (round bilged steel boats have lower wetted surface but can be very costly to build), and the ease with which tanks can be added and fittings attached wherever you want them. Steel gives a tremendous feeling of strength, especially when you realize the whole hull acts as a chainplate for the rig. The other side of the coin is maintenance. Modern epoxy hull coatings and sand blasting are amazingly expensive. Rust, dents and scratches must be primed and repainted as soon as possible or they will become bigger pitting problems. Any wood you attach to the exterior of a steel hull will cause rust as it holds moisture against the metal. Resale value drops by almost half once a steel hull is ten years old. If you doubt this, call almost any broker, he will confirm this.

This resale problem is one of the main disadvantages of ferrocement construction. The man who builds a ferro hull will rarely get more than his material costs back when he sells the boat. The second buyer will often get a real bargain. We met the new owner of a 35-foot Hartley designed ferro hull here in New Zealand who told a common story. He bought the ready-to-sail boat for $7,000 (U.S.) from the original builder /owner who had been trying to find a buyer for two years. With another $4,000 investment he turned the boat into a ready-to-cruise home. If you try to build a ferro boat to the same quality as a glass or wood boat, the only savings will be in hull material costs. The hull, deck and cabin equal one third of the cost of the average yacht so your savings would be only about 15 percent on the total boat. The one real advantage is that ferro construction is less intimidating for the amateur than other methods. Maintenance problems and materials seem to be similar to those of steel hulls. But, it is hard to get and keep a new appearance on a ferro hull. Fracturing of the concrete causes rusting and bleeding problems that are hard to cure, especially around chainplates, toe rails or bulwark to hull connections.

Aluminum looks like a fine solution for cruising hulls at first; it is light, tough. But the initial cost is a big factor, plus the need for extra hull insulation just as steel hulls. Hull coatings are expensive and require careful application to stick. Electrolysis is a constant worry as is the bubbling that happens near attached stainless steel fittings or if any moisture at all gets under the surface coatings.

With so many considerations is it possible to get a near perfect cruising boat? We think near perfect cruising boats evolve, they don't just happen. You have to build on a foundation of experience, form your initial parameters and use what you learn from each boat you own to plan improvements that will work on the next one. To do this well, it pays to stick to one basic type of boat, a type you find generally pleasing to your senses, then refine it. We do know that people who switch from one extreme of design and construction to the other from a super heavy boat to a super light displacement type, almost invariably find they traded one set of problems for another.

When it came time to choose *Seraffyn*'s design I had come to prefer the long-keeled, moderately heavy displacement boats I'd owned and sailed. I put windward sailing ability first on my list of priorities, light air ability a close second. I chose a size of boat I felt confident I would have the funds and patience to complete and maintain once I was cruising. I wanted to be able to carry a hard dinghy amidships. I wanted safe non-skid teak decks. I wanted a boat that acted and looked seaworthy. Every other consideration was secondary. After three years of searching I narrowed my choices down to two boats, one, called *Little Dipper* was designed by Gene Wells of California. It had a sweet bow and low sweeping sheer. The other was Lyle Hess's *Renegade*. I decided *Renegade* looked like the tougher boat, almost like a tom boy, while *Little Dipper* seemed such a lady I'd worry about pushing her too hard. So I built to Lyle's design and was amazingly satisfied with the results.

When *Taleisin* became a dream, Lin and I had a few extra parameters. We wanted a boat we could live on in cold, wet climates. One that would be a powerful machine to windward (i.e., more ballast) plus have room for two bicycles, a shower tub, a kerosene heater, work bench and vise plus the wet area I mentioned earlier. We had enjoyed *Seraffyn* and felt confident her designer could do a good job for us again. So in our very conservative way we asked for an improved, modified design to our slightly improved financial limits. We did not go for a boat that was a completely new concept, a complete departure from what we already knew worked for us. We are delighted with the results we got, even though as the next chapter explains, we made some compromises in interior design and displacement.

To start this evolution you first have to decide on your cruising plans. Look at the boat you have now and see if it can be modified to suit your needs. If it isn't right, list your priorities then get out sailing on every different type of boat you can. Charter in cold climates like Maine as well as in the Caribbean. If you see a boat you like hauled out, offer to help paint the bottom. You'll learn about maintenance costs and the labor involved on larger or other types of yachts. If you offer to trade a day of labor for a day of sailing you'll probably find lots of takers. If someone tries to sell you on one type of boat, one type of construction, go find another experienced sailor who prefers the contrasting type. Then compare their arguments. Offer to crew for deliveries if you can get time off. This will give you not only sea time and experience you will need to make wise choices, it could take you to sailing centers where cruisers congregate so you can see their boats.

When you have narrowed your choices down to half a dozen, locate a surveyor who is very active in your area, one who does surveys for insurance companies, new owners and builders. Offer him fifty dollars for a couple of hours of his time and show him your list. Then ask about his experience with these brands or types of boats. He will probably have surveyed a few like the one you are interested in. His information could help you finalize your choices, plan future modifications and know the weak points of particular types of boats. We know of one Californian surveyor who keeps files not only on boats he surveys, but on those surveyed by people he knows and trusts. With these files he has been able to give prospective buyers information and suggestions for other brands of boats they might find worth consideration.

When you find a boat that seems well suited to your needs, remember that it usually costs 25 percent of a boat's purchase price to change it from a ready-to-sail boat to a ready-to-cruise offshore yacht, especially if it is a new boat. Secondhand boats may only need 10 to 15 percent extra if they are well outfitted when you buy them.

After you acquire or launch a new boat, you are in for an exciting period. At least this is one part of cruising I really enjoy. This is the time you spend adding the hundreds of details that make a cruising boat convenient and efficient. As you do this don't forget to go out sailing regularly, at first for day sails, later for short trial cruises. That way you can be sure your modifications are working properly, you will be able to plan the next step of your adventure and make changes you find you need while you are still close to chandleries and shipyards. You'll also come to trust and rely on the boat that is hopefully the finest passagemaker your planning and compromises could produce.

2
From a Wish to a Design

We've all played the game, the one that starts off, "If I could have just one wish . . ." Our wish was to have a cruising boat designed just for us. Nine years ago it seemed like ours was on the verge of becoming reality when Lyle Hess offered to design our dream boat. "Just tell me what you want," he said. So we did and within a few weeks we received a package that reminded us that wishes are just that, and the happily-ever-afters fairy tales tell of are probably as full of compromises as the process we encountered while our new boat grew from an idea into a full-fledged, buildable design.

We thought our desires were extremely simple: the beamiest possible boat under thirty feet on deck with the largest possible sail area so she wouldn't need an overlapping genoa until the breeze fell to less than eight knots; outboard rudder, cutter-rigged, easy on the helm and beautiful (to our eyes) with a profile similar to *Seraffyn*, our first cruising boat.

That package with the original drawings arrived like the magic "wish." But when we opened the cylinder and unrolled the beautiful pencil sketches we learned the first lesson about working with a yacht designer. Right from the beginning you must be explicit about any

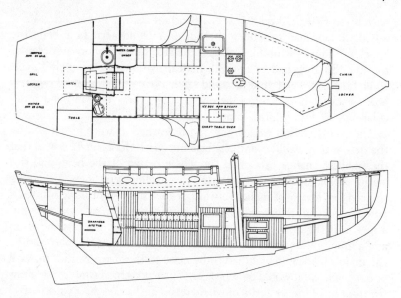

FIGURE 2.1   Profile and interior of *Taleisin* of Victoria.

Courtesy Lyle Hess

details that could affect the underwater profile of the hull you hope to have. Lyle had drawn a beautiful hull with a fair sweeping keel profile just like *Seraffyn*'s. The forefoot wasn't too deep so she could come about smartly; it had the lateral area aft necessary for good directional stability. But we'd forgotten to remind Lyle we wanted a break in the keel line with a long flat area so this boat could easily take the beach and stand on her own keel supported by simple supports or leaned against a dock or wall while the tide went out. We'd hauled *Seraffyn* in enough primitive yards to know that a flat keel could have saved hours of shoring and nights of discomfort when the rounded keel profile let her settle bow down on any ways-car unless we convinced the yard manager to let us arrange the blocking beforehand. We'd discussed this with Lyle over occasional dinners when we'd happened to be in the same country at the same time. We'd thought he'd remember but we were not the only people on his mind, and our boat, as important and special as it was to us, was not the only one on his drawing board. We should have listed that flat keel as a very important feature in our letter. As it was, Lyle now had to redraw the hull to include what he called "the knuckle." This new profile changed the area of the underwater plan of the hull. So Lyle had to re-think his calculations. Fortunately for us, while he did this he found he could safely increase the beam of our new boat by five inches. Unfortunately for Lyle, the redrawing and recalculating cost him a lot of time.

The second lesson we learned and re-learned as work progressed on the design that would eventually become our 30-foot *Taleisin,* was that the smallest change can affect the whole design of the boat, and this always seems to affect the rig. Lyle's first sketch of our new cutter's rig showed her mast just inches forward of the cabin front. Lyle wanted a powerful staysail that would balance against the mainsail when we put a reef in it (figure 2.3). We wanted a deck box for our propane tanks and a gravity water tank between the mast and cabin. We also wanted the main bulkhead which had to be close to the mast, farther forward or our main salon would be too short. To us it seemed simple, just draw the mast in 14 inches ahead of where it was in the sketch. "Not so easy," Lyle explained. In order to have a boat with an easy helm, one that has a tendency to safely head into the wind if a gust heels the boat sharply, the center of effort of the sail plan should be between 15 to 19 percent forward of the center of the lateral plane of the keel. (This center is the point where the boat should remain broadside if a tow line is attached and you try to drag the hull sideways through the water.) If the center of effort is farther forward than this the boat could develop a potentially

FIGURE 2.2

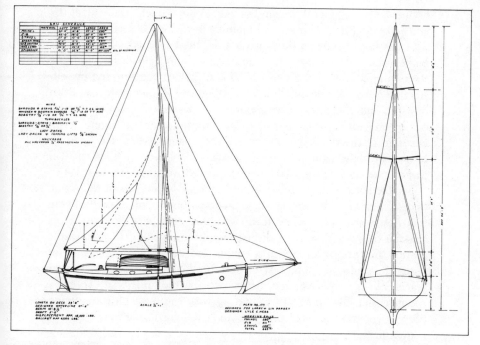

FIGURE 2.3 Final rig for *Taleisin* of Victoria. Courtesy Lyle Hess.

dangerous lee helm. If it is farther aft, she would develop weather helm
and could become tough to handle in heavy winds.

We threw another curve into Lyle's calculations by asking him to
increase the length of the bowsprit from six feet, as he sketched it the
first time, to eight feet. Lyle preferred the short bowsprit because he felt
it was less formidable, especially for newer sailors. But this boat was to
be just for us and our reasons for wanting the longer bowsprit were based
on our sailing experience with *Seraffyn*. We'd found her bowsprit was
a wonderful light weather sail extension. The big sails we could set
because of it didn't have to overlap the mast at all to keep us driving
to windward in a light breeze. So they were easy to tack, easy to see
under. Going to windward we always took the jib off the bowsprit after
the wind piped up to 22 knots. The boat with reefed main and staysail
became just like a knockabout sloop, all sail inboard, easy to handle. Our
longer bowsprit could be completely forgotten in heavy weather. A final

bonus was for light air downwind sailing. When we set the drifter at the end and lead it to the vanged out mainboom so it worked wing and wing with our small genoa on the whisker pole, the two sails pulled our boat by her nose on an amazingly steady course. This helped the windvane steer through one of the most difficult situations encountered by self-steering gears. We definitely wanted those two-and-a-half feet of extra bowsprit but the design considerations of the small seeming change combined with moving the mast forward meant some very careful recalculations of the rig or hull to achieve the balance we wanted. Lyle set to work juggling again and one of the main changes on our new sail plan was a handsome 30-inch rake in the tapered wooden spar.

That led us to the most important lesson we learned about the magic of designing a new boat. The whole process is one of compromise. There is no design that is exactly what you want in every aspect. You can't have the speed of an ultra-light displacement surfing hull, the sea-kindly motion and cargo capacity of a long-keeled heavy cutter, the interior space of a six-foot-high topsidy modern production boat, and the sweet graceful lines of a classic ten meter yacht on the same boat. To enjoy the give and take necessary to end up with the most pleasing design possible you must list your priorities and carefully decide where you can compromise.

One of the most difficult design situations occurs when a potential owner sets the interior plan of his boat as the top priority. Inevitably the owner wants more in the interior than can comfortably fit. So the designer is forced to suggest a larger hull, or he raises the sheer to provide more headroom under the deck area which makes climbing on board more difficult; or worse·yet, he increases the size of the cabin until there is virtually no side deck area left for safe, easy sail handling. All of these changes contribute to building a boat that is less fun to sail, less handsome and much more expensive. The best evidence of the fallacy of choosing accommodation space as the first priority in the ultimate design of a dream yacht can be seen in the less expensive production boats offered today. The salesmen want an interior spaciousness all out of proportion to the size of the boat so reluctant families can be lured on board. The boats they sell are tubby, the cabins are too high, the topsides tower and the decks are dangerously narrow. We decided we'd never have all of the interior space we'd like to have. We'd been able to enjoy living in 24′4″ *Seraffyn* for eleven years of cruising. She only had nine feet of beam, so 29'6" *Taleisin* with 10'9" of beam would definitely provide the extra that seemed like luxury. So we put interior accommodations at the lower end of our priority list, and performance, ease of handling and appearance at the top. Then the design started to fall together.

Once we had a hull, rig, and general deck plan we began dreaming of the interior we'd slip into the seemingly huge space of the new boat. Like most potential design customers, we frustrated Lyle by forgetting that the shape of our hull meant there would be no room for our heads if we put the settees too far outboard. Lyle tried to sketch some of the interiors we thought we wanted. Finally out of sheer frustration he came up with a solution that let us make our own decisions based on solid information. He drew out sections of the hull representing the complete view you would see if you took a thwartships slice every 27 inches. He drew in the frames on each side of the hull, the deck beams, planking and cabin, so we could see the exact volume we had to work with as the shapes changed from the narrow V of the bow to the wide U amidships and smoothly fined into the Y shapes of the stern. We cut these out and began to draw our own interior ideas guided by Skene's *Elements of Yacht Design*, a book that has a list of normal body lengths, counter heights, and comfortable seating measurements. Within two hours we began to sympathize with every yacht designer who'd tried to draw a comfortable, easy-to-live-with interior in a boat less than 35 feet.

If we found a perfect place for the dinette-type table we thought we wanted there was no floor space left for the cook in the galley. If we gave the sit-down shower tub we wanted a space where there was headroom, we had no place left for a good dinette. The cut-out hull sections began to get ragged as we arranged, rearranged, made people shaped cut-outs, bathtub patterns, paper tables, stoves and bunks then trimmed corners so they'd fit into the space we could now visualize. We spent two dozen evenings this way, listing interior priorities, measuring friend's boats, lying down on the floor to pretend we were in different sized sleeping areas just to convince ourselves we'd made the pilot berths large enough. Just when we'd convinced ourselves we'd figured it all out we'd look at our drawing and find we'd put too many of our heavy items on one side of the boat, too many big storage lockers, too many water tanks to port, so it was back to the cut-outs.

The day that the hull was completed, the decks and bulwarks finished,

A—Light weather sails storage between water tanks

B—Trim tab for self-steering

C—Folding bike storage, under deck

D—Workbench with vise. (The vise is actually closer to the hatch.) Headroom is supplied by standing in the hatch opening.

E—Wood-burning stove converted to round wick "Valor" type kerosene heater

F—Sit-tub with pump up shower tank under sink. Tub drains into gray water tank in the bilge.

G—Head bucket under port seat. Starboard locker opposite holds foul-weather gear.

H—Split table supported on two 1½" OD bronze pipes which reach from the deck head to the floor timbers. The table is inclinable when *Taleisin* is heeled.

I—The triple use area—navigation table, extra galley counter area, and ice chest. The ice box is under the table and can hold 5½ cubic feet of ice and food.

J—Tongue and groove deck box for gravity water and propane tanks

K—Oil lamps fitted to dinghy chocks for easy removal and replacement from sliding hatch

L—Wide coaming seats with storage inside for stern anchor rode, diving gear, mooring lines, fenders, etc

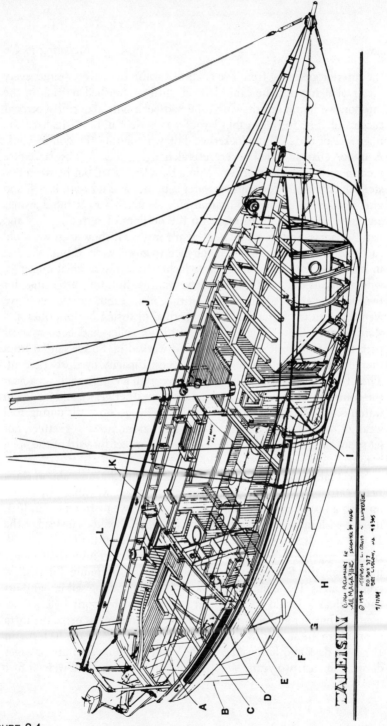

TALESIN

ROUGH RENDERING OF AIL MAGAZINE SKETCH BY N/C ILLUSTRATE
© 1984 JOSEPH L. DAVIS ~ ILLUSTRATE
P.O. BOX 377
PORT CLYDE, ME 04855
7/17/84

FIGURE 2.4

the interior gleaming from five coats of varnish over every frame, every bit of planking but the cabin left off until we finished putting in the interior, we found our drawing time had been only about fifty percent successful. The forward cabin layout was perfect until we realized the huge size of the clothing locker we'd drawn opposite the double bunk. A minor change added a very useful hanging locker. The lazzerette section with its storage for two folding bicycles, its sail bin between two stern quarter tanks for cruising water supplies, and its work bench and vise, needed no changes. But amidships we finally forgot the drawings and used scrap timber to mock up the outlines of settees, galley and bathtub areas. This was well worthwhile in that it showed us we could successfully raise the cabin sole one inch to give a wider cabin sole, and in turn lower the cabin sides three inches from the original drawings, which gave us the sweet low profile we wanted. But, time after time, for two days we changed our minds on that main cabin interior until we went back to the boringly obvious method of listing our priorities and starting with those as guidelines. *Seraffyn's* galley had been as near perfect for a boat of her size as any I'd worked in. So we started from there, enlarging the counters and ice chest capacity by thirty percent. Then the interior began falling into place with a comfortable area near the companionway where a person in wet weather gear could lounge in watch seats port or starboard to be ready to go on deck during foul weather, yet not worry about dripping salt water onto velvet settees, nor let spray onto the pilot berths which were four feet forward of the open hatch.

Now that *Taleisin* has been a home and magic carpet for almost three years, carrying us over 9,000 miles during that time, we can see we ended up with a boat that is a bit different from what we pictured in our first, make-a-wish innocence. *Taleisin* displaces 17,400 pounds instead of the 16,000 pounds we originally budgeted for (see *Seraffyn's European Adventure*, appendix). She draws five feet three inches. This is three inches more than the five feet we originally felt was optimum for shallow cruising areas. Her eight-foot bowsprit makes handling sail in light airs harder than it would be if we had the five-foot bowsprit Lyle recommended, but her amazing speed in light to medium airs make the extra effort seem most worthwhile, especially when she regularly turns in 165-knot days and has averaged 149 knots for three separate passages during the past two years. We asked for an easy helm and were at first uneasy with the amazingly balanced boat Lyle drew for us. She has an almost neutral helm in any winds under 18 knots. Her interior is not what we first dreamed of, but it works nicely, seating six to eight for drinks in reasonable comfort, four perfectly for dinner, two in lounging luxury all the time. But we didn't get the up-all-the-time table we once dreamed of; ours has to fold in half to allow passage fore and aft.

We spent a few pleasant evenings with cruising friends who had had the same type of dreams as we did when we first talked to Lyle Hess about our wish. This couple had commissioned a new design for their third cruising boat and had just finished telling us of the long drawn-out process of modifying their new boat once it was launched. It had taken them almost two years to change the balance of the rig, moving the rudder aft and adding deadwood to the underbody to improve the sailing qualities of the new design. This had cost them several thousand dollars. Now they asked, "Would you go through the conflicts, decision making and potential disappointments of having a boat designed again?"

We too had had to make some modifications to *Taleisin* once she was launched. The most expensive was a builder's error—our rudder warped due to poorly seasoned timbers. There was no one to blame but ourselves for that problem. A sister ship built on the East Coast had floated three inches lower than Lyle had originally planned. He brought this to our attention just before we launched *Taleisin* but it was too late to raise her waterline, move her bobstay fitting and adjust the rudder fairing to cover this, so we had to do it later. These were admittedly small and inexpensive changes compared to our friends. Yet as they asked this question, I thought back to the days after we launched *Seraffyn*. She'd been near perfect, floating within a half inch of where we expected, trimming as we expected. But she had also been the second boat built to Lyle's original *Renegade* design. Lyle and his partner Roy had built the *Renegade*. Hale Field, her first owner, had raced and cruised on *Renegade*, changing her rig, experimenting and telling Lyle of any improvements he made. We had sailed on *Renegade* several times and knew what modifications we needed to make her suit our needs. This had saved us from any surprises. Those memories almost made us agree with our cruising friends. It might have been easier to build a proven design like *Seraffyn*. But as the evening progressed, they told us of how they had chosen a designer who had previously designed very different boats from the one they wanted, how they'd chosen a builder they

hadn't known well. They'd asked for a design that was a distinct departure from any boat they had previously owned. "Next time we'll find a
boat we think we like, we'll sail on it as much as we can. Then we'll ask
the designer to make a few changes if we think we need them."

Compared to them we'd been super conservative in our design project. We chose the same designer, the same builders, the same type of
boat. We sailed on several boats of similar types designed by Lyle. Our
only real changes involved increasing the amount of ballast to displacement, and increasing the dimensions from *Seraffyn*'s size and the size
of Lyle's successful 28-foot Bristol Channel Cutter design (we sailed on
six of these boats while we watched *Taleisin*'s drawings develop) to get
the exact boat we wanted. So we felt comfortable investing most of our
life savings and four years of our labor building a custom design.

In spite of the occasional headaches and doubts we had, in spite of
some temper flair-ups caused because three strong personalities were
working together to build something each of us wanted, I think we'd do
it again (if Lyle could stand it). *Taleisin* is wonderfully ours. We have
the bonus of feeling we were part of her creation from the beginning.
And we have the bonus of knowing how a boat grows from a concept
to a design. We have also learned some invaluable lessons about the care,
calculations and compromises that go into any well thought out sailing
yacht.

3

What Does Cruising Cost?

In 1983 we spent a delightful evening listening to a lecture by Bernard Moitessier, the well-known French singlehander. He'd just sailed non-stop from Tahiti to San Francisco to earn cruising funds by showing his excellent film about the first singlehanded around-the-world race. During the discussion period following the film, someone asked the question that is dominant in most prospective cruising sailors' minds. "How much money does it cost to outfit a boat, then go cruising?"

Bernard brought a roar of laughter from the audience when he answered, "Just as much as you have." We laughed as loud as everyone else then and still do now because a review of our average yearly cruising costs for fourteen years of voyaging reads like the bottom line of our yearly income sheet.

When we set off in 1969 with $4,000 set aside, we spent between $250 and $300 per month. In 1974 when we landed a plum of a delivery job and also sold a few thousand dollars worth of magazine articles, our expenses shot up to $700 a month. The next year our income declined and so did our cruising expenses. Inflation seemed to have little to do with it. In 1978 when we spent a large portion of our cruising money on 2400 board feet of Burmese teak timbers at a bargain price so we could eventually build a new boat, we found ourselves cruising for less than $400 a month.

John and Cottee Ross cruised from 1983 until 1986 on their 38-foot home finished, fibreglass sloop, *Skye II,* for a monthly average of $300. They had two fast growing teenaged sons on board and may have been, as Cottee said, "the most spartan cruisers out here." But all four on board were healthy and enjoying life. (See end of chapter for an analysis of their costs.)

Another friend on a 28-foot glass boat has had to cut his cruising short by almost a year because he spent fifty percent more than the $6,000 a year he'd allotted for a three-year voyage through the South Pacific. Even with occasional jobs as a day charterer, he's now having to take a full-time, year-long job to earn money to continue his voyage.

We've done some serious thinking on this question of cruising costs. During 1976 we surveyed 76 cruising sailors regarding their costs. All of these people had been away from their home port for at least twelve months. That survey showed that boat size plus the complexity of the equipment each sailor chose, had a direct bearing on cruising costs. Since then we've asked other sailors about their expenses and found that the areas you choose to visit and the amount of time you spend in major yachting centers will affect your costs.

In our 1976 survey, cruising costs for boats under 30 feet averaged $350 to $500 a month for crews of three or less. But the people on boats 31 feet and over averaged between $500 to $900 a month. The obvious reasons for this are higher haul-out costs, higher mooring charges and higher spare parts and maintenance bills. People who own larger yachts tend to motor more and have higher fuel bills. With a bigger boat there is more room for so called luxuries such as radio transmitters, freezer units, water heaters and radar. These all require maintenance and repairs. The further you move away from your own port, the higher these repair costs climb. We know of one voyager who sent to the United States for a $46 spare part to repair his refrigeration compressor since no one in Fiji carried what he needed. When he finally received the part three months later he computed its cost at $210. The telegrams, freight costs, duties and customs which were figured at one hundred percent of the value of the part and freight, plus agents' fees to clear all the paper work, and finally taxi charges to rescue his part from the airport quintupled the cost of his part.

Even with a boat under 30 feet, this problem of maintaining complicated equipment can double your cruising costs. The difference between John and Cottee's $300-a-month cruising expenses with a family of four and our $900-a-month friend on the 28-footer who had an average of two to three people on board could be traced directly to their attitudes toward equipment. *Skye II* had only a very small 10 horsepower auxiliary motor. *Skye II*'s motor only pushed the boat at 2½ to 3½ knots, so was rarely used and so far never needed spare parts. *Skye II* carried the simplest of electronics. Our other friend was convinced that since he had a ham radio on board it had to be working. I watched his girlfriend rushing around in California spending over $1,000 on parts plus a special antennae unit. We can appreciate his frustration at having something on board that wasn't working correctly. But when costs matter, it pays to question whether your so-called cruising conveniences are worth the price.

Where you cruise plays a large part in determining cruising costs. If many of your ports-of-call are deserted island anchorages where the joys of skin diving and quiet walks ashore fill your days, you'll spend a lot less than if you voyage to exciting social centers like Athens, Monaco, Papeete or Singapore. It's almost impossible to avoid the money gobbling night clubs and cafe's. Tourist shops with stunning jewelry and glittering yacht hardware are hard to resist. Furthermore, places commonly frequented by cruising sailors often have small yacht harbors where moorings cost $5, $10 or $15 a night. Although with a little planning you can find a place to anchor for free, it's attractive to be in the center of the action occasionally.

The countries where we noticed our cruising costs were lowest often weren't those places where living costs were considered low: England, Sweden, Finland, Spain, Japan, and the United States. We spent time in each of these places and lived more inexpensively than we did in the Caribbean, Singapore, Malta, or Gibraltar. I know the main reason was that we could get away from normal yacht harbors and meet locals who helped us find real bargains in entertainment and food. We could also avoid the delightful but expensive cycle of parties that happen everywhere a dozen foreign yachts happen to congregate.

We've been absolutely amazed when a casual afternoon gathering of voyagers completely depleted our liquor supply along with a generous portion of snacks and soft drinks. Then we personally compounded the expenses by saying, "Sure we'll join you at Antonio's for dinner." There we'd spend another $15 or $20 on a meal that may not have been as good as we'd get at a less glamourous cafe for half the price. After a week of afternoons like this we've often found ourselves and our cruising funds exhausted. Don't get me wrong, these rendezvous in favorite cruising ports are a special part of our lives. But to keep both our budget and our reason for cruising to foreign countries in the proper perspective, the socializing has to be rationed.

Another way to cut the rendezvous costs is to make sure there are no cafe's or bars near your anchorage. At Rangiroa in the Tuamoto Islands, our costs shot up when five other friends anchored nearby and we all seemed to meet each evening at the very welcoming bar on shore run by the Kia Ora resort. One or two beers for each of us at $2.50 a beer, plus the almost inevitable, "It's raining, let's eat dinner here and wait for it to stop," doubled that month's expenses. Two later rendezvous that same year, with several of the same cruising sailors in the lagoon at Suvorov and at a quiet, out of the way beach in Tonga, cost us almost nothing. Since we had no shops or bars nearby, we shared fresh fish we caught and were more conservative with the limited amount of wine we carried. I think we may have had more fun, too!

There are several budget items that will cost less than prospective cruisers expect. Medical expenses seem to drop drastically when you head offshore. Possibly this is because its more difficult to find a doctor so you solve your own problems. But more realistically its because cruising is a very healthy way of life. Furthermore, doctors and medicine cost less when you get away from the United States. Not only that but usually someone you meet on shore or someone in the cruising fleet knows a doctor friend who'll help you in exchange for a day sail and a picnic.

Your clothing costs will drop by 50 or 75 percent when you actually set sail. No more suits, ties, and nylon stockings. Except for a possible biannual replacement for your foul weather gear, clothes purchases will drop to occasional souvenir shirts, a hand-painted evening frock, a straw hat or pair of sandles. Even if you are a clothes horse on shore, the space limitations of a boat will usually control this habit.

Insurance is another expense that usually drops out of your life if you become a long-term cruiser. Few of us can afford the type of insurance that would cover voyages to far-off places. The lowest price for total loss coverage for worldwide cruising we've heard of was offered at 1.5 to 2 percent of the boat's value per year. This means to cover a $100,000 yacht for a year of leisurely cruising through the Marquesas Islands you would pay $1,500 to $2,000 a year, or $167 a month. On top of this you need $5,000 cash somewhere to cover the deductible insurance policies like this require. For wider coverage, costs escalate until you'd have to double your cruising kitty just to insure your boat and its equipment. That is why most of the long-term cruisers we've met prefer to spend their money on extra ground tackle, excellent charts, and the best possible sailing equipment instead of formal insurance. (See chapter 6 for more on insurance.)

Eating out, renting a car or taxi for a bit of touring, even buying a used vehicle for an extended tour, are the cruising expenses we'd never skimp on. If you use the same care and research techniques that went into planning your boat and cruise, you'll find these on-shore pleasures can be had for a surprisingly low cost. If you search out a local policeman and ask where he eats lunch, you'll find fine ethnic dining that will probably cost half the price of the picturesque cafe closest to the waterfront. A bit of research will turn up someone willing to lease you a motorcycle for only dollars a day. One enterprising cruising couple took their folding bicycles on the local buses and rode to the highest point in each of the European countries they visited. Then they peddled down hill, knapsacks on their backs, staying at pensions and eating at simple cafes. They had great touring and downhill bicycling for about $20 (U.S.) a day, complete.

Another approach is one we took. After careful shopping in the Balearic Islands of Spain, we spent $1,000 on a popular model 350 motorcycle (secondhand). With two sleeping bags, a tube tent, two wine bottles and three changes of clothes we toured Europe for six weeks. We ate at a nice cafe each evening but snacked on cold cuts and fresh country bread during the day. Our average touring costs were $110 a week. When we returned we sold the motorcycle for the same price as we originally paid. This experience away from seaports, high in the Swiss Alps and along the rivers of France, was worth any price.

There are several other ways to keep cruising costs down. Do your entertaining on board, not in restaurants. If its a gathering of a large group of voyagers, suggest potluck. If your guests are people whom you've met on shore, suggest a sail to a nearby anchorage and anchor there away from the hustle and bustle while you serve a special meal.

That's an evening few shorebound guests would trade for dinner in the finest restaurant.

Avoid buying souvenirs in tourist towns. You'll usually find more momentoes than you can carry right on the beach. You'll find better, less expensive local handicrafts in the isolated villages you visit and the natives will probably be willing to trade for old clothes, a few cans of meat or a piece of line. Carry trading goods. These have to be carefully suited to your intended cruising goal. This year all along the Mexico, South Pacific route, good popular music cassettes (Anne Murray, Sade, old Beatles favorites) T-shirts with well-known mottoes on them or fun silkscreening are good; inexpensive plastic jewelry, fishing tackle, canned meats and canned chicken, nice fabrics, liquor and, if you smoke, cigarettes, make useable trading items. In Tonga and Westward almost anything you carry will be a potential trading item. We were given a highly prized Ta'valo or ceremonial mat when we gave a family on shore in Northern Tonga a tupperware container and new bath towel. I had meant them as gifts for a fine dinner, but my Tongan hosts insisted on giving the mat to me in return.

Good paperback books are also worth trading almost anywhere in the world. So are yachting magazines. But the more sophisticated the area, the less successful trading will be.

If there is something that really strikes your fancy, take color transparencies. These photos will mean more in the long run than any other kind of souvenir. I remember when I was drooling over a lush reindeer pelt in Finland. It was only $100 or a week's living expense. But after Larry took some photos of me hugging my treasure then suggested I think about it for a day or two, I left satisfied. Now when I see that slide I wonder—was I conned?

Do buy, trade or pick up a few dozen special handmade souvenirs in each place you visit. They make excellent hostess gifts as you visit homes in the next country. The shell necklaces we bought for two dollars each in Tahiti's street stalls, made great gifts for the Tongan ladies who couldn't find the same type of shells on their islands. The Tongan baskets we bought for one dollar in Vava'u are a fine, inexpensive gift when we are invited to dinner here in New Zealand. We just fill the basket with some fresh cookies or a shell necklace instead of the soon forgotten bottle of wine most guests bring. That way our hostess has something she can use again and again.

FIGURE 3.1 Tongan baskets like these are great values and make wonderful gifts. Storage can be a problem, however.

Buy stores when they are cheap. Stock up and keep your boat stocked even if you aren't going on a passage right now. In the Azores fine Portuguese canned hams were 60 cents a pound. I filled the forward locker and was still enjoying this bargain a year later when Danish ham cost $4.00 a pound. This is even more important in the South Pacific where quality peanut butter costs $1.70 a jar in American Samoa, but $3.00 in Tahiti.

Trade charts or take tracing paper and carefully copy details of gunk-holing anchorages. You'll find this gets easy once you are out among the cruising fleet. We have charts that have been used by six different boats for the voyage up or down the Red Sea. Each voyager marked his favorite anchorages so we had lots of places to explore if we wanted to. Charts you borrow or wish to share with someone else are cheap to mail. Simply roll them tightly in bundles weighing less than 20 pounds then wrap the charts in an old chart with the ends of the package open for inspection. Packaged like this they can be shipped under what is called the printed matter or educational matter rate. In the United States that is about 27 cents a pound, overseas it costs even less.

Take care of your sails. We lay each one of ours out twice a year and check every stitch on every seam. We mend even a single broken stitch. Then if possible wash the sails in fresh water. Our small genoa on *Seraffyn* lasted an average of 18,000 miles of pulling.

Our nylon sails were still okay after 11½ years with this treatment.

Don't buy any new piece of equipment until you learn to repair it yourself. This is an important money-saving rule. That satellite navigation system could become a double expense if you buy it then have to hire someone else to install or repair it. That motorcycle might seem like a good idea until salt water turns it to a mass of corrosion and you find you are doing more fixing than riding. You might find it would have been far cheaper to rent a motorcycle when you needed one.

The list of money-saving techniques for offshore cruisers can go on forever. But in the final analysis the question still stands: What does it cost to cruise? We've come up with a rough formula that seems to work. This formula assumes that few people will really change their basic tastes and desires drastically once they settle into cruising. People who liked wine with dinner will still drink wine, people who were avid magazine readers will still buy fresh magazines, people used to living like graduate students will know how to continue living at that level. So if you take your everyday, on shore living expenses and subtract all of your automobile costs, two thirds of your clothing expenses, your house rent or mortgage payments, and your mooring costs, then add one third to your food costs, you'll come up with a close estimate of your eventual cruising costs over an extended period.

Your first year of cruising will probably cost less than your second year. This is because your boat is freshly outfitted, full of stores and you are so thrilled to be free of shoreside hassles that your desire for entertainment will be satisfied by simpler pleasures—clear sparkling skies, the public markets, or a new pair of sandals. But if you last that first year and if you find cruising gets in your blood, you'll discover ways to extend your funds year after year.

One of the main facts we've learned about long-term cruisers is that very few of them are wealthy. Maybe its because people who can always afford the best don't feel the need to spend weeks on their own boat just to get to a hideaway island. The frustration of maintaining a boat and its gear without outside assistance may not appeal to people who have the funds to hire specialists. Or maybe the complications of maintaining the investments that are the basis of their wealth pulls these people back to a shore-based life.

Most successful long-term cruisers come up with some kind of work-to-cruise ratio that satisfies their sense of freedom. We are only willing to spend four full months a year working to earn money. If this isn't enough we either work harder or cut our expenses. This gives us flexibility in our spending. We can be rich or poor according to the proximity of enjoyable fund-earning work. People who start cruising after they retire don't have this same feeling. Since their earnings are static, their standard of living seems to change with the cost of living for the places they visit. In places where life is inexpensive such as Turkey, the Bahamas, or Tonga, they glow. But if they want to sail to more costly areas like Tahiti, Scandinavia or France, they hesitate far longer than those who earn as they cruise.

If you are working now to save up money to insure five, ten or fifteen years of trouble free cruising, you may never reach your goal. Inflation, illness, changing world conditions, can all defeat you if you try to take every risk out of selling out and going. Instead, work for a few years of cruising money in the bank, then get an efficient little cruiser, stock it well and plan for a year at a time. Leave some money squirreled away back at home so if you feel like you'd like to go back you can. But if you like what you see out here, you'll find a way to keep on going.

TWO EXAMPLES OF CRUISING COSTS FOR 1986—SOUTH PACIFIC CRUISING.

Cottee and John Ross on *Skye II* provided the following breakdown for the middle year of their three-year cruise. Cottee kept careful financial records and said this was a more typical cruising year than their first when they were stocking up in the United States and their last when they were using up their stores and making far more passages than normal. Cottee and John had cruised previously, sailing through the Pacific for two years with the children. They did not work along the way, preferring to live off money they earned before they left. John's reasoning was this, "I can sail back to Canada and work at my own profession as a steel fabricator, twelve hours a day, seven months straight, Cottee can do the same as a nurse and we'll save three years cruising funds again. Besides, if I get work out here it means the family is stuck in some port they probably won't like and I'll be working at something I don't like as much." Their living costs support their theory—they probably could save three times as much as the average person when they both worked full time.

Month	Cruising Area	Cost	Special Circumstances
July	Baja California	$385	bought solar panel
August		340	$50 for medical expenses
September		90	
October		440	haulout
November		220	parents visiting, they took us out and paid for it
December		270	
January 1985		500	stocking up, shoes, clothes, souvenirs
February		500	
March		15	at sea
April	Marquesas	220	
May		100	
June	Papeete	430	
July		420	medical $110
Total for 13 months		$3,900	
Monthly average $300			

Cottee explained that their haulout—the first in two years—cost $350. Repairs over two years cost $270, diesel fuel, 65 gallons for the year. Visits to the dentist the previous year were an extra expense of $200.

Cottee and John told us they rarely eat out. But the family occasionally bought tacos at a road side stand in Mexico. The big treat was to buy a gallon of ice cream and eat it all at one sitting.

The boys were both keen and very successful fishermen. Fish made up most of their meals. They bought chickens occasionally, meat less than twice a year.

Cottee and John both stressed that their cruising expenses were atypical among the people they met. "Remember, our boat is new, and neither of us likes to drink much. Cottee doesn't like restaurants, and we'd do anything to stay out here because we'd rather be cruising than freezing and working in Canada," John said.

When I asked if either of them wished they had more funds for any particular item only Cottee could think of anything she'd add to her cruising life. "If I had some extra money I'd spend it for more reference books." She told me. The boys didn't seem to feel any lack. They earned a bit of money or traded for items they wanted by fishing and by offering to help other cruisers occasionally. They seemed to find that most of the youngsters they met in the villages they visited didn't have spending money either. What money Dean and Toby did spend seemed to all go for yet more fishing gear.

We spent the year of 1985 along a similar route. *Taleisin* was, like *Skye II,* an almost new boat, and so needed few repairs. We did, on the other hand, buy some equipment including a Honda two horsepower outboard motor, some water jugs, extra line, special batteries, for our EPIRB, so we spent an extra $500 on boat equipment that first year of offshore voyaging. We left the route the Rosses took at Tonga and sailed south to New Zealand. Our costs were definitely in the upper range for couples cruising on a 30- to 32-foot boat. I must admit we were feeling wealthy during this period and splurged on a lavish twentieth anniversary celebration for ourselves, and sent many gifts home to relatives and friends who had helped us as we built *Taleisin.*

January 1985	Mexico	$ 800	offshore stores cost $300
February		1,282	Shipyard $460, final stores $600
March	at sea two weeks	305	
April	Tuamotos	491	
May	Papeete	904	
June		885	
July		913	
August	Samoa	1,270	Reprovisioning
September		427	
October		823	$400 of this was spent on Tongan gifts for friends
November		347	
December	New Zealand	560	
Total		$ 9040	
Monthly average	$753		

We both felt we cruised and lived extremely luxuriously for this sum. We ate out two or three times a week in port, purchased a whole new wardrobe and put on a feast for a Tongan family of sixteen.

Our cruising costs shocked us and we are now back on a more austere budget. But we proved Bernard's adage: Cruising costs as much as you have. When we looked over these costs we found we could easily have cut the monthly average from $753 to a more affordable $500 by changing our restaurant choices from candlelit cafés to Le Truck's in Papeete, by choosing street side pareao shops instead of artist galleries for the hand-painted lengths of fabric that made up my tropical wardrobe and by entertaining less lavishly. The costs I feel we couldn't cut were, offshore stores which totaled about $2,000 for what amounted to almost 7,000 miles of sailing. This included canned and paper goods, treats and necessities. Cottee and John cut this in half by depending mainly on beans, lentils and grains for their protein, but, as we said in the beginning of this article, none of us really will change our living styles as we cruise. Cottee and John have always eaten as they please, on shore or afloat, tending towards vegetarianism. We've been the opposite, being great fans of a good canned ham, a tinned brie cheese on a cold night at sea.

Another cost neither of us could cut were haulout charges. In Mexico where tides were too small to let us dry out against some pilings, the ways charges for *Taleisin* were $249 for three days; bottom paint, purchased wholesale from an American friend was $160. The Ross's paid nearly the same. French Polynesian prices would have been dearer. New Zealand haulout prices are half, but delaying haulouts for lower prices could be false economy.

4
The Question of Children and Cruising

One question always comes up after we've spent an evening showing slides and talking about cruising at a yacht club or cruising center, "What about children?" Although we've never sailed with young people on board for more than a week. Our experiences with cruising families we've met in foreign ports and anchorages have always been positive. But I wonder if that's because happy cruising families draw us like magnets. Almost every time we see a boatload of cheerful youngsters drop anchor nearby, it seems that Larry ends up sailing off with one or two of them in our dinghy while I dig out the ingredients for a chocolate cake or a batch of cookies.

So our answers to concerned parents come from the success stories of twenty or twenty-five families we've met along the way, stories that could be the envy of any shore-side family.

John and Maureen Guzzwell set off from England on 45-foot *Treasure* when their twin boys were just becoming school aged. During the next ten years the Guzzwells cruised and taught the boys with correspon-

dence courses. When we last saw John, Jr. and James they were almost
twenty years old. One wanted to be a boat builder like his father; the
other applied for medical school and was accepted immediately.

A favorite story of ours with a bittersweet ending is about the Forrestal family. Tom was in his mid-forties when his doctor told him he had
only two or three years to live. He kept this a complete secret and asked
his wife and nine daughters (yes *nine*) if they'd like to buy a cruising
boat. Since they all remembered the good times they'd had sailing as a
family around Long Island, the girls soon talked Tom into quitting work
to go off for two or three years. Jo and Tom sold out, bought a 51-foot
boat and set off with the girls aged 12 to 23. We met them a year and
a half later. Each of the girls had taken over some area of the boat's
management and maintenance. One was the mechanic, one learned
navigation, another basic electronics. The oldest girls spent the winter
at their jobs or colleges, the youngest six were on board full time. When
Tom died suddenly one morning in a tiny Greek village, the girls and
their mother decided the finest tribute they could pay to Tom was to
use the skills he'd taught them. So they continued on and cruised for
two more years including an Atlantic crossing. Education was obviously
a success on board because each new letter from Jo includes the name
of a top school that's accepted yet another Forrestal girl.

The very young cruising children we've met not only seem to thrive
on board, but provide an instant attraction wherever they go. Laddie,
the thirty-eight-year-old mother of a beautiful three-year-old girl and
four-year-old boy, laughingly lamented, "I'm getting an inferiority complex. Everywhere we go locals rush up to meet the kids and ignore me!"

Our stories all seem to be the same. Boat size didn't affect the kids
we met. One family of four, including two children in their early teens,
explored the Mediterranean for a year on a 28-footer. Another couple
brought their infant son on board their 29-foot Trimaran, two days after
he was born in Costa Rica, and set sail for the Marquesas three months
later. We heard stories of the sun-browned, sturdy youngster rowing a
borrowed ten foot skiff four years later in French Polynesia.

One of the few semi-unhappy youngsters we met in fifteen years afloat
was a fourteen-year-old girl who resented being torn away from the
friends she'd made at school. She also felt a bit like an outsider since
her two younger brothers charged off together through the streets of
every new village the family anchored near and always came back with

local friends within hours. But we met this same young lady four years later when she'd entered a prime East Coast college and her memories of the family's two year cruise were exceptionally rosy. In fact it was hard to believe she'd found so much pleasure since she'd been down in the dumps during most of the three weeks we spent cruising in company with them.

Schooling is, of course, the big question. We met the Bushnell family after they'd completed a seven-year circumnavigation on their 31-footer with two daughters aged nine and eleven. Six years later the oldest girl left to marry another cruising sailor and the Bushnells stopped in South Africa to have another child so they wouldn't have to cruise alone. We later met the older daughter and asked her about correspondence school afloat. "Great for me, lousy for my sister," Kim said with a twinkle. "I hated real school, always got in fights with the teachers. My sister was the opposite. She was so happy to come back to regular school after seven years. She'd kept up with her class okay. Me, I'm never going to school again. I got my high school diploma from correspondence classes. But it sure was a drag having to be down below studying half the day while the folks were up on deck enjoying the Mississippi."

Some cruising families we've met who plan to voyage for only one year and then return to their home port, find the time and emotions spent fighting to keep children involved in their correspondence courses may not be worthwhile. They instead encourage their children to learn everything they can from the cruising experience, then catch up with their classes when they get home. The three children on *Pegasus*, Bridgit, Brendan and Tim Metherall, set aside most of their school work, yet were constantly learning by writing letters to friends back home, drawing boats, maintaining their 38-foot ketch and meeting new friends ashore. Their latest letter from their Melbourne, Australia, home indicated their one-year holiday only made them more eager to get good grades so they could dream of sailing off again, on their *own* yachts.

That same letter had an amusing aside that may answer the question that most worries potential cruising parents—health problems. "Bridgit has been down with the flu for the past three weeks," her mother Jan wrote. "She was definitely healthier when we were off sailing. Guess she wasn't closed up in a class room with so many germs." The relative healthiness of cruising children is amazing and I think Jan's reasoning is the best answer. Staph infections from coral scratches and ear infections are the two most common complaints among cruising children who are constantly playing in the water. Both can be avoided with a bit of pre-planning.

Skin diving ear infections can be prevented by putting two drops of baby oil in each ear before diving to seal the sensitive skin of the eardrum. Then, after each day's diving, rinse each ear with two or three drops of alcohol to kill any bacteria. The French doctor in Papeete who is an ear infection specialist recommended a twice daily alcohol ear rinse —once at midday and once after the last swim of the day—for both children and parents.

The staph infections, which can keep young people out of the water for weeks if they are not prevented, can be minimized by a conscientious vitamin supplement program and then treating each and every scratch and cut immediately with an antibacterial cream and bandages until it is completely closed. Carry Silvadene cream for deep cuts which need to be allowed to ooze. Silvadene is antibacterial and will let even deep wounds heal without becoming infected. (Silvadene creme is only available by prescription and is usually used to cover burns as they heal, but handles this tropical need perfectly.)

Safety is a far bigger worry with children afloat than health. The worst tragedy we heard of during our cruising years involved a nine-month-old baby who crawled through an opening in the lifeline netting and drowned while her parents were having coffee below. The baby had never before been able to climb out of the cockpit alone. I have only heard of this one child drowning, though we've been around cruising families for years, yet many young parents are so afraid that they insist their children wear flotation vests constantly, morning to night. The children grow to hate the cumbersome gear, especially in the tropics.

Doreen Samuelson, a wonderfully matter-of-fact French mother who cruises with her English husband, David, and seven-year-old American-born daughter Nikki on their 43-foot sloop *Swan II*, said, "Until Nikki could swim, she had to wear a vest if she went out of the cockpit. Once she could swim, we had to take our chances and teach her to be careful, just as we had to teach ourselves. We wear harnesses when it is rough at sea. So does she."

When I asked about that pre-swimming age, Doreen said, "We didn't start cruising until after that." This lead to a discussion of what age children adapt best to cruising.

Vicky Carkhuff wrote a fine article about her experiences cruising with children, in which she said, "Three to fourteen are the 'operable ages.' " Her reasoning was that younger than that the child can't swim, can't recognize danger, and can't be bundled below out of the way and ignored by parents who have to handle a sudden sail reduction as a squall rushes down on the boat. Couples who have a child under three on board usually find the husband has to sail as a singlehander while his wife works full time as mother and safety officer. Martine and Benoidt, two young French sailors who had a baby in Tahiti after two years of voyaging, set sail as soon as their daughter was three months old. They had been in Tahiti a year and wished to get out of the South Pacific hurricane area rather than suffer through the hot, still, humid season again. They sailed towards New Zealand at the same time we did and each time we met, Martine looked more tired, Benoidt, lonelier. "When we are anchored, life is very nice," Martine told me. "But at sea, I get sea sick, I can't take medication or it will affect my baby's milk. So Benoidt has to take care of the baby, the boat, and me." Martine and her five-month-old baby flew from Fiji to New Zealand and Benoidt sailed singlehanded. When we met again, Martine was angry. "I sailed through all of the worst weather, then the one time I decide to fly, Benoidt tells me the sailing was perfect, never more than 15 knots of wind." They now plan to sail to New Caledonia and stop for two years until their daughter reaches the age they agree is more operable.

After the age of three, children can find tremendous interest in all aspects of sailing. I've seen four to six year olds sailing the family tender alone, taking over the helm on their cruising boat for 15 to 30 minutes at a time. Older cruising children can become valuable crew. The three children from *Poganua* were a wonderful crew for us on *Taleisin* in the first annual Neiafu-Snafu regatta. Their father, who raced with his wife and a family friend, said he really missed their sail changing help.

Vicky Carkhuff went on to say, "After fourteen, children want to start planning their own dreams." I agree with her. Unless you set sail before your children reach the end of the "operable age years," unless your children are keen sailors who want to go cruising just as badly as you do, chances are fifty-fifty that they'll desperately miss their friends back home and be restless afloat for more than a one-year, extended holiday.

There are several things that parents who cruise enjoyably with children all seem to do. They all provide each child with a separate, private

space somewhere on board, out of the way. This area can be left neat
or untidy, crammed or empty, according to the child's whim. It usually
can be closed off and is private territory so the youngster can escape and
be by himself when necessary. Mike Saunderson's children on *Walk-
about* had a curtained-off pilot berth to call their own. Nikki Samuelson
on *Swan II* had the luxury of a curtained-off after cabin under the
cockpit that was stuffed with woolly animals, but was neat as a pin. The
two boys on *Pegasus* had one side each of the forepeak and were forever
trying to locate things in a typical boy's room chaos. On board *Skye II*
the Ross's sons, Dean and Toby, who were 13 and 11 when they left
home for a second extended cruise, had private, tiny areas each side of
the cockpit. "I wouldn't go into Toby's cabin," Cottee warned me one
day. "It stinks from all the shark's jaws he's cleaning."

Every family cruising with two children or more carried two tenders
on board. Usually one was a solid tender with sailing gear, the other an
inflatable tender. That way no one became stranded on board or stuck
on shore because someone was off in the dinghy. Some families also
carried surf sailors which served as yet another tender in the warmth of
the tropics. Although many families provided a small outboard for their
children to use occasionally with the tender, one thing I would avoid is
a high-powered outboard. One cruising family became almost pariahs by
providing their children with a high-powered runabout which they used
for joy riding all day. They disturbed everyone's peaceful anchorage.

On each of the satisfied family boats we noticed the parents took turns
being responsible for the children. Doreen felt free to spend an afternoon showing me her favorite shopping spots in Papeete while David
took Nikki bicycling off towards Maeva beach. Quiet tea times with Jan
were always a treat while Peter set off shopping or exploring with his
youngsters.

There is no way around the fact that cruising with children is harder
than cruising without them. But I think the same can be said of shore
life. With children on board you'll need more room for provisions and
stores, you'll have more people to organize for forays ashore, more
personalities to contend with. You may get fewer invitations to have
dinner on board other boats because cruising friends are reluctant to say,
"leave your children at home." But some of the parents we met said they
couldn't imagine sailing as only a couple. Cottee and John are that way.
They've stretched their intended two-year cruise to cover three. "It

won't be as much fun when the boys grow up and go their own ways. They are always finding interesting new things to show us, new friends, keeping us supplied with fish. Besides, they're the ones that keep the boat moving at sea. They love to sail, to trim things and make a faster passage than their friends do."

Cottee and John have given Toby and Dean far more responsibility than shorebound youngsters would have. We felt comfortable hiring 15-year-old Dean to live on board *Taleisin* in La Paz harbor for four days in early 1985 while we went away whale watching. His father's boat was moored 300 yards away in case of emergencies beyond Dean's capabilities. But he handled the situation just fine, leaving our boat perfectly clean, the dinghy spotless and waiting for us just when we said we'd be back.

This maturity (some call it pre-maturity) found in long-term cruising children is one thing many shorebound people have commented on. Shipboard life does breed conscientious children. They know the chores they are asked to do are important contributions to their families lifestyle, not just "make work" gambits to keep them busy. They spend far more time than normal around adults and far less among children their own age. They are told time and again that they are special by people they meet along the way. To combat the adjustment problems this might later cause, some parents stop for every second year and have their children attend local schools while they earn more cruising funds or refit the boat. Some parents plan their cruise to spend as much time as possible with other voyaging families. In almost every case, children who voyage long term are more adultlike, more serious, more observant of the outside world. Maybe that is why we enjoy their company so much.

I guess that explains the ulterior motives for this chapter. The reason we like to encourage parents to say yes to cruising in spite of the extra planning, the extra work, is that children usually love it, and usually love their parents for being determined and different enough to go cruising.

5

Medical Preparations for Cruising

I thought it would be simpler the second time. We'd been out there before so we knew what to expect. We had the mistakes and lessons of eleven years of cruising and a lifetime affair with sailing to draw on. Then, as *Taleisin*'s interior started to fill the boat and her sails stopped being work objects and began to be stored away one by one in the finished equipment room, our preparations for the second phase of our offshore cruising life began in earnest. That's when we were reminded once again that the joy of sailing as a life style is that, no matter how long you do it, there's always something more to learn. Each time you go, there are new skills that you feel will help your cruising life flow more smoothly. So as we worked through the winter of 1982–83 finishing *Taleisin*, as we scrounged through hardware stores, catalogues and plumbing supply houses for the last bits of gear we needed to launch a sailing home, we also took time to study and make decisions we hoped would help us as we set off cruising again.

In the excitement of finishing our first cruising boat we forgot completely about the health and medical aspects of cruising. I had taken first aid and advanced first aid courses with the American Red Cross as part of one of my college jobs. We had a first-aid kit for our shop that we planned to carry on *Seraffyn*. But that's as far as we went. Then the doctor who'd cared for us while we built *Seraffyn* came by soon after we launched and gave us a gift that set us thinking. He'd found an excellent, compact book called *Being Your Own Wilderness Doctor* by Kodet and Angier, published by Stackpole books. Then he filled a small fishing tackle box with the prescription drugs the book recommended. We did read through the book and enlarged our first aid equipment to include the items it recommended. Three months after our launching we set sail for six months or a year or until we ran through the $5,000 that represented our total cruising fund. Of course the taste of freedom we had that first year made it seem impossible to return to a shore-based life so we found ways to earn as we sailed. During those first nine years of our cruise, a period during which we rarely sailed over 4,000 miles or spent over 50 days a year away from towns or villages, we occasionally had to dip into our medical kit when we were out of reach of local medical assistance to cure minor ailments, an upset stomach, a deep splinter, a mild allergic reaction. More often we dug out the kit when someone we met had problems. Larry assured us of a summer's supply of ice by lancing and cleaning an abcess on a Mexican fisherman's foot by following our *Wilderness Doctor* book instructions. A fellow cruising couple made us a fabulous dinner after our supply of drugs had exactly what the lady needed for a painful bout with cystitis. In both cases the nearest doctors were two or three days away even by power boat. Things changed during the tenth year of our cruise when we decided to sail from Malta to Victoria, Canada over what turned out to be sixteen month period. We spent over 200 days at sea to cover 16,000 miles. During that period we had two potentially frightening medical problems. Larry had an abcessed tooth during the North Pacific crossing twenty days out of Japan and I had severe salt-deficiency cramps as we wound our way between the hostile shores of north Yemen and Ethiopia's Eritrea coast in the Red Sea. Those problems convinced us that it would pay to know a bit more about the bodies we lived in since our future plans included extensive voyaging. That is when we began looking for some kind of emergency medical course we could take while we were ashore building our new, more sophisticated cruising home.

Our first idea was to sign up for a paramedics course at the local college. But the course outline proved that was not the best solution.

The whole emphasis was on handling accident victims for the first hour or possibly two while medical assistance is reached. There was no discussion of extended care, medicines to use for illness, or solving problems. The whole basis of the paramedics course is, rightfully, to keep the patient alive and get him to a hospital.

Another choice was to join a ham-radio network which offered advise from consulting doctors. This meant carrying a wind generator and ham radio, two complications we weren't quite prepared for but would have considered until a physician we met discussed the shortcomings of relying on radio assistance for emergency medical care. "First and foremost," he stressed, "you can't contact anyone on a radio immediately." Even on days when transmission is good, phone patches, tuning, getting someone to give you advice can take anywhere from thirty minutes to an hour. In most real emergency cases, that's too long. An allergic reaction, massive bleeding, near drowning, all require basic, immediate action. Secondly, if the physician you contact does not know what medication you carry, or if you do not have the appropriate supplies, radio help will not solve the problem. And last, if you do not know how to observe and record the information a doctor needs, if you do not know how to take vital signs including blood pressure, pulse, temperature and pupil reaction to describe to the advisor, he or she can be of little assistance.

Our final choice and one we feel comfortable with, was a three day, 28-hour intensive survey of the medical emergency course offered by a well-recommended emergency room physician, Bob Kingston, 25381 G Alicia Parkway, Suite 104, Laguna Hills, California, 92653. (See end of chapter for other medical course contacts.) The course turned out to be a guided and well-illustrated trip through a two pound, on board, medical manual that Bob had compiled over several years of local sailing and ten years of emergency room work. We were amazed at the thorough coverage of the course and realized the accompanying manual meant we didn't have to memorize anything more than the basic ABC rule that was stressed time and again by Bob and the four emergency room nurses who worked with us during the practical sessions: check airways, breathing, and circulation. We did learn how to use a stethoscope and take all other vital signs and record them. We did learn the importance of having a crew card for each person on board listing special medication, normal blood pressure and allergies. But most important of all we learned to stem the initial emergency, then sit back, slow down, check the manual and remember that most of the time it is safest and best to do nothing other than make an injured or ill person comfortable until professional help can be reached.

This differentiation between what is a medical emergency and what is only a medical problem was one of the more interesting aspects of the course. Some of the doctors we spoke with about this course voiced their concern over the danger inherent in untrained, would-be saviors prescribing potentially dangerous drugs for themselves or their crew instead of seeking assistance. Dr. Kingston stressed several times that doctors, even in the most primitive countries, are a safer bet than relying on your own limited knowledge. "They might not have qualifications to please the American Medical Association," he said, "But they'll have seen enough sick people to be able to differentiate between serious problems and minor ones. So go see the local doctor if you are in or near a port. But out at sea, you are on your own even if you can reach radio assistance because *you* have to be able to make the final decision!"

I think this awareness that on an offshore vessel you are on your own to handle any emergencies was one of the most important aspects of the course. If the sight of someone's badly mashed wrist would put you out of commission, you'll be of little help to your partner even if you can reach radio assistance.

The one weakness of the course we took was the lack of suggestions on how to prevent illness or injuries. From our own experience we've learned that most of the serious injuries on board sailing boats can be avoided by eliminating potentially dangerous gear, such as wire, reel halyard winches, cross cockpit mainsheet travelors and un-vanged booms. But Dr. Kingston assumed that by the time a sailor has decided to set off on a voyage he has already learned about safety, and the course time could be put to better use discussing the best ways to use the medicines you could carry on board.

After we'd taken the emergency survey course we were left with four basic questions: Who should take it? Is it worth the cost? Is it enough? And finally, how can you be sure a course you'll take from another doctor will satisfy your needs as a cruising sailor?

The first three questions all depend on considering the odds. If you are a new cruising sailor setting off to wet your toes and test the water for six months or a year, the odds are that you'll encounter no medical emergencies worth mentioning while you are out of reach of competent doctors. You would probably make better use of the $500 per couple tuition plus travel costs by buying a storm trysail or taking a shake down cruise to practice your sailing skills. Even for people who plan to cruise for two or three years, exploring the bays of Mexico or gunkholing along the Caribbean's windswept island chain, the odds are that a carefully selected medical guide, a well-thought out kit and a Red Cross first-aid course will probably serve your purposes quite well. It's when your cruise lasts longer than a year and you are likely to spend three or four months of each year on passages or in isolated areas where doctors are unavailable that the odds turn against you.

If we had children, extra crew or a person with special medical needs, on board for a voyage of over a year I'd once again feel the odds begin to tilt toward encountering an emergency or illness that required treatment on board. In this situation I think I would like to combine a Red Cross first-aid course for at least two members of the crew with a more advanced emergency medical class and participation in a ham network doctors assistance program.

No class can prepare you for all of the emergencies your imagination can find to worry about. But any first-aid training will help you cope with the emotional stress of being alone with an emergency. By knowing the most logical steps to take to bring the emergency under control, you gain the time you need to find further assistance, either through books, the radio or by reaching land.

Life afloat is amazingly healthy. As we look back over more than twenty-one years of racing, cruising, charter work and delivery work, and review the accidents and illnesses encountered by our sailing friends, we find that most occurred on race boats or onshore in towns or cities where sea-tuned cruisers forgot the dangers of motorized traffic. In both situations help is usually available. The most serious injuries we have heard of at sea, on a cruising boat or during deliveries, have been leg or arm fractures or burns, and these are well covered in the first-aid courses offered by the Red Cross and in the course we took.

The question of cost is relative. If you must decide between this type of medical course and an anchor windlass, you'd be wiser to choose the gear your boat needs to make it and you safer and settle for the two Red Cross first-aid courses which cost $7 per person. On the other hand, if a $75 evening out once or twice a month doesn't destroy your budget, by all means take an emergency medical course, after you've taken the preliminary first-aid courses.

The final question—are all courses offered by all doctors the same—must be answered by a definite no. They can't be. In fact the nurse supervising the practical session of our course said the attitude of the students in each of the ten seminars she'd worked with determined how much could be taught. "The enthusiastic groups like this one get us excited and we do a more detailed job," Mary said. A look at the course outline and the credentials of the doctor who is in charge can give you a good idea of whether the course you are looking at will suit your purposes. Does the doctor offering the course know what would most likely be of concern to the yachtsman, does he consider the special circumstances you'll have to work under? An emergency room specialist would probably offer a better course than a heart specialist, a doctor who had been sailing would be more likely to relate to your situation. A doctor who has previous teaching experience is more likely to be able to organize a course so it progresses logically. Final aspects to consider when taking a course are the visual and study aids used. Drawings, charts, and slides where shown during almost half of the lectures we attended, they were keyed to the instruction book we took home. Medical supplies and instruments such as we would eventually carry on board were available to use and handle so that each of us could practice taking vital signs at least six times during the three-day course.

A few months after we'd completed our course, we went out for a day race with a friend on his 55-footer. The clew on the genoa needed an emergency repair early in the day. Larry used the skills he'd acquired during four months of work in an English sail loft and had it ready to use within twenty minutes. Late in the day a crew man who had had a bit too much to drink, fell and dislocated a finger. I used my basic first-aid training and what we'd learned in the course to handle that situation until we reached shore. That day put the emergency medical course lessons in perspective. They are like anything you can learn to broaden your skills as a sailor. Like mechanical repair skills, sailmaking skills, maintenance skills, or seamanship lessons—every time you learn more about caring for your vessel, your crew, or the body you live in you swing the odds more in your favor.

To find an emergency medical course to fit your needs check in the classified sections of your favorite sailing magazine or contact Health on the Water, Inc., P.O. Box 24, Bar Harbor, Maine, 04669 or Emergency and Safety Progress, P.O. Box 161412, Miami, Florida, 33116, or of course, Bob Kingston. These courses seem to be available if enough people are interested, if not, you may have to travel some distance to attend one.

6

Medical and Boat Insurance for Offshore Cruising

We carried no health insurance during our cruising years on board *Seraffyn* nor during the time we spent building *Taleisin*. Instead we kept a $3,000 emergency fund which fortunately we never had to touch. But as we listened to talk of rising medical costs and heard news reports of personal financial disasters caused by health problems, we began to reconsider insurance for our next cruise. After all, we were past those normally healthy young years and into the more dangerous middle-age zone where we can expect some maintenance problems. So we began a search for an affordable plan that would cover us as we cruised beyond American waters.

Our search proved more difficult than we expected. The best plans we found had some worrisome if, and, and buts. The most affordable, a Blue Shield plan, required a $2,000 deductible* per year to cut the premium below $1,000 a year. Furthermore, the coverage did not apply to transportation from a foreign country back to the United States nor

*Deductible is the American term for what British firms call excess.

did it cover costs other than initial emergency treatment in any foreign hospital facilities. The only way to cover "trips," as the broker explained, was with separate riders added to this policy at an additional cost for each two weeks, for periods of no more than two months in any one year.

The fine print plus the idea of spending two months' cruising funds each year "just in case," made us sit back and reconsider our previous medical history. We'd enjoyed pretty normal health during our stays ashore in foreign countries, an eye injury from working in a sail loft, a broken leg while day sailing in Canada, pneumonia and amoebic dysentery during a work period in Costa Rica, an allergic reaction in Portugal. In each case we were able to find excellent medical assistance even though translation problems often added a bit of confusion to the situation. As we reviewed those flat tires in our lives we began to realize why we'd never thought of buying health insurance while we cruised. In every case, the cost of fine medical care was less than one third of similar costs in the United States. The complete costs for an emergency hospital visit to x-ray a broken leg, bandages, three follow-up visits plus crutches in Canada during 1979 was less than $100. A friend's stay in a Mexican hospital during the spring of 1983 for a malarial attack cost $5.00 a day, the doctor charged $3.00 a visit. To this realization we added two other facts: first, we would be eliminating the largest single cause of accidents in the United States when we sold our pick-up truck to go sailing; and second, we'd be eliminating another potential health hazard when we closed down our boat yard, sold our house and simplified our life again. No longer would we have the constant nagging tensions of shore-based modern American life, an irritant some doctors claim is the root cause of fifty percent of the medical problems they treat. So instead of paying $1,000 a year in premiums and keeping aside $2,000 to pay the deductible expenses plus $1,000 for air fares to return to an American hospital, we decided to put $3,000 into an easily accessible, interest bearing investment and add $1,000 per year as we cruised. Then we would not only be insuring ourselves, but if illness interrupted our cruising, we'd be more inclined to search for the best medical care offered in the country we were visiting, instead of abandoning our boat and our cruise when it might not have been necessary. It's been almost three years since we set off on *Taleisin* and we are still comfortable with this decision. Better yet, our fund has been growing well ahead of inflation, because of the interest it is collecting and compounding.

We've had a few of the middle-aged sailors' medical problems as we voyaged around Mexico and the South Pacific, but again are reassured by the lower costs and fine treatment we've received. Larry had an eye infection diagnosed and glasses prescribed by a gentle, Spanish-trained, Mexican opthamologist for a total cost of $125 including reading glasses. An ear infection, picked up from diving in French Polynesia, was cured by a French doctor in Papeete for under $50 including medication and a kit to prevent further "diver's ear" problems.

But remember, our reluctance to pay health insurance premiums is a personal one based on our own health histories. Each family or couple who plans to set off should review their past medical costs and consider their financial resources, the earning ability of each of the permanent crew members should a prolonged illness incapacitate someone on board, plus the area in which you plan to cruise. If your cruising grounds are mostly around the U.S., you may feel far more inclined to carry insurance than if you plan to spend much of the year around a place like New Zealand where a visit to the doctor costs just $8.00. If you do decide to buy medical insurance, talk to representatives of several insurance plans. The important questions to ask beyond those mentioned before are, what documentation is necessary to prove foreign hospital or medical costs, and how long will repayment take if you cover the costs from your own funds? Few foreign facilities will accept your insurance company card as proof of payment. You will have to cover costs and file for reimbursement, so check into these procedures before you consider a particular medical plan.

BOAT INSURANCE

If you are thinking of insuring your boat for offshore voyaging, many of the same questions have to be considered. Is it affordable? Does it cover the problems you'll most likely encounter? Should you self-insure?

The growing popularity of offshore voyaging has had one interesting side effect. It has decreased the cost of offshore cruising insurance for experienced sailors by as much as 400 percent. In 1968 when we set off on *Seraffyn*, the brokers searched their files for a policy to cover our proposed wandering. In spite of having a brand new, well-equipped boat, in spite of Larry's previous good sailing record, the lowest premium rate offered was approximately eight or nine percent of the value we wished to place on the boat and then we would only be covered for total loss, not repairable damage. *Seraffyn* had cost us approximately $8,000 in material plus our labor and her estimated replacement value was around $28,000. We found we spent an average of $250 a month to live and cruise through Mexico that year. So if we had bought insurance, we'd have been paying $200 per month, this would have almost doubled our cruising costs. We spoke to a lot of other cruising sailors about this question as we wandered on *Seraffyn* and found only one full-time cruiser who carried insurance for a boat under 40 feet. We'd occasionally meet people on a six month or one year cruise who were able to get a rider attached to their regular insurance for a reasonable sum, but they had to specify their cruising itinerary in advance and stick to that plan or call and inform their brokers of any changes. They were restricted to areas they could visit and seasons they could sail in.

So we voyaged for eleven years uninsured and our worst problems with the boat was a broken boomkin caused by a careless Spanish power-boater. That made us feel very much like we'd beaten some invisible odds maker. Instead of working three months a year to earn enough extra to insure the boat, we'd been free to roam and explore and technically had saved $2,000 a year.

Maybe it was the conservatism that comes as you grow older, or maybe it was the shock of seeing 27 cruising boats stranded and wrecked on the beach at Cabo San Lucas in late 1982 (see Section VI), but as *Taleisin* grew closer to completion, we began looking at insurance. Things have changed dramatically since 1968. Some people say it is because people are financing boats for cruising and the banks are demanding coverage, others say it is because many more boat owners are buying insurance so the risk is more widely spread, but now insurance policies with only a five percent deductible (you pay the first five percent of any damages in any accident) are available from companies like Lloyds of London for just over 1.5 percent of the boat's insured value. This covers ocean passages to almost any place that is not in a war zone. It covers boat equipment spars and sails but not gear failure due to wear. This rate is based on the owner's experience as estimated by the broker, on the condition and construction of the insured boat and the intended goal of the cruise on a yearly basis. To get this rate we'd still have to provide an approximate itinerary and inform our broker of major plan changes. But, "We'll be in Mexico for five or six months then sail for the Marquesas" was, we were told, enough of a plan to secure this rate. We almost jumped at what seemed like an unbelievably low rate until we began looking at the replacement cost of *Taleisin*. Inflation and our own more demanding specifications, plus her larger size drove material costs to an amazing $40,000. Our labor costs are hard to value. But total replacement to the same quality was estimated so high if we sat back and let an American or European boatyard do it, that to insure her properly would have cost close to $2,000 per year. Then because of the five percent deductible, any losses would have to be paid by us until they reached over $7,000. That combined $9,000 figure set us thinking back over the type of accidents that we knew happened to offshore cruising boats.

The most worrisome accident of all is for your boat to founder at sea. We knew of only two such losses among our friends other than those who sailed singlehanded and/or in multi-hulls. In one case our friends, sailors who said they never kept a watch once they cleared the coast by 200 miles, were lost with their boat. In the second case, our friend's boat was over 30 years old and would have been hard to insure. He hit a log, holed the boat and had to sail his tender the last 200 miles to land. In the first case the insurance money would have done us little good. In the second case the owner would have had little chance of having insurance, and possibly the age and condition of the vessel contributed to her loss. We'd have a new boat under us, with fine new equipment and the memory of the thousands of hours we'd worked to build her. This we felt would make us more eager to keep watches and anchor with care.

Non-total loss situations came under our careful scrutiny. As we remembered the people struggling to salvage and rebuild their boats after the Cabo storm, we reminded ourselves that at least eleven boats pulled up anchor and left for the safety of the open sea that night. Another two dozen boats were able to remain safely at anchor because they'd used more discretion in their choice of gear or position or just because they had luck on their side. Although some of these boats suffered damage, repairs cost far less than five percent of their boats value.

This set us thinking about the other side of the insurance and sailing coin. Could it be that asking someone else to protect us in the form of guaranteed money if me made a mistake in seamanship, would allow us to relax that extra little bit and actually cause us to make mistakes? We've heard this question posed by many cruising sailors who cover many more miles than we do and the answer always seems the same. "If my boat gets damaged I'll still have to do all the work to fix it. So I might as well save the premiums to buy better ground tackle." This was a sentiment repeated by many sailors we have met.

So in the end, our boat insurance choices changed right back to those we'd had with *Seraffyn*. We kept her insured while she was under construction and unmovable. With *Taleisin* it was the same. Forest fires, unexpected storms and floods are disasters we couldn't plan against as she stood immobile in her building shed. So she was insured. Careless drivers on California's freeways could and almost did create an accident as she was moved along the 60 miles of highway between her boat shed and the shipyard where she was launched. Our own inexperience with a new boat could possibly cause accidents that would damage other peoples' boats as we did our seatrials. So our builder's insurance policy was extended to cover the first three months of *Taleisin*'s life afloat. But

FIGURE 6.1 *Taleisin* was fully insured while she was under construction and when she was being shipped overland. Here she is being taken off the truck at Lido Shipyard, Newport Beach, California.

once she became a cruising boat and we headed offshore we reverted back to our own skills to protect our home and our major investment. Then we added another $2,000 a year to our self-insurance fund, hoping it would gather interest and cover that future accident. We set a $1,000 deductible on our insurance fund, excluding labor, since we still expected to do that ourselves. Two years after we set sail we had our first major loss in twenty years of voyaging and delivering boats. We lost our lapper (no. 2 genoa). Replacing that jib cost one hundred dollars less than our self-imposed deductible. So our boat insurance fund is growing along with our medical insurance fund.

Of course not every one has the skills to rebuild his own boat or repair someone else's boat as we would have to do if an accident occurred, so some type of boat insurance could make the difference between losing a whole life style or setting off again. If your boat represents almost all you own in the world, it might also be a good idea to remain insured as you cruise, especially until you gain sailing confidence and navigating experience and can evaluate your own insurance needs. I remember one very sad couple whom I met at Cabo San Lucas who had sold everything they owned and set sail uninsured with their last few thousand dollars on board in cash. They were in their fifties and the loss of their boat put them back to the same financial position they had been in when they were both only 25 years old. If your boat is over 45-feet long, insurance might be a wise investment for two reasons. First, it is much more possible to do serious damage to other vessels with a larger cruising boat than it is with one only 28- to 32-feet long, so third party insurance might be quite important some day. And second, the total loss of a $200,000 yacht could be much more financially devastating than the loss of even a $60,000 yacht.

To cut your voyaging insurance costs, consider either a higher deductible or look into harbor and coastal insurance coverage only. Some companies will reduce your premiums considerably if you, in effect, cancel your insurance once you are 150 miles offshore and only reinstate it once you are again close the land. The reason the insurers are willing to lower the rates is that a large portion of casualty payments comes from the cost of long distance towing if a salvage vessel must be called in. Insurance payouts are much lower if accidents happen closer to port. We feel this is a reasonable gamble to take since only about two percent of all insured boats file accident reports during any one year of cruising or sailing locally, according to two brokers we spoke to, and less than a tenth of a percent of these boats are damaged by accidents that happen more than ten miles offshore.

If instead you decide as we did to start your own insurance fund, you can offer far more comprehensive coverage than any commercial company. Your fund can cover not only boat repairs, health emergencies and flights back home to be with your family during their health emergencies, but if you never have to use it, the money you save could someday be used to build the next cruising boat or start the next phase of your life. To keep this fund separated from your cruising kitty and to make your yearly payments even though they are to yourself, requires discipline. But that's probably one of the main traits that got you out of the normal shorebound life and off for a cruising adventure in the first place.

SECTION II

Choosing the Gear to Go Cruising

Once you've bought or built a new boat, or decided to update the boat you already own to go cruising, your ability to look at each piece of equipment, each sailing system you want to modify or install through the eyes of a seaman will be constantly tested. Ideas and gear that look great in the marine store might not work well in the harsh salt-air environment that lies ahead. Rigs that look beautiful on a cruise up the bay to your permanent mooring might be beyond your crew's capabilities as you try to maneuver in a strange, coral-strewn harbor during a sudden rain squall.

The decisions you make as you outfit and personalize your boat must each be carefully considered without letting your landsman's values interfere. The first chapter in this section gives some guidelines to help you make your choices. The later chapters show how complex each decision can be and how we came to make some of the major outfitting choices that have worked well for us.

7
Buying the Gear to Go Cruising

There are few sailors, ourselves included, who couldn't make up a page-long list of "I'd like to have's" after wandering through a well stocked chandlery or reading a marine catalogue. As we cruise we are invited on board other boats and almost always come back to *Taleisin* saying something like, "Did you see those great fair leads? They'd work perfectly here. Did you hear the quality of the sound on their compact lazer disc player? We could install one there."

The desire to acquire new gear, to add to your pleasures by purchasing yet another item, is thoroughly American. But it must be controlled. It could be what is tying you to the nine-to-five, work, buy, work, buy, syndrome. The lack of cash this buying syndrome causes will stop you from ever going cruising. Even more important, (as you will see from our chapter on solar stills) purchases that are not considered carefully, inspected, researched and custom planned for your boat and your cruising life style could actually leave you unsafe in an emergency.

Although Thoreau once said, "Most men go through life dragging their furniture behind them," even he at times found he desired and needed tools and a few home comforts. It was easier for him, to control his impulse to buy than it is for us and our sailing friends today, there

was much less available "off the shelf" in his day, and far fewer catalogues and consumer magazines offering tempting tidbits.

So, to keep not only our budget but our boat's waterline in sight, we've
had to re-think the purchasing patterns we learned before cruising became our dream. We had to learn ways to make sure we purchased only
the gear we absolutely needed, gear that was well suited, long lasting and
well priced. The rules we learned, sometimes the hard way, might help
you along your path to adventure.

I remember the first marine store we walked into in Falmouth after
our voyage across the Atlantic. We hadn't been near a chandlery for six
months. Our pile of five months' worth of mail contained a check worth
over a month's cruising funds, the chandlery prices seemed low after
American prices. We spent half of that check on ten items. Seven of
them never got used on *Seraffyn*, they lay in a might-come-in-handy box
in the lazzerette until we eventually gave or traded them away. That was
when we declared a new regime. Keep a shopping list of gear for the
boat, the galley, and for our personal gear. Don't buy anything the first
time you see it unless it is on the list, excepting toiletries, food and
magazines or items under $5. When we are away from shops of any kind
for four or five months we don't carry more than $40 with us that first
day ashore to help us stick to the list resolve. If we do see some wondrous
item we think we can't live without, we wait until we go back to the
boat, if it is still a memorable need, we add it to the list.

Once an item actually gets on the list, if it will cost over half a week's
cruising funds, we don't buy it until we have researched the item
thoroughly, checking not only quality, suitability and prices, but questioning our need for it as well. This is often the most enjoyable part of
the purchase. We now have an excuse to prowl the new and secondhand
shops, to discuss the item with other owners.

Getting information as you do your research can be difficult. I remember the problems we had getting dependable information for three
purchases in particular as we cruised, our stereo for *Taleisin*, our folding
bicycles, and a simple short wave radio receiver. They were all on our
list for a long time, we had conflicting advice from individual users, but
finally sorted it out by visiting repair shops and talking to the people who
maintain these items professionally. The stereo repair man in Newport
Beach had several good recommendations when we told him our price
range. He said, "The Sanyos would suit you best. The ones that come

in for servicing off boats don't ever have any rust in them. Every other brand in that price range does." Try to find a nonfactory affiliated repair person to talk with. But if only factory repair people are available, ask for their maintenance recommendation, what spare parts you should carry, problems he's seen that make units come back for servicing. You'll be able to tell from his attitude whether he is a salesman in disguise or a person who is giving you semi-unbiased information.

A second source of good information comes from consumer testing agencies and publications if you are buying a non-marine item that is sold in large quantities, such as electronic gear. But remember, they do their testing based on shore side home use, not offshore cruising use. A third is people who have used various brands of the item you want, but do not own it. Good information can be gained by comparing products at boat shows or, as we did for our folding bicycles, at a bicycle dealer's show case. The three least dependable research sources are magazine articles which show overviews of what is available without testing or giving pros and cons of each available brand, people who now own the brand they are recommending, and finally, advertisers.

Magazine editors are caught in a quandary. They'd like to come flat out and say, this is good, this is bad. But unless they have funds to do complete tests, this information could be just opinion. Editors and magazine publishers must always be aware of the threat of lawsuits. Even if their disparagement of a particular piece of gear is proven correct in a court case, they will have had to spend time and large amounts of money defending their position. Finally, they'll probably lose the advertising funds that keep them able to produce a magazine at a reasonable price if they are too negative toward equipment and boat manufacturers. Good editors try to overcome these problems by taking every chance they can to praise high quality items, give clear-cut examples of how and why a piece of gear failed, yet praise its good points or show how the owner was partially responsible for the failure. And finally, we know a few editors who simply refuse to review boats, equipment, and books they feel are inferior. "It's better to say nothing at all, than to be too negative," one of these editors told us.

At present the market for most marine equipment is too small to support a well-financed, gear-testing publication. *The Practical Sailor,* a small publication that tries to evaluate gear without the restrictions of being advertiser-supported, can only evaluate as much equipment as they can afford to purchase or gear that is donated by manufacturers. They cannot pay people to do full-time, in-depth studies of boats, or equipment. So opinions often creep into their otherwise helpful reports. I'm in no way saying magazines are giving poor consumer advice, only that they should not be your main or only source of advice. (Books can be a less biased source of information than magazines in one way: the writers do not have to worry about the sensibilities of advertisers or editors, and so can make candid judgments in print, as long as they avoid libelous statements. But, they can also state opinions as often and strongly as they want. So look for careful research, and decide if the author's biases and experiences give him a good basis for his conclusions before you put too much weight on his ideas.)

Advice from people who tell you the brand they now own is the only, the best, you'd be crazy to buy another should have their information discounted a bit. We've found they are often unaware that their choice suits their needs, but might not suit yours. We've been shopping for a new shortwave radio receiver for about two years. At least a dozen people tried to convince us the one they had was the best, (three of these people offered to sell us their radio discounted because they now want a fancier, or newer model. This did make us suspicious.) Finally we met Harry, an American radio specialist cruising on his 45-foot sloop *Whale Song.* "Let me think about that for a while," he said after questioning us thoroughly on our power source (none), our budget and needs. It was four days later when he said, "I looked through my catalogues, thought about it for a while. The Kenwood R-600 would suit your needs." He owned a completely different brand of ham and receiving equipment. He hadn't suggested a radio with one feature more than our absolute minimal needs. Therefore we gave his suggestions and his reasons, a lot of thought and after further research, decided to order this radio. (Unfortunately, when we finally placed our order, the model was discontinued so we are back to square one.)

When you've done your research, try one last time to talk yourself out of buying any expensive items unless you have a large budget and are already afloat and outfitted and ready to go. Look at the list of priorities for safe voyaging in our book *The Self-Sufficient Sailor.* If the item isn't on the list, if there are other items on that list you still need, remember anything you buy beyond the basic necessities could keep you from leaving, or having enough funds when you do.

We know of one couple who chose a fine boat, outfitted it well, then ·
kept finding items they thought would make cruising easier, more comfortable. During the six months before they set sail they spent $14,000
on a word processor, electronic navigation aids, fine china, matching
sleeping bags and sheets. When they set off their cruising kitty was down
to $5,000. The money they hoped to earn with the word processors (they
were both free-lance writers) didn't come through and they had to spend
eight months of their planned year of cruising, working for funds to pay
boat insurance and boat mortgages totaling $700 a month. To add insult
to injury, the word processor's memory failed and lost half the manuscript for a new book. Three of the electronic navigation aids malfunc-
tioned and the replacement of the alternator which kept everything
working cost another $1,000, since they felt, as most of us do, if we have
it on board, it has to be useable. These people may sound like an extreme
example, but from our observations they are only a bit past the norm.
*The urge to have the best, the latest, and every possible convenience, can
be very hard to resist.*

A trap people who are building a boat to go cruising often fall into,
is buying a piece of equipment for "when we move on board," even
though the money spent this way could be more useful sitting in the
cruising kitty. We know it is fun to fondle, play with, and even use these
eventual fitting out items when boat building seems so slow and cruising
so far away. But we have seen the purchase of a ham radio grow into
the installation of a full-on ham station that eventually became a stum-
bling block for the whole boat-building project. Not only did the $2,500
reappropriation from the more urgently needed materials fund bring the
boat building to a halt, the time spent talking to ham contacts was stolen
from the boring hours of finish work the boat needed, until the boat-
building project was finally forgotten.

Electronics gear is the most frequent culprit in this steal-your-cruis-
ing-funds assault. Other than a reliable dry-cell battery operated short
wave radio receiver, none of it is absolutely necessary. It is also the worst
possible equipment investment you can make. The secondhand market
for electronics gear is constantly being undermined by companies introducing newer models, by advances in equipment design or function, by
an overabundance of secondhand equipment and by the discount selling
of new equipment in foreign duty-free centers. One sailor offered us his
ICOM radio receiver at half of what he'd paid for it in the United States

eight months previously. Tongan friends contacted the duty-free agent in Fiji and found we could buy the same unit brand new, for 5 percent less than his half-price offer.

Another skilled ham operator told us "don't buy any used electronic equipment that has been on board a cruising boat unless you can take it to a good service depot for full testing. Voltage variations and salt air might have caused deterioration." He said this is especially true of any Ham equipment since it is only designed for shore side installation, it is not built to withstand the rigors of a marine environment.

Several repair men advised us to buy individual units to do each electronic function, and not to buy multi-purpose units. If you lose one function on these units, you may lose them all. When we interviewed the Sat-Nav repair men in Papeete, Samoa and then New Zealand to find the success/failure rate of these magic units, each said, the simpler the unit, the fewer bells and whistles, the less prone to failure it is. The same can be said of mechanical devices from your main engine, to your outboard motor.

A final comment on buying electronic gear is not to buy the fanciest gear there is, but buy the gear that is good enough to fulfill your purpose. When we were shopping for our stereo we asked the repair man, what type of speakers do we need. He sent us to a huge stereo outlet store that had boards full of different speakers mounted and ready to hear. We listened to $29 speakers, we listened to $300 speakers, we found we could hear little improvement in sound when we went past $49. So that is what we purchased in spite of the urging of our more electronically oriented friends. To this day three years later, we are delighted with the reliability and the sound our $130 total investment stereo unit puts out.

If your shopping list has nonelectronic gear on it there are several pointers we can give you based on our 95 percent thorough satisfaction ratio, as opposed to our fifty-fifty ratio with electronics. First and foremost, before you buy any gear, try a mock-up on board. Make a plywood or cardboard pattern of the gear, then take it on board and see if it fits, note what will have to be changed to accommodate the new gear, and if it will do the job well.

Remember that boat gear gets exceptionally hard use, so look for metals that will withstand time, abuse, and saltwater immersion. Bronze is always our first choice. It does not tend to work harden, it is malleable, it turns a particular shade of green we find acceptable so we don't have

to polish it. Stainless steel would be second. Because it is more prone
to work hardening, be careful if you use it where it is in a constantly
moving or flexing situation. Although metalurgist friends of ours have
told us using a magnet while we shop will not guarantee the stainless
fittings we buy are of higher quality alloys just because our magnet
doesn't stick to them, they did agree that those fittings that had the least
magnetic attraction would stain or bleed rust less (it is only stainless not
stain proof.) The reasons for this vary from better, more weather resistant alloys to better electro-polishing and pacifying. Avoid aluminum
wherever possible for deck hardware; regular washings down with salt
water will corrode alloy fittings no matter how well anodized they are.
In the case of fittings like windvane gears, be sure you take each piece
apart, then reassemble every part and bolt with waterproof grease protecting the joints to minimize what we call the white madness. Otherwise the aluminum corrosion could cause swelling and expansion that,
if left uncontrolled, can actually cause cracking in the cast parts. Some
joints will be impossible to separate if they are left unprotected for too
long. The manufacturers of the new, fold-up model aries wind vane have
boiled the cast alloy parts in oil to control this corrosion.

One way to find long-lasting, dependable equipment is to look for gear
that has been used on an active, older boat. If after twenty years that
gear is still in good condition, if the same company is still offering a
basically unchanged unit, put it at the top of your prospective fitting list.
That company probably stayed in business because they offered a good
product, good service, or both. Two items come to mind immediately
as I write this, our Edson bronze, pump-a-gallon-a-stroke bilge pump and
our Merriman bronze boom castings (the gooseneck and outhaul
fittings.) Tried, true and perfect for the job we asked them to do, we
sailed with them on boats that were twenty years old, twenty years ago.
Least you think we are saying, don't buy new, let me assure you that we
are presently testing the newest in cruising sail cloth on *Taleisin,* a mylar
reinforced dacron laminated jib (two layers of dacron with a mylar core).
Only after it proves itself for two or three years would we have all our
working sails from an experimental cloth. The same goes for any equipment we buy that is essential to the sailing safety of the boat. Be
conservative when you are shopping for any newly designed gear which
must keep working in extreme weather conditions.

Once you've learned to ruthlessly control your urge to buy what you see as soon as you see it, you'll find some of the joys of this simpler life style. Careful, limited, I-can-live-without-it shopping let's you buy the very best of anything you do finally purchase. If you are like us you will sit back and savour each separate acquisition, secure that it will give you few future disappointments because you know you have done your homework. If your research convinces you to cross an item off your list, you'll have the pleasure of watching the money you left in the bank increase as interest compounds instead of the hassel of trying to fix broken down gear that ends up with little resale value. Then if your non-spending program works, you'll either go cruising sooner, need to work for freedom chips less often or have some extra funds to spend for dinners on shore, to rent transportation or buy some special long lasting momentos of your cruise. In our case, we had used the money we saved to build up a small collection of affordable original art work and signed, numbered prints as we cruise. The dozen we bought during our voyage on *Seraffyn* were used to adorn our cottage while we built *Taleisin*. These lasting treasures gave us and our guests ten times the pleasure of any thing we might have missed by curbing our impulse buying.

8

Positive Flotation— Is It an Option for Ballasted Boats?

Seraffyn sat safely at her mooring in Newport Beach after eleven years of cruising while we read of a far less fortunate vessel. *Spirit,* a 40-foot ketch, had hit a submerged object late at night while she close reached at six knots, headed home from Hawaii toward San Francisco. As the badly holed ketch began sinking, her crew split up. Half climbed into a life raft and half into an inflatable dinghy. In the confusion of abandoning ship, the emergency pack was either lost overboard or left behind. Four days later the first raft was found, the next day the other was located. Half of the crew had died due to exposure, shock or dehydration. That article brought to the forefront a fear almost every sailor harbors in the nether regions of his mind. Any ballasted boat, any boat with heavy engines, lives only a hole away from sinking, and sinking means abandoning ship and climbing into flimsy dinghies or rafts with the most minimal of survival equipment. We think this fear, more than the quest for speed, may be the reason some people have chosen catamarans and trimarans. For even if these boats are holed or capsize, their nonballasted, foam or wood cored construction should keep them floating.

Less than a week after we read of *Spirit*'s demise, a friend in England sent us a page of a French yachting magazine that offered a new way of assuaging this age-old fear. A major French inflatable equipment company was introducing a system of CO_2 bags that fit under berth cushions or floor boards so that in the case of a capsize or holing, all you had to do was pull a rip cord and 30 seconds later your boat became unsinkable, its life raft inside instead of outside. This idea intrigued us. The advantages seemed obvious. If you could keep your whole boat afloat until assistance arrived, you had all of your supplies around you. Better yet, since the boat flotation would give you time to find the cause of the leak and very possibly time to effect temporary repairs, you could continue sailing and save your boat and its equipment. This idea seemed like a big plus for people like us who sail offshore and find insurance costs more than we can afford. By adding boat flotation we'd in effect be paying a one-time insurance premium and getting something we could pump up occasionally and caress, something we could actually see, not just a piece of paper issued by some unseen company, promising us we could collect some money if we lived to claim it. The idea definitely appealed to our prevention, not cure, philosophy. So as we worked building *Taleisin*, we began researching the idea of positive flotation, writing to our network of cruising friends and manufacturers, and our file slowly began to grow.

Donald Street, who has sold marine insurance as he sailed the Atlantic and Caribbean over the past 22 years wrote to us, "Maybe if people weren't afraid of their boat sinking, they'd stick with it until the last second. Do you know that the insurance companies have documented dozens of cases of sail boats abandoned by their crew, life rafts gone; the yachts have water in them but they are still afloat. We rarely find the crew or life raft." We added this to our list of pluses as we began to learn about other types of boat flotation which were beginning to be more frequently discussed, as manufacturers and magazine editors became worried about the loss of life during the Fastnet Race disaster. The flotation bags were the newest systems being discussed. Watertight bulkheads and double bottoms had been touted since the days of the

Titanic and we found that foam, both molded into hulls or packed into lockers, had been used by various boat manufacturers in the U.S. and Europe for almost twenty years.

The more we researched, the more the problem began to resemble that found by people who begin to look at life insurance policies. Each option has its pros and cons, each option can only be fully appraised in the final analysis. Fortunately for insurance buyers, there are legal guidelines, legal advisers to help narrow and explain your options. With flotation systems, it's your own research and the calculations of your boat builder that you must count on to insure your boat and life.

The first and simplest part of the whole question is, how much flotation must I have to keep a boat buoyant if it is holed? The calculations to reach this figure are simple but time consuming, since you must know the weight of the materials that comprise your boat in its "at sea" condition. Since salt water weighs 64 pounds per cubic foot, anything that weighs less per cubic foot will float by itself; anything that weighs more will need assistance to keep from sinking. Fresh water weighs 62.4 pounds per cubic foot, so in your calculations you can count on each gallon you carry assisting just a tiny bit. The average foam, single berth cushion will add 60 pounds of buoyancy per inch of thickness, if the foam is a closed cell type or is sealed in plastic, and if the cushions are secured in place so they are kept below deck level in the event of flooding. If they are free to float up into the cabin top cavity, their potential lifting power comes into play too late to be useful. So if, like on *Taleisin,* you have cushions that are four inches thick and the equivalent of five and a half single berths, that's 1400 pounds of positive buoyancy. Wooden interior joinery has positive flotation, food stores are usually close to neutral, engines are negative, but the biggest negative factor is ballast.

Taleisin's 6,200 pounds of lead ballast at 710 pounds per cubic foot requires 5,642 pounds of positive flotation to keep it at the surface of the sea. (6,200 pounds of lead equal 8.73 cubic feet at 712 pounds per cube, less 64 or the weight of a cubic foot of saltwater per cube, or 558 pounds to equal 5,642.) If your boat has a glass hull instead of wood it will require more positive buoyancy. A foam or balsa cored glass hull would fall somewhere in the middle, depending on the volumn of glass to the volume of cored material. The Olson 30, a super light dis-

Taleisin's basic flotation calculations for buoyancy bags. Salt water weighs 64 pounds per cubic foot. Anything that weighs less is a positive flotation factor, anything that weighs more is a negative factor.

Positive flotation factors:

Hull buoyancy due to wood construction, 166 cubic feet of teak at 48 pounds per cube for an average reserve buoyancy of 15 pounds per cubic foot	2490
Cushions (plastic sealed) or closed cell at 60 pounds lift per inch of thickness (see text)	1400
Water tanks empty 10.6 cubic feet	667
Ice chest insulation—foam, four cubic feet	240
Total positive factor	4797

Neutral buoyancy:

Food stores (these tend to average out at neutral because fruit and vegetables float, noodles float, plastic containers float; these offset bottles and canned stores which have negative buoyancy)

Books

Fresh water

Sails

Negative buoyancy items:

Lead keel	6200
Cooking stove and heating stove	90
Deck structure	1500
Fastenings, bronze strapping and floors, rigging wires and deck hardware	1000
Anchor equipment	860
Spare parts and tools	1000
Spars	500
Total negative factor	11,150
Positive factor subtract	4797
Basic flotation necessary	6353
25% safety factor	1588

Extra flotation necessary to keep *Taleisin* up while we repair her or wait for assistance computed the long way	7941

Manufacturer's recommendation:

Ballast 6200 pounds plus 25% safety factor or 7,755 pounds of added buoyancy. This divided by 62 pounds means we should have 125 cubic feet of buoyancy bags or foam, using the shorter computation method.

placement hull, has positive buoyancy if you eliminate the keel weight.

All of the companies we contacted who offer flotation systems, simplify this process for their initial calculations, by figuring that a formula of 1 to 1.6 covers minimum flotation requirements for glass hulls with up to 35 percent lead ballast. In other words, for every 1.6 tons of displacement, you will need a minimum of 1 ton of added buoyancy to keep even with the surface of the water. They then recommend a 25 percent safety margin which brings their figure to 1.25 to 1.6. If your boat, fully laden, displaces 18,000 pounds, they recommend adding foam or air bags or air tight compartments that will support 11,500 pounds. For a vessel like ours, which has the buoyancy of a wood hull, the recommendation is to add buoyancy equivalent to the ballast and engine weight plus 25 percent.*

Air bags such as these systems use offer about 63 pounds of lift per cubic foot. Watertight areas offer the same if they are not used for

Weights of some common materials used on boats in pounds per cubic foot.

Aluminium, cast	165	Kerosene	51
Bronze	509	Lead 712	
Cedar	31–35	Mahogany	35
Concrete (cement, stone and sand)	144	Oil, diesel	53
		Potatoes	42
Fiberglass—30% glass, 70% resin	96	Spruce	27
		Steel—structural	490
Fiberglass insulation	3.5	Steel—stainless	500
Fir	32	Styrofoam	1.3
Fir plywood	36	Teak	48
Ice	44	Water—fresh	62.4
Iron, cast	450	Water—salt	64

*It may pay to contact a marine engineer before investing in any flotation system. He can confirm that you are, in fact, going to float if your boat is holed.

storage; foam is usually figured at 62 pounds lift per cubic foot. So to keep a 25-foot glass boat that displaces 6,000 pounds afloat if it is holed, you need 96 cubic feet of buoyancy aid. For an average 18,000 pound 35-foot offshore voyager, you need about 185 cubic feet. This takes a lot of space, and leads to the trickier second problem of adding positive flotation in the proper position in an offshore sailing boat.

As one manufacturer cautioned us, if the flotation is in the wrong place, the flooded boat becomes unstable. "Take a drop keel, light weight beamy boat with an aluminium mast," he said. "If the spar fills with water, it might add just the right amount of weight to keep the boat upside down. That's why I'd recommend stuffing foam inside the mast, and designing the flotation placement to combat this tendency. A boat like your *Taleisin* with its ballast almost like a shoe at the very bottom of the keel, its hollow wooden spar, would always try to float upright no matter where you add buoyancy." To complicate this problem, buoyancy too close to deck level is less effective than buoyancy added near the bilges, since the boat will be allowed to settle lower in the water before the added flotation begins to work. The obvious seeming answer of keeping all buoyancy close to the keel is an over-simplification since you want your boat to be a stable platform if it does fill. To achieve this, the buoyancy must be well spread throughout the depth, length and width of the boat.

With these basic problems in mind, the final questions that must be considered before you assess the pros and cons of different flotation systems, are ones that cannot be answered with mathematical formulas. What circumstances are most likely to cause a boat to fill with water and sink, and how much time will you have to react? Our first worry as offshore voyagers is collision with unmarked objects, either whales, jettisoned truck-sized shipping containers such as might have sunk *Spirit*, concrete docks that have broken their moorings and set off to sea on the tide, trees washed down monsoon-swollen rivers, or even other cruising boats running without lights. This is the hardest type of holing to prevent, even with a careful watch. Fortunately, most collisions with flotsam do not take place during storms. *Spirit's* crew reported winds of 25 knots, the Baileys and Robertsons, both famous survivors of whale collision sinkings, were holed when winds were under 15 knots. This means the odds are, any flotation system that would be able to be put into action within sixty seconds to two minutes would probably be workable for most collision problems.

Offshore boats actually rolling over in a storm and sinking seems to be less of a risk, especially if hatches are well designed and stay in place. Instead, the research we've done in the past three years shows the three most common causes of sailboat sinkings are knockdowns, hitting reefs or rocks and sinking right at anchor, or at the dock when a through hull fitting fails or a marine toilet begins to back syphon. Knockdowns are the biggest threat in the under 28-foot, weekend-type boats, especially those with companionways that open lower than deck level. Any water in the cockpit goes directly into the boat in this situation. We know of two 20-footers that sank instantly less than half a mile off Chicago's waterfront on a sunny Sunday afternoon, when a gust of wind funnelled between two tall buildings and caught the unaware sailors with sheets cleated. An inflation type buoyancy system probably could not have worked quickly enough to solve this problem. On larger boats, the volume of the companionway hatch is rarely much larger than that of the average 28-footer, and the interior volume is much greater. So this quick loss situation is not as much of a worry. These larger boats are more likely to have multiple through hulls that could endanger them when no one is on board to activate an inflation bag system, so an automatic system of some sort becomes important.

Given all these basic parameters, a look at the problems and benefits of each type of buoyancy system will begin to show why there is no simple solution that will work for all boats.

Watertight bulkheads sound like the simplest, least expensive solution, and if you are building a metal boat they may be easy to install. But to retro-fit an existing glass or wood boat is difficult. An efficient watertight bulkhead system requires enough individual flotation compartments so that if any single compartment is holed, the others will support the boat. This means bolt closing hatches, bulkhead doors that seal and can withstand a substantial increase in water pressure. This not only limits your access and ventilation to different parts of the boat, but means more plumbing since each compartment needs its own bilge pump system. In the knockdown with open hatches situation where the boat fills quickly on a nice afternoon sail, or at the dock when no one is on board, this watertight bulkhead system probably won't work because most sailors will not keep their boat sealed and compartmental-ized, except in rough weather at sea. In head-on collisions, watertight bulkheads would be at their most effective. But if a collision produces a long gash down the side of a vessel, and if the gash extends to both sides of the watertight bulkheads, the boat will sink. In other words, if several watertight sections are breached, you are no longer protected.

Closed cell polyurethane foam figured in the design stages and built right into the boat is probably the best flotation system. The French government, which controls and licenses pleasure sailing craft, is so impressed with this system that boats such as those built by the Belgium Etap company can legally carry crew and passengers with no life raft on board. We have seen photographs and results of the tests these boats must be subjected to get an unsinkable rating. Not only must they retain almost half of their original freeboard when flooded, but they are tested in a mast down condition to make sure they prefer to stay upright. Furthermore, a maximum crew (in the case of the Etap 26, four crew of at least 165 pounds each), were required to move to all parts of the flooded boat to test its stability in a fully flooded condition.

The English have followed this lead, producing a 26-foot Sadler, racer-cruiser with the same flotation system. An American company, Wellington Boats, has offered positive buoyancy as an option on their 44- and 57-footer. The cost on the two smaller boats is about five percent of their total value, less than half the cost of a life raft. On the Welling-ton, the cost was about six percent of the base price of the boat. Space loss on the Etap and Sadler was about 15 percent of the storage areas. On the Wellington, the manufacturer estimated the space loss was six percent of the storage areas (not volume). With careful design work, the foam could be worked into less accessible areas such as below tanks and engine mounts, behind deep lockers, and therefore interfere less with the storage that is like a sacred cow to us cruising sailors. It must be remembered that all of the flotation must be added to the hull, as flotation in the deck will not become effective until the decks are awash. If the decks are awash, the boat becomes difficult to pump and salvage, and is no longer the refuge we are seeking.

This built-in foam not only serves as an always working, fail safe flotation system, it also adds insulation and sound deadening to the glass hull, and theoretically, stiffness and impact resistance at the same time. Two insurance brokers we spoke with, said built-in flotation would probably reduce insurance premiums, since total loss claims would be less likely. Does this foam eliminate the need for a life raft? The French government says it does; at the moment the Royal Sailing Association of England and the worldwide IYRU haven't agreed with the French.

On the down side is the obvious problem. Closed cell, molded-in foam cannot be easily added to any boat that has an interior in place. So it is mostly a new boat option. The foam must be protected from abrasion, or it will crumble into dust, so either a liner or ceiling is necessary, so to add a fitting to the hull means putting in compression sleeves or pads for each and every bolt. Furthermore, since this foam will be behind cabinetry and liners where plumbing and wiring usually run, it could make repairs and renovations more difficult. It also adds expense both during tooling and construction. It is highly flammable, more so than solid glass fiber and resins. Urethane foam is also worrisome because it produces cyanide gas when it burns. The final problem with this built-in foam is the mathematical one. If a builder allows a 25 percent safety factor using the displacement figures his designer shows on the plans, what happens when a cruising family actually sets off to sea with a boat that may be laden three to six inches below its design waterline? Throughout our 22 years of voyaging we have found 90 percent of all cruising boats are down on their lines, some are over 25 percent heavier than their original designed displacement. How would, or how much should builders compensate for this very common overloading problem?

Roger MacGregor, owner of MacGregor Marine and a firm advocate of positive buoyancy, has one solution for this problem. During the past twenty years he has built over 20,000 boats, his most popular model being a light weight, trailerable drop keel 21-footer aimed at the cost conscious, first-time boat owner market; his newest, a sophisticated 65-foot line honors racer. All of his boats have styrofoam blocks filling major parts of the areas usually reserved for stores. "In my 65-footer I force people to keep weight out of the ends of the boat by filling them with block foam. It's better for performance. In the smaller boats the foam is behind the cockpit, under the forward bunks, all places where people store junk they rarely use." Of course owners can unscrew the retaining panels and remove the foam, but according to MacGregor, few do. "My wife and I knew our boats were some of the least expensive ones being sold in the American market. We knew they would attract a disproportionate number of first-time buyers, the less experienced sailors. We added buoyancy as a standard item so we could sleep at night, not worry about people losing their lives or boats because of a knock-down."

Roger chose 6- × 6- × 12-inch blocks of styrofoam for several reasons. It is easy for an inexperienced low cost labor force to put into his boats. The foreman orders a certain number of styrofoam blocks from the materials department, and counts as they are added to designated lockers, 1,520 blocks in his 21,000 pound ultra-light 65-footer, 120 blocks in his 21-footer. The workers don't have to mix catalysts, glue, cut or fasten these blocks, they just arrange them inside the various compartments and screw the covers in place. The styrofoam is cheap. MacGregor is the most cost control conscious man I've ever met, and his figures show this positive buoyancy costs him $40 on his 21-footer, and $400 on the 65-footer. "I'm not sure how many extra sales we get because of it, but I'm sure it helps," he told us. Styrofoam such as he uses can be added to existing sailboats quite easily, and has one big advantage over built-in foam—it is removable. If you must reach an area to check or repair your boat, the blocks can be removed. They can be replaced if they crumble, and more can be added at any time.

Unfortunately, this buoyancy option is not a good choice for anyone who wishes to voyage offshore for longer periods. The space loss is more than most of us will accept. Roger admits his 65-footer has about the same interior space as the average 52-footer by the time buoyancy is added. His 25-footer loses 50 percent of its storage locker space to foam blocks. He feels a quarter of this space could be retrieved if the owner wanted to spend the time shaping each block so it fits the compartments more compactly, but then you again run the risk of adding too many stores, so the boat becomes heavier than the designer originally planned. Styrofoam blocks do not add insulation, sound deadening or structural strength to the hull. We doubt insurance companies would consider rate reductions for offshore boats fitted with styrofoam, since an owner could easily remove the flotation once the insurance surveyor was gone. But for the person who is introducing a timid spouse to the joys of bay sailing on their first boat with a ballast keel, the emotional lift (pun intended) of styrofoam blocks could make a big difference.

Buoyancy bags have been used in racing dinghies for years. They are inflated before the boat is launched and strapped in place. The same type of buoyancy is used for helicopters that operate over water. B.F.

Goodrich builds an emergency helicopter flotation system activated by a water sensitive switch that opens a CO_2 and Nitrogen filled container, which causes sponson shaped bags to inflate in less than twenty seconds. This system must be serviced and packed by professionals, but with the other costs associated with running a multi-million dollar helicopter, this cost is acceptable. Now this same technology is being considered for pleasure craft, and is the option that first caught our attention. This system would take little storage room; Myriad Marine, one company exploring this market, calculated that the three bags needed to offer a 30 percent safety margin for *Taleisin* plus the necessary plumbing and inflation tanks, would take the same space as four beach towels plus a diving air tank, and weigh about 77 pounds. The cost for their system and those offered by Mountcracken Marine of England, Pegasus Co. or Avitari, Inc. of the United States, came to between $1,700 and $2,200 for *Taleisin,* or the same as a life raft and canister. The system does not interfere too much with storage, as the uninflated bags can be folded under bunk cushions or attached to bulkheads like sausage rolls, and the pressurized tanks can be stored in any out-of-the-way place. It's relatively easy to calculate the buoyancy you need using the manufacturer's rated lifting power for each size bag, and adding a spare bag if your boat begins to float lower than its lines. You can test these bags manually once each year by inflating them with a dinghy foot pump. Best of all, this system can be retro-fitted to any boat.

FIGURE 8.1   A fully flooded 5.5-meter yacht being sailed back to port supported by two Boat-a-Float inflation bags made by Pegasus Marine.

But as we began to research this option, the only one actually feasible for us, we learned that buoyancy bags for pleasure craft are in an embryonic stage of their development, and there are problems to be solved before they will work in the majority of emergency situations that can cause ballasted sail boats to sink. Furthermore, the head of research at B.F. Goodrich Company said he felt this development would be slow and difficult, because "Big companies can't afford to get involved with items that must be custom fitted or specially installed in each boat. We like products that can be built in three sizes to cover all contingencies, products that don't require installers, designers and engineers once they are on the retailers' shelves." He also implied that the product liability involved with these systems might present an insurance problem for the manufacturer.

Ted Mangles, a marine engineer who willingly discussed these systems with us, agreed with this liability problem. "Consider the guy who inflates his bags inside a boat with a lightly designed hull to deck connection. His deck pulls loose and that's the end of the boat. There aren't many decks designed to hold the ballast of a sail boat, and in effect that's what will happen once you pull the cord." So for safety and to get the buoyancy lifting power pulling in the right direction, these bags must have strong, custom-made tie downs fastened in a direct line to the ballast keel.

Chafing is a second major problem. No matter how strong the fabric

FIGURE 8.2
Mountcracken marine conducted this test on a J-24 using two of their square bags plus a bow bag.

used, none will withstand the rubbing raw-edged glass, exposed screws or bolt heads for more than a short time. In the event of a holing at sea, the sloshing of two or three tons of seawater inside the hull is likely to begin breaking up interior joiner, so this chafing problem cannot be played down completely. One manufacturer suggested that the bunk cushions be velcroed to the deflated bags so they would act as protection when the bags inflated. This would definitely help.

What type of compressed gas to use presents another problem. The most common choice offered at the moment is CO_2. It is easy and inexpensive to obtain. But it is stored under high pressure, so a defective bottle is a potential danger. A leak could be hazardous to your health. Halon 401 is offered as another choice since it is stored under relatively low pressure, and is not as potentially dangerous to your health. But this gas is more costly and not as widely available. In either case, a cylinder the size of the average diver's tank will fill the 110 cubic feet of buoyancy bags needed to offset our 6,200 pounds of lead ballast.

Inflation speed is another unanswered question. The B.F. Goodrich Company adds nitrogen to their CO_2 to act as a propellant so that their helicopter bags inflate almost instantaneously. On the other extreme is the recommendation by Myriad Marine that the valves be regulated to fill the bags over a six-minute period. B.F. Goodrich figures every second lost could see some valuable electronics ruined by salt water. Myriad Marine justifies their slow fill by saying people are afraid of being trapped in their bunk by the inflating bags. Boat sinkings happen at

FIGURE 8.3 The various shapes of bags offered by Mountcracken Marine.

different rates. The Maxi racer, 72-foot *Sirus Maximus*, was knocked down and sank in front of spectators in less than 30 seconds. A 45-foot ketch moored five slips away from us took five hours to take on 900 gallons of water from a syphoning head, and probably would have required another five hours to sink if someone hadn't noticed the lack of freeboard. So a choice must be made, and we think we'd be for the 30 second inflation, since we can think of no situation where the violence of collision or knockdown would leave someone sleeping, and 30 seconds would give most awake people time to exit from a bunk.

The biggest unanswered question with buoyancy bags is how to activate them so they work quickly in emergency situations, yet are not set off accidentally; so they can be shut down immediately if the emergency is averted, yet work if no electricity is available, and no one is on board to activate them manually. Most of the systems being offered use the simplest possible inflation devices: a rip cord or pull switch. Avitari and Pegasus Company both pack each bag with its own inflation cylinder. This is fine on smaller boats where one or two bags are sufficient to

FIGURE 8.4   Two bags with one ton of lifting power. One bag is rolled, the other inflated. Note the CO_2 cylinder alongside. These are Mountcracken marine bags.

obtain positive buoyancy. But on larger boats where four or six bags are required, an interconnected system such as the French Insub is necessary. Their bags are all filled by the same gas canister, once again activated by a pull handle. Unfortunately this pull handle system has several draw backs. To inflate the system, you must be able to locate the handle in a hurry. If it is near the helmsman and he is below making a cup of coffee at the time of flooding, precious minutes could be lost. More important yet, this manual type of inflation does not cover the two most probable causes of sinking, knockdowns where crew will be busy with sails and steering, and possibly unable to reach the rip cord, and unattended sinking, those that happen when you are tied to a dock and have gone off to a party.

Myriad Marine has come up with an electrical automatic inflation system that uses a self-contained battery and solanoid type switches with a water level sensor. This is an improvement, but adds the complication of electronics to an otherwise simply maintained system. No manufacturer we have found so far uses automatic or pressure sensitive valves such as those used by the B.F. Goodrich Company, or pressure sensitive

FIGURE 8.5   Mountcracken marine bow flotation bag.

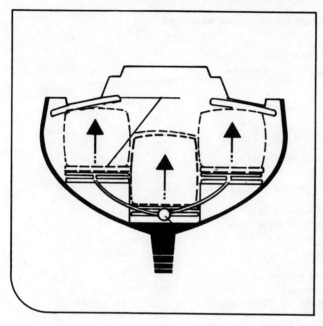

FIGURE 8.6 A linked buoyancy bag system, inflated with bunk cushions providing chafe resistance.

valves such as used on life raft canisters (see end of chapter for list of companies and addresses). This inflation device problem may eventually be solved if buoyancy bag systems become popular and draw more manufacturers with higher research budgets into the market.

Who will spend money for these systems we've discussed? Obviously, for new sailors the security offered by stuffing $10 worth of styrofoam into various lockers on their weekender is worth having. For weekend racers on super-light, high-speed boats, buoyancy bags could be better than insurance. For people building a new boat, watertight bulkheads might be a wise investment. If we were building a new glass offshore cruising boat, we'd definitely consider spreading closed cell foam through less accessible parts of the hull. But will many sailors install a positive buoyancy bag system in an offshore racer or cruiser? We think that once a positive, nonelectric dependent automatic bag inflating valve is developed and tested, many of us will become very interested in this lightweight, easy to stow and relatively inexpensive positive buoyancy system.

Addresses for companies mentioned:

Avitare, Inc.
4681 Tajo Drive,
Santa Barbara, California 93110   (805) 967-3589

Insub,
Hutchinson Mapa,
2 Rue Balsac,
75008 Paris, France.   261-51-04

MacGregor Marine
1631 Placentia Avenue
Costa Mesa, California 92627   (714) 642-6830

Mountcracken Marine,
Brighton Marina,
East Sussex BN2 5UF
England.   (0273) 698957

Myriad Marine,
P.O. Box 144,
Crystal Lake, Illinois 60014   (815) 455-0405

Pegasus Floatation,
Boat-a-Float,
P.O. Box 932,
Port Townsend, Washington 98368   (206) 385-5038

Wellington Boats,
11544 Normandy Boulevard
Jacksonville, Florida 32221   (904) 781-1055

Float Pac Pty Ltd
P.O. Box 67
Rushcutters Bay 2011
NSW Australia   (02) 331-1195

9

Getting More Out of Your Cruising Staysail

There are practical reasons why the cutter rig has dominated new cruising designs during the past ten years. It gives you better performance to windward than a two-masted rig. You have less rigging to buy, only one mast, one mast step and one boom to build. A windvane for self-steering can be installed more easily on a cutter than a ketch because the boom usually doesn't overhang the transom. The three smaller sails of a cutter are easier to handle and reef than the two larger sails on a sloop (all things being equal). Most important of all, the cutter rig gives you the most versatile sail found on a cruising boat, the staysail. But to get the full potential from this special sail requires careful attention to rigging details.

The staysail on our cutter *Taleisin* is heavily constructed of eight ounce U.S. dacron. It has two rows of reefs and is set on a movable stay (figures 9.1 and 9.2). This gives us a sail which can be used in a wide variety of wind conditions from force two all the way to storm force ten.

When either Lin or I are alone on watch, it's easy to keep the boat

FIGURE 9.1

FIGURE 9.2

moving well by using a combination of the main and one hundred percent lapper with the staysail set in between. The staysail can be simply dropped on deck if the wind increases or conversely we can hoist the staysail when the breeze drops. This easy increase of sail area improves our average passage times. Compare this to a single headsail sloop rig. One sail has to be taken off, another hanked on in its place, whenever you want to change the sail area. Needless to say, everyone has to reduce sail area as the wind increases; but when I am sailing on a boat with a single headsail rig, I usually find myself putting off sail increases, especially when I am alone on watch at night. This reluctance to change up can easily cut ten or twenty miles off a day's run.

Your staysail gives you flexibility. If you are reaching at top speed with the full rig as you come into the lee of the land, and you find you have to short tack into the anchorage, the cutter gives you two quick easy sail change choices. You can drop either the staysail or the jib and tack easily into the bay. In gusty williwaw conditions like those that are often found in the lee of steep headlands, or to work through narrow channels, we usually choose to drop the jib and use the staysail and main. If we find we need more power once we get inside the anchorage, the jib is lying in the jib net ready to go back up.

Your staysail can also be hoisted or dropped easily for use with any sail you carry, the genoa, any jib, the nylon drifter and even a spinnaker on a beam reach. But it is in strong winds that the staysail really pays its keep.

When you use your staysail with a reefed down mainsail, it reduces your sailplan proportionately, so it becomes a smaller triangle with the fore and aft balance or lead similar to that of a full rig (figure 9.3). Compare this to the deeply reefed single headsail sloop (figure 9.4). Note that the reefed sail area on the sloop moves forward. This often causes lee helm. A boat with lee helm has difficulty holding her bow up to the wind and seas and therefore is a poor windward performer.

About 90 percent of our sailing on *Taleisin* is done with three sails, the seven ounce, 100 percent lapper, which has one row of reefs in it, the eight ounce staysail with two rows of reefs and the eight ounce mainsail with three rows of reefs. (This gives us about the same total sail area as a sloop would have with a 150 percent genoa and mainsail). To do this we depend on our staysail, which unreefed can be a heavy weather staysail, reefed once, a storm staysail, or in a hard flog to

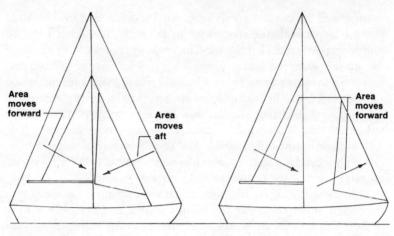

FIGURE 9.3   FIGURE 9.4

windward it works double reefed as a spitfire staysail that is set with the triple reefed main, or in extremely heavy conditions, our trysail. This may seem like a lot of reefs to some sailors. But I was once down to triple reefed mainsail and single reefed staysail on *Seraffyn* as we reached into Malta on a storm-force northwesterly wind. I was thinking to myself, "Damn, I could use a trysail and another reef in the staysail just in case the wind increases or I am headed and have to beat into Marsaxlokk Harbor."

The most likely damage to sails usually occurs along the highly loaded leech or clew area. This leads to an added advantage to these extra reefs. If any sail is damaged along its lower section you can simply tie in a reef and sail on using the undamaged upper section. If the leech or clew is torn on a roller furling sail it is completely out of business. For this reason I would not have roller furling on any sails which the yacht or crew rely on in heavy weather.

The main reason our staysail is loose footed with no club or boom, is so we can conveniently release the staysail stay and move it aft when we wish to short tack. Clearing away the staysail stay allows the jib to pass across the foredeck without hanging up on the staysail stay. This means one person can tack the boat easily in light winds, freeing the other crew person to navigate and watch for coral heads or rocks.

Another advantage of our boomless staysail is that it can overlap the mast a bit. This gives you a little more sail area and an increase in slot efficiency compared to the shorter footed boomed staysail.

If you eliminate the club on your staysail you will save the expense of sheet, tackle, traveler, gooseneck and the spar itself. It will also keep your foredeck clearer and therefore make it easier to change sails, work the anchor windlass and ground tackle. (For more on club footed staysails see Don Street's *Ocean Cruising Yacht,* Vol. 11).

The day sailor or coastal cruising sailor is usually in love with his self-tending staysail. It allows him to tack in and out of creeks, rivers and narrow inlets with only the jib sheets to handle. But the boomless staysail works fine for the open water cruiser for whom short tacking is not the norm. Our solution to the occasional short tacking we have to do is, as I said before, to use one headsail at a time. It is safe to sail with the staysail stay released in flat water or until the mast begins to bend aft towards the mainsail. (A straight mast is a safe mast). Then the staysail should be set up again. This is especially true if you are rail down, punching into a head sea.

The question now is, if I had a sloop which met all my other cruising needs, would I go to the trouble and expense of converting it to a double headsail rig? I most definitely would add a staysail with a release lever if it met the following requirements: (A) It was a masthead rigged sloop for maximum luff length on both staysail and jib; (B) it had a generous distance between jib stay and mast (J measurement), a distance at least as long as the mainsail boom; (C) it had a healthy beam so the staysail would breathe easily in the open slot between main and jib; and (D) the staysail could be designed so that it was at least 22 percent of the total working sailplan (main, working jib and staysail). Otherwise it would not have sufficient drive when the staysail and main alone were used. With these parameters, a staysail could be added and the extra sail area forward might even reduce that common fault, a weather helm.*

The addition of the staysail stay would require a tang and halyard connection aloft along with two intermediate supporting shrouds led to chainplates aft of the mast. On larger, more powerful boats, ones 35 feet and over, running backstays would be required. The connection at the

*If the sloop had a stiff weather helm I would even consider the addition of a bowsprit, to correct the bad balance and effectively lengthen the J measurement.

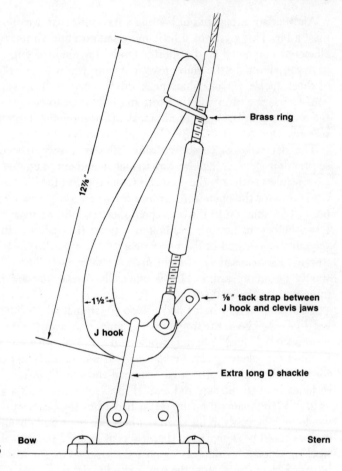

Brass ring

12⅞"

←1½"→

⅛" tack strap between
J hook and clevis jaws

J hook

Extra long D shackle

Bow   Stern

FIGURE 9.5

lower end of the staysail stay should be attached securely to the stemhead on a bowsprited boat, or if the stay is attached to the middle of
the foredeck, a rod or wire below decks should tension the stay to either
a bulkhead or the forefoot. Add to this some deck fairleads and you've
got quite a hardware bill, not to mention the cost of labor. But I think
it is worthwhile if the boat you now own can gain the subtle but
important advantages of a staysail.

In any case, get professional advice on this standing rigging addition.
Be sure to ask about the position of the staysail stay, how much overlap

FIGURE 9.6

you can have on the sail and where the sheets should lead (inside or outside the lowers). These details are important in getting a double headsail rig to work well close hauled.

A racing sailmaker is usually your best bet for getting a double head rig set up to work efficiently. He will probably have to come down and measure the boat so the staysail will sheet correctly. He'll know how to cut a bit of extra hollow in the leech and adjust the sheet leads athwartships and fore and aft to give the staysail the correct twist aloft, so the leech falls off a bit to minimize backwinding the mainsail.

A short lanyard on the tack of your staysail can eliminate the need for expensive fore and aft track and adjustable staysail sheet cars. This lanyard will let you adjust the sail up and down the stay. This moves the clew and effectively tightens or loosens the leech. This lanyard can also be used to secure and adjust the tack when you reef. We have simple deck fairleads without blocks on *Taleisin* just as we did on *Seraffyn* and they work fine because we have this adjustable lanyard.

Our sailmaker helped us eliminate the need to adjust the staysail sheet

FIGURE 9.7

leads when we reefed by angling the reef patches so they are higher at the clew and lower at the tack. (See figure 9.1).

To move our staysail aft we use an over-center tension release device (staysail stay release lever or Hy-field lever), with a drop down ring to keep it from opening accidentally (made in the U.S. by Merriman Yacht Specialties or ABI Industries). At the bottom of Figure 9.2 you can see the stainless steel fast pin secured to the lever assembly with a lanyard. We use this pin to disconnect the stay assembly from the gammon iron. Another type of release tension device called a J hook, can be homemade from a quarter inch plate of bronze, aluminum or stainless steel (listed in order of my preference and ease of working). (See figure 9.5.)*

The best wire for the staysail is 7- by 7- stainless steel, which is more flexible and less likely to work harden than $\frac{1}{19}$ wire. The staysail stay

*Ready-made J hook levers are available from Eisenlohr Enterprises, 18600 Quail Hill Drive, Corona, California, 92647. Schaeffer Marine also makes a clean simple release lever for boats with staysail stays of up to ¼" diameter. Schaeffer Marine, Inc., 14 Industrial Park, New Bedford, Massachusetts, 02745.

FIGURE 9.8

will flop around when it is moved aft. This will bend the wire back and forth, side to side, and eventually cause metal fatigue right where the wire enters the swage fitting. A toggle or shackle at the mast tang aloft in conjunction with a shock cord, secured with a rolling hitch to hold the stay tight when it is brought aft (figure 9.6), will help minimize wire bending and the subsequent metal fatigue.

In figure 9.7 you can see the clear plastic hose and brass luff hanks (sail rings) we slid on before I spliced the wire on *Taleisin*'s staysail stays. We did this because when we tacked the light weather genoa on *Seraffyn* and left the staysail stay set up, we used to get mysterious quarter-inch semi-circular holes in the genoa. When I finally changed to hank rings and plastic-covered wire after seven years, there were no more holes, no more chafe and no more wear on the hanks against the bare staysail stay wire. The rings and plastic hose can easily be passed over a threaded turnbuckle end if you use swages instead of splices. This would give the added advantage that the staysail could be removed for repairs or stowing below. All you would have to do is unscrew the turnbuckle body and slide the rings off the stay. I have to cut the seizing on the rings to get the sail off, so therefore I keep it bagged permanently on deck (figure 9.8).

The staysail is the most versatile sail on our cutter, and because of this it is subjected to a lot of wear and tear. I tend to watch it more closely than any other sail on board because I know it is the sail we will depend on in extreme conditions. So I would suggest that once you notice signs of wear (it usually takes three or four years, or 15 to 20 thousand miles of sailing), have a new staysail made, check it to be sure it fits, then stow it below so that you have two strong sails in reserve; your rarely used but vital storm trysail, and your multipurpose storm and spitfire staysail. These two rugged sails could allow you to beat free of the classic sailors' nightmare, storm force winds blowing onto a lee shore.

10

Bowsprits for Offshore Voyaging

I've had at least a hundred visitors on board our two well-endowed cutters ask, "Isn't going out on that bowsprit in heavy weather difficult and dangerous?" or, "Don't marinas charge you for the bowsprit?" I usually give these guests a two-sentence answer. Afterwards I feel dissatisfied because I know it was too glib, too simple. Although I know a bowsprit definitely adds an element of danger and occasional extra expense, I choose to have one for several reasons, which I feel far outweigh these obvious disadvantages. So a complete answer must be balanced with a discussion of why we choose to have a bowsprit, the advantages it gives us, such as increased sailing performance, easier tacking, simpler anchor handling, and other in-port conveniences. Then later I'll discuss ways to effectively minimize the problems, so you can safely and efficiently use the bowsprit on your existing boat, or feel more comfortable about buying one of the many voyaging boats with bowsprits that are being offered today. The final part of the discussion will be about the addition of a bowsprit to improve the cruising and passagemaking qualities of the boat you now own.

Length on deck is almost always the first parameter a customer gives a designer. "I want a 35-foot performance offshore passagemaker . . ."

By the time the designer has listed several thousand pounds of the necessities, options and luxuries his client wants, he mumbles to himself, "What this guy really needs is a 50-footer." But the budget restricts the designer, and he produces drawings for a beamy 35-footer with buoyant ends and a long waterline. To make this heavily loaded boat perform well, he needs sail area.* He now has three choices: add overhanging ends, increase the mast height, or add a bowsprit.

The disadvantage of designing a boat with overhangs, i.e., a longer boat, is that this increases the cost of the boat without increasing the living space relative to the length on deck. It does increase the storage space in the ends, but this is resented by the designer, because he knows cruisers will fill these ends with heavy gear like anchors, chains, and tanks that slow his boat down. The disadvantage of a higher aspect rig is that it is harder to support than a shorter rig with a bowsprit. Furthermore, to increase the sail area by increasing only mast height, you need an extremely tall rig. To give 17,400 pound 29'6" LOD *Taleisin* the same 730 square feet of working sail area without her eight foot bowsprit, her mast height would have to be increased from 43 feet above the load waterline to a towering 55 feet. Of course designers must balance these thoughts against the fact that the taller rig is usually faster close hauled, but the lower aspect rig is usually faster on a reach and because of its shorter mast is stiffer in a breeze. So, bowsprits are often a designer's solution, the cheapest, easiest way to get extra sail horsepower.

Another less recognized but important reason to include a bowsprit on the design of a cruising boat, especially a beamy one, is that it gives you a closer headsail sheeting angle. This dramatically improves an efficient hull's pointing and windward performance (figure 10.2). The chainplates on modern racing boats are placed inboard so the genoa can be sheeted flatter. This lets the boat drive closer to the wind, especially in light to moderate sea conditions. But inboard chainplates are a pain on a cruising boat. They are a source of deck leaks, and they usually end up in the middle of the side decks, which makes carrying sails fore and aft a hassle. Moving the chainplates inboard increases all the loads on the mast, rigging and chainplates, which proportionately increases the chance of mast failure. Finally, the inboard shrouds and their underdeck supports can take interior space, the sacred cow of small boat cruising

*In our experience, a cruising boat needs at least 80 to 84 square feet of working sail per 2,000 pound ton of fully loaded displacement to sail well in light to medium winds.

FIGURE 10.1   An example of what I call a light/medium weather bowsprit.

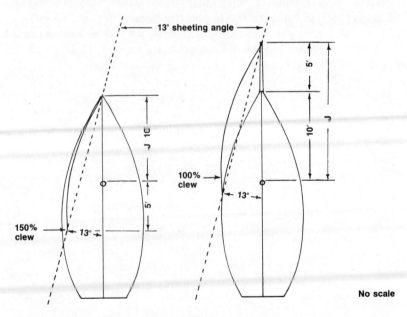

FIGURE 10.2

sailors. The bowsprit offers you the same tighter sheeting angle without moving your chainplates inboard, because it increases your J measurement, by moving the jib and headstay further away from the mast.

A bowsprit simplifies shorthanded tacking. If the sloop in figure 10.3 has a ten-foot J measurement, it would have to carry a 150 percent overlapping genoa, to equal the sail area of a 100 percent jib on the same hull with a five-foot bowsprit. A 100 percent jib will tack easily and unaided past the front of the mast. Quite often you can sheet it home before it fills on the new tack. In moderate winds, with a bit of coordination, you can dispense with the winch handle. Compare this to tacking the 150 percent genoa alone on a stem headed sloop. Its sheets will be 50 percent longer and the clew will have to travel 100 percent further from tack to tack, so you will almost always have to use the winch handle to sweat in the last bit of sheet. This 150 percent genoa will chafe against spreaders, shrouds, lifelines and pulpit. It will tend to lose its airfoil shape in fresh winds, it cuts visibility to leeward, and finally works poorly downwind, wing and wing on a pole. This is because the foot of a 150 percent genoa is 50 percent longer than the standard length spinnaker or whisker pole (J measurement). The pole is not long enough to fully extend the sail so its area works efficiently. This extra sail sags forward to chafe against the headstay and pulpit. Even worse, the baggy, nonextended part of the sail can flop from port to starboard, which exaggerates any tend-

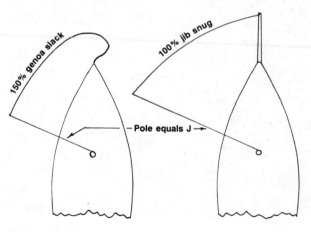

FIGURE 10.3

ency your boat has to roll downwind. In short, by having a bowsprit, you can enjoy the advantages of high cut, generous sail area, without the myriad problems associated with overlapping sails (figure 10.4).

In port, bowsprits really shine. They are a natural place for a chain roller and bowsprit ended nylon anchor pennant. This system keeps chain away from your topsides and bottom paint when the wind is blowing opposite to the current (figure 10.5). The nylon pennant is rigged to a fairlead or single block at the very end of the bowsprit then hitched to your chain. The stretch in the line acts to absorb pitching shocks, and can minimize yawing. The amount of this yaw and pitch control is relative to the length of your bowsprit. The eight-foot bowsprit on *Taleisin* holds her bow down comfortably in a two-foot windchop. She never tries to sail at anchor, and only yaws slightly in strong winds. A boat with a shorter bowsprit might yaw more; one without a bowsprit ended pennant would have a tendency to move around even more. Comfort at anchor is *all important* since most boats out cruising spend 85 to 90 percent of their total time in port. If your boat is tacking back and forth at anchor you may get a lot more miles under your keel, but you won't get much peace of mind or rest. You'll also threaten the yachts near you, because you'll have more of a tendency to foul your anchor and drag, and you'll take up more room in the anchorage.

A nylon pennant rigged to the end of the bowsprit is stronger, safer and more effective than one shackled to a bobstay fitting or waterline

FIGURE 10.4 *Taleisin*'s 100 percent lapper fully extended by her spinnaker pole.

FIGURE 10.5   An example of an all-weather bowsprit. Note the nylon snubber attached to the chain.

stem fitting for several reasons. The line rigged to the bobstay fitting gives you none of the yaw and pitch controlling leverage to help your boat lie comfortably head to wind. More important, it is harder to let out scope quickly in a dragging situation. It is more difficult to buoy your anchor line and let your gear go if another vessel starts dragging down on you. To get the line free, you have to winch up the chain to relieve the strain on the chain hook, or the rolling hitch that connects the snubber to the anchor cable. This time lag could be vital, especially if an untended barge or ship is dragging down on you during a storm. If, instead, your shock absorber is attached to the chain with a rolling hitch, then rigged to the end of your bowsprit, lead aft and secured on deck, you can simply cast off the nylon line and let the chain out to increase scope, or buoy the bitter end of your chain and cast off both the pennant and your gear quickly and completely. The attached pennant can be retrieved when you pull the chain back in. Few bobstay fittings on wood or glass boats are designed for the violent side loads exerted by a snubber when a boat is yawing or sailing at anchor. (The welded bobstay fittings on metal boats can usually take these loads quite well.) So the only real advantage to using a snubber on the bobstay fitting instead of at the end of a bowsprit applies to all boats, the pennant attached near the waterline keeps the cable below the level of your topsides so there is little chance of marring your topside finish. But your boat can still override its cable and chafe its bottom paint.

The question that will naturally come up now is, will the bowsprit support the nylon preventer pennant (shock absorber) without breaking. A bowsprit which is stayed properly is designed to take the violent, intermittent strains caused by a jib while the boat is crashing to windward through steep seas. To do this, the headstay wires and whisker stays are usually two to three times stronger than the anchor chain the same boat will carry. The safe working load on ⅜ inch BBB chain is 2,750 pounds, the normal breaking point is 11,000 pounds. These same limits for ⅜ inch diameter 1 by 19 stainless steel wire are, safe working load 8,750, breaking point, 17,500 pounds. This means the chain will part before the wires that support the bowsprit do. If the bowsprit itself is properly stayed, it will take almost none of the loads from the snubber; what little it does take will be compression loads, the loads this spar is designed to take easily.

This bowsprit ended nylon pennant should not be used on gaff-riggers or any boat without a permanent backstay unless the supporting running back stays are set up firmly. The nylon pennant does most of its work by absorbing shock loads. If the pennant is lead through a fairlead at the end of the bowsprit, its stretch is combined with the stretch in the backstay and headstay to further absorb anchor cable shocks. I would feel secure about using this system while lying to a single anchor. In storm conditions where I would set more than one anchor, I would be reluctant to use the pennant to the end of the bowsprit, because I would like to watch for chafe and have easy access to tend chafe protection gear. My second bower is mainly nylon and I would use the two rollers on the inboard end of the bowsprit and rig a deck-length snubber behind the chain rode in this multi-anchor situation.

Installing anchor rode rollers on either side of the bowsprit instead of on the stem, allows you to store dual anchors, hooked up and ready to go, without having toe-stubbing anchors on deck (figures 10.6 and 10.7). These rollers should not be further than 14 inches from the stem of the boat. If they are in the middle of the bowsprit they could cause the spar to break when extreme loads come on the anchor chain. To clear your deck even more, especially in port, your working jib can be left bagged and stowed on the forestay.

The bobstay and whisker stays of your bowsprit can be shock absorbers in minor collisions with docks, flotsam or other vessels. It is usually easier to repair a broken bowsprit than to fix a smashed stem or holed hull. Your whisker stays can be built as a continuation of a metal covered rub-rail from bowsprit end to the aft end of the boat. This is very useful in fishboat harbors or where you will be coming alongside pilings. The bobstay can be used as an instant swim step for agile swimmers. And finally, a jib net is a romantic place to lay watching the dolphins skimming the cutwater as you slice through the dark blue southern seas.

And now on to the other side of the discussion. Headsail removal and marina charges are the two most obvious disadvantages of a bowsprit. Let's get into jib removal first. If someone who had never ridden in a car suddenly found himself as a passenger in an MG, roaring down a winding canyon road, tires squealing on each turn, cars flashing by only four or five feet away, barely missing each other at the speed limit of 55 miles per hour, he would probably turn white with fright. And I believe that is the way bowsprit jib removal must appear to someone who has never gone out on one at night. Sailing is just like driving. You don't learn on winding roads, at night or in extreme conditions. Instead you develop skills and self-confidence in moderate or easy conditions. These skills will allow you to remove the jib with speed and safety yet still retain the thrill of doing something which is potentially dangerous. Both sports, driving and sailing, can give a great feeling of satisfaction if you do them well and smoothly. The occasional extra physical effort and excitement of removing the jib is the trade-off we are willing to accept to get the advantages we discussed previously.

Our bowsprit is rigged for convenience (figure 10.8). It is not a macho long slippery pole with four bare stays, the kind Charlie Barr preferred for the lowest windage and the least weight in the ends. But Charlie Barr had a big advantage. He just sent a couple of his super-tough Grand Banks fishermen out to pull down the luff of the jib and change it. If I asked Lin to change sails on a spar like that she would look me straight in the eye and say, "You've got to be joking." That's why we have a jib downhaul, lifelines and a jib net. The jib downhaul is a line that attaches to the halyard and is led through a fairlead or single block near the tack of the jib, then aft to a cleat on deck, preferably near the jib halyard.

FIGURE 10.6

FIGURE 10.7

FIGURE 10.8

(See *Self-Sufficient Sailor.*) Let go the halyard, pull the downhaul and
if you are either heading into the wind or running downwind slightly by
the lee, so the mainsail is blanketing the headsail, it will usually pull
easily down into the trough of the jib net. If you are reaching or going
to windward, the downhaul will still pull the flogging sail down. It may
go into the water, but it will be down and you can use the sheets to pull
it on deck. Your major problem is solved. The sail is down and held down
by the downhaul line. Now you can use the technique I call the "non-
macho" or "cream puff" method of removing a jib to go out on the
bowsprit and change sails.

Adjust the self-steering vane so you are running downwind. It won't
be necessary to let the mainsail out while you run off because you are
only going to be on the bowsprit a short time. Once you are running
downwind, the bowsprit will hardly move up and down at all compared
to when you are closehauled, so going out to change sails will be much
easier. (If you are close to a lee shore, you might not want to run off.
Instead you can use a modified "cream puff," reaching off with the wind
just slightly aft of the beam.) When I am alone on deck, I tie the end
of the main halyard around my waist or use a rough weather harness,

whichever is handiest, before I go out on the bowsprit. I take a sail gasket with me and straddle the spar, feet on the whisker stays, hand alternately holding the lifelines while I slide out towards the headstay. I furl the sail loosely into the jib net, tie the gasket around the foot and leech near the hanks, then hang onto the headstay with my left hand and unhook the hanks with my right. We use easy opening snap shackles at the tack and halyard and have a pull line on them to further facilitate jib removal. Once the sail is free, I slide aft, pulling it by the luff containing gasket until I can get on deck and lift the sail out of the jib net onto the foredeck. I leave the jib sheets rigged with figure eight stopper knots in the ends so the sail is always attached to the boat. Only when it is bagged and secured do we remove the sheets from the jib lead blocks.

To put the smaller jib back, I tie a gasket around its foot and leech so that the tack and jib hanks are in order, ready to be attached to the headstay. I lead the jibsheets and tie the stopper knots to secure the jib to the boat. I reattach my safety line and reverse the removal procedures. (I have used the word "I" instead of "Lin or I" for easier reading here. Lin changes the jib alone as a matter of course, without disturbing the off watch.)

After reading these procedures, some people will ask, why don't you have a roller furling jib out on that bowsprit? This is something I have researched and thought about for a long time. My personal conclusion is, if I were using *Taleisin* for coastal cruising where furling gear repair facilities and replacement parts and new headstay extrusions were available, where a jib that didn't roll up properly would only be an embarrassment, and it could be easily repaired or replaced if it was damaged from flogging in a semi-rolled condition, I'd have a roller furling. (The more moving parts you have, the more chance of failure.) But since we use *Taleisin* for extensive, shorthanded voyaging, we need the absolute safety of sails that will come down no matter what conditions we encounter. Offshore, sail shortening methods must be Murphy-free and as reliable as the steering or brakes on the family station wagon.

With a cutter rig like ours which has a good sized staysail, you probably won't have to go back out on the bowsprit once you remove the working jib. Your stem-headed staysail and main will become your heavy weather rig. This means the bowsprit becomes a moderate to light air rig extension only. So going out in winds over 25 knots can be avoided by normal prudent sail reductions—reductions that take place before you are "way over-canvassed."

When you are cruising offshore, headsail changes become far less frequent. During the last two and a half years of voyaging with *Taleisin* in California then out to New Zealand, a distance of over 9,000 miles, 80 percent of it downwind in the trades, we've only changed the lapper for the reefed lapper at sea four times. When it was time to beat into harbors in the 22- to 25-knot trades, we usually dropped the lapper and left it tied in the jib net while we sailed with the main and staysail. As a rule, jib changes are more common with the wind forward of the beam. But once again for offshore voyaging, these changes are far less frequent than you would expect.

Setting light weather sails is slightly harder with a bowsprit. But even here you can make things easier by setting your nylon sails on their own luff, i.e., without jib hanks. Then you only have to carry the tack of the sail to the end of the bowsprit to attach it, then hoist the sail with a spinnaker halyard. If you run by the lee, this sail will drop back onto the deck behind the mainsail when you ease the halyard.

I feel there are two categories of bowsprits: the first is what I call the light/medium weather cutter rigged bowsprit, like the one we have on *Taleisin*. On this type of rig, the staysail becomes the storm jib and all sails are carried inboard in heavy weather. The weight and complications of a long platform and pulpit are not absolutely necessary for use in these conditions. The other category is what I call the all-weather bowsprit. This is one on a boat rigged so that storm canvas must be carried on the jibstay to balance the rig when you are going to weather in heavy conditions. Since it will be necessary to go out on the bowsprit to change to a spitfire or storm jib on the all-weather bowsprit, you need not only a jib downhaul, jib net, and "cream puff" methods of sail handling, but in addition, the safety of a platform, grating, pulpit, and lifelines lead out to the end of the bowsprit as in figure 10.5. All-weather bowsprits are usually short. Therefore a strong, rigid platform pulpit combination is relatively light, cheap, and easy to build compared to one for the longer light/medium weather bowsprit.

The bowsprit can be a financial problem in marinas. But when we are out cruising a marina berth is rarely available. Instead we anchor for little or no charge at all. When we need to be in a marina we can shop around and if slips are not scarce, a sympathetic marina manager can arrange to put our boat in a place where the extra appendages don't get in other sailors' ways. Then we only pay for our on-deck measurments.

There may be no free lunch in marinas, but there are in shipyards. We have never been charged for anything but our length on deck during haul-outs or for harbor dues in any of the hundreds of foreign ports we have visited. If we were putting our boat into winter storage in a boat house, ashore or afloat, and the charges included the bowsprit length, we could remove it with a few hours' work.

The bowsprit and its gear definitely require maintenance and inspection. A stainless steel bowsprit could cut this to a minimum. But once again, if you had extra overhangs instead, they would have to be polished and painted, especially if your anchor cable were rubbing on the topsides.

If you have a bowsprit you should inspect the bobstay fittings as carefully as you do your rudder fittings. Your bobstay fittings should be of a metal similar to that of the other underwater hardware, to minimize electrolysis. I met the owner of *Le Gamin* (figure 10.5) in Tonga, and he said the stainless steel bolts in his bobstay fittings corroded and pulled part way out of the stem on a trip from the U.S. to Hawaii. He has now replaced the bolts and attached a flat piece of zinc to the fitting, to combat the electrolytic action.

Your bobstay fitting takes strains that are similar to, or more than those of your upper shroud chainplate. So it must be strong. If it lets go at sea, it is very hard to repair or jury rig.

It is a good idea to put a plastic hose over the bobstay wire so your anchor chain will winch in smoothly. This hose will also minimize chafe on nylon anchor rodes and protect the bobstay wire from anchor chain chafe.

With a bowsprit you will need a longer whisker/spinnaker pole because your J measurement will be longer. Using this pole can be made easy if you rig an instant uphaul/downhaul arrangement with the inboard end of the pole sliding up the mast on a long track and an endless hauling line controlling the inboard end of the pole. (See *The Self-Sufficient Sailor*, pp. 223–29.) I feel any disadvantages of this longer pole are offset by the advantages of a non-overlapping jib.

You have to be more careful when you maneuver in a harbor with a bowsprit. Unless it has a platform, it will be harder to get out to the end to fend off pilings, other boats or docks. But skills acquired by practice in moderate, uncramped quarters, just like you would use when you are learning to park a motorhome, will help you judge the turning radius of your extended bow.

Docklines are harder to handle with a jib net and whisker stays messing up fairleads to dock cleats. And finally, your bobstay fitting is a real tattle-tale if your true love is overweight. The fitting will be under water and this will point out the weight problem for the whole world to see. Leaving the bobstay fitting and stainless steel wire end under water can cause serious electrolytic pitting in as little as four or five months.

Since bowsprits definitely have advantages for new cruising boats, some owners might be interested in adding one to the boat they now have. The CCA inspired sloop *Le Gamin* shown in figure 10.5 was converted to a live-aboard ocean cruiser by the owner, who told us he added the bowsprit to his production sloop for two reasons: first to increase her sail area, and second to cure a weatherhelm. His bowsprit was a good solution for what was only a relatively minor overloading problem. But care and commonsense should be exercised before over-loading any boat for cruising, especially light displacement, ex-racers. A 35-foot sailboat that is down six or eight inches from its designed load waterline is much stiffer than its designer planned for it to be, because its ballast is now on a longer lever arm, i.e., it is deeper in the water, which makes it more effective. This stiffness is further accentuated because major cruising weights like water, fuel and canned goods are stored low in the hull. This also increases the yacht's stability. This increased stiffness puts strains on the hull, rigging, mast and chainplates, that cut down the safety factors originally used in the computation of the design. This overloading/stress problem becomes most acute if the ex-racer was designed close to the strength limits of the construction materials. I'm sure many of you have noted the increase in gear and mast failures among racing boats lately. We have seen a corresponding in-crease in failures among the cruising fleet, including five dismastings in 1985, just around the French Polynesia. Strains caused by overloading may have been a significant factor in these failures. So before you think of adding a bowsprit for its benefits in increasing sail area, consult a designer to make sure the rest of your rig can support this increase in stresses.

The addition of a bowsprit, or even an increase in the length of an existing one, is a time-honored way to correct a weather helm. The term "weather helm" means your boat is hard to steer, because it constantly wants to round into the wind. A jib at the end of the bowsprit will exert a powerful leverlike effect which will hold the bow so it won't try to head up into the wind. If the bowsprit is too long, it will over-correct and cause a lee helm. The idea you are seeking is one-finger control on the tiller to hold a steady course in any but the roughest seas. For safety and good performance, your boat should have a tendency to head slowly into the wind when you let go of the helm. The extra leverage of a wheel can disguise the feel of a weather helm. But it does not change the fact that the rudder is angled off center, causing constant speed-robbing drag if you have a weather helm. But once again before you spend the money to add a bowsprit to solve your steering problem, it would pay to contact a designer, sailmaker or rigger and take him out for a sail on your boat so he can feel your helm. Then he can estimate the correct length of bowsprit for your boat and eliminate the expense and frustration of a trial-and-error conversion.

A bowsprit is definitely a compromise. To get the sailing and cruising advantages you have to pay a little more in marina charges and handle sail out over the water. Light-weight race boats which rarely lie at anchor don't need bowsprits. But since most passagemaking cruising boats turn into miniature cargo carriers, their owners will bless the anchoring advantages, the extra sail power and performance a bowsprit provides.

11

Cruising Tenders: Choices, Improvements, and Storage

La Paz, Baja California is the first major provisioning and repair spot voyagers reach after leaving San Diego, 900 miles to the north. On a busy winter afternoon there are often 50 to 70 dinghies, inflatables, hard dinghies, even Fold-A-Boats and tenders with Add-A-Buoys on the beach near the Los Arcos Hotel. Many have modifications and patches. Their owners are most willing to explain their latest improvements or bitch about the recent repairs. The owners agree on only one absolute: a reliable, convenient, ready-to-use dinghy is a must when you go cruising in Mexico, the Caribbean or the South Pacific. These are places where the average cruising sailor is only at sea ten percent of the time, tied to docks five percent of the time, the rest of the time he is at anchor. So a dinghy becomes more important than the family station wagon. This little work boat carries everything, including food, water, laundry and party-goers from shore and back again. Your tender needs to be tidy and seamanlike, since it quite often forms the first impression you give locals in foreign ports, anchorages or yacht clubs. It should be quick and easy to launch for those times when you anchor in beautiful, out-of-the-way coves, or you may miss those special experiences that rowing ashore provides.

So what are the choices for the cruising sailboat? Basically you have two types of available tenders: soft and hard. Both come in planing and rowing models; each type has its pros and cons. The decision you make should fit the kind of cruising boat you have, the amount of crew you sail with, the area you cruise in, and your style of cruising.

The number of crew you normally sail with is the first factor to consider. A crew of one or two people can get by with a six- to eight-foot tender; a larger crew needs an eight- to twelve-footer. Two tenders is a good option for larger families. One could be an inflatable with an outboard motor for the parents, the other a rowing, sailing boat for the children. Carrying two tenders would be handy even if there are only two people on board, but unfortunately many of us not cannot afford the space or cost of this solution so a choice must be made.

Many sailors buy inflatables because they are convenient and easy to store below. No special chocks or davits have to be fitted and fastened to your cruising boat to hold them. For the small cruising boat they are quite often the only possible choice. Since they are lightweight, a child can pull the smaller ones up on deck or up the beach. The pneumatic topsides are easy on shiny new paint jobs. These same low topsides with their concentrated buoyancy tanks are perfect for skin diving. A wet, gear-laden scuba diver can clamber back into the inflatable with ease.

Many soft dinghies will plane with only a 10 to 12.5 horsepower outboard. This is very handy if you like going off to distant skin diving holes, or have to commute in a large harbor with strong tides. This combination of planning ability and soft forgiving sides makes the inflatable especially useful in sloppy, rough weather conditions. During the winter of 1983, Newport Beach was racked with 80-knot Santa Ana winds. *Taleisin,* in her downwind slip on Balboa Peninsula, was seriously threatened by the waves that built in the one-mile fetch across the harbor. The waves were hitting her right on the port quarter, the dock our port stern lines were attached to was breaking in half. Ernie Minnie spent the whole day in his 12-foot transom-type inflatable with its 12.5

motor, kedging out *Taleisin*'s 65-pound storm anchor, taking lines ashore, then going to the assistance of the 65-foot yawl *Troubador* which had broken away from its mooring. Ernie's inflatable was great for this work because it was stable and its soft sides minimized the risk involved in coming alongside *Taleisin* and *Troubador* in the three-foot wind chop. On the other hand, the reliable 12.5 horsepower outboard was absolutely necessary for these strong wind conditions where rowing the same inflatable would have been impossible.

Another plus for the soft dinghy is towability. English sailors tow them over the transom with just the aft end of the dinghy touching the water. This seems to work better than towing ten or twelve feet astern, where a strong gust of wind can flip inflatables over.

If you do lose or wear out your inflatable, replacement is not difficult. Most chandleries carry a wide selection of models. They can be collapsed and air freighted to out of the way places. Because they require no chocks, a new model will almost always fit where the old dinghy was stowed.

Though the soft dinghy has many good points, it also has serious drawbacks for the live-aboard cruiser. The most important, in my opinion, is its determined refusal to be rowed to windward in winds of force six or above. A two-foot wind chops stops it dead. This is *extremely dangerous* in open roadstead anchorages. If your motor quits, a fresh offshore wind could blow you out to sea. This has happened several times right at Catalina Island in California, and some of the unfortunate people have perished. If you happen to run your cruising yacht aground, this lack of windward rowing ability combined with the time required to pump up an inflatable, then put on and start its outboard motor, could keep you from kedging out an anchor fast enough to haul your home off a reef or shoal before the ebb tide locks it in its dangerous grip. Because of their skegless, flat bottoms and light weight, inflatables make considerable leeway when you try to row in a beam wind. That is why I feel an inflatable without a reliable outboard motor is only safe in good weather and well protected harbors.

Soft dinghies stow neatly in the trunk of a car, and this leads to one of the other problems owners of inflatables have encountered. Since serial numbers are usually the only thing that distinguishes one eight-foot Avon from the other, theft is a problem.

If it is used on a year-round basis, the soft dinghy usually has a life span of about three or four years. This is because it is hard to do major repairs on a soft dinghy. A cruiser in La Paz showed us how the plywood transom on his inflatable had delaminated and was threatening to break. The materials and heat bonding equipment required to replace the transom made it necessary to return his dinghy to a well equipped repair shop, in this case 900 miles away in San Diego.

Dragging a soft dinghy up beaches wears the bottom out quickly. I have yet to see anyone find an efficient way to add extra protection to combat this problem, nor have I seen an effective way to patch holes caused by this wear.

Leaks in a soft dinghy will be magnified by the hot sun once you are in the tropics, and these minute leaks will cause your buoyancy tanks to become flabby at the end of the day. Returning to a cruising boat after dark in a half-inflated dinghy with no air pump, has cooled the ardor of many a potentially lively cruising lady.

The fabric and rubber buoyancy tanks are susceptible to tears. Fish hooks, broken glass, even fish spines, can cause holes. You can fix them, but eventually it becomes a case of patch on patch.

On a basic rowing inflatable model, without floor boards, the slightest bit of water in the bilge will accumulate where you step. Soggy shoes are the result. This can be avoided with plywood floor boards, but these present their own problems. They take time to assemble, require storage space on your cruising home and add weight to the dinghy. In addition, sand often gets under the plywood and grinds at the bottom fabric of the dinghy, especially at the inaccessible corners under the buoyancy tanks. Some of the new dinghies have a series of four-inch diameter longitudinal inflation tanks along their bottom. This minimizes the problem, but the grooves between the floor tubes collect sand which is hard to wipe out.

A final disadvantage with inflatables is that it is not uncommon to see one flip over at anchor when a strong gust of wind gets under its buoyancy tanks. Many oars, gas tanks, shoes and outboards have been damaged or lost in this manner.

You probably won't encounter most of these disadvantages unless you use your dinghy on a year-round, day-in-day-out basis. The yachtsman who can manage only weekends and annual holidays afloat will probably find his inflatable can last ten or fifteen years. But weekend or year-round, your inflatable's lifespan and usefulness can be improved by some of the suggestions cruising people gave us as we took the photos for this article.

The most common improvement we have seen is eliminating the light, two-part oars usually supplied by the inflatable manufacturers, and using longer, huskier solid oars in their place. This will improve rowing headway in stronger wind and sea conditions. A small anchor with 400 feet of ⅛-inch nylon line kept in the dinghy should solve the problem of being blown offshore from a roadstead anchorage.

If you are harbor hopping, it could pay to keep your inflatable stored on deck inflated or partially inflated. This would definitely speed up any anchor kedging operations.

Some people have reduced the problem of ultraviolet deterioration by fitting a white protective cloth cover over the buoyancy tanks (see figure 11.1), and securing it to existing fittings. This cover is left on during use and also when the dinghy is stowed on deck. The cover solves the problem of burning your bottom on hot sunny days. White hypalon paint (figure 11.2) also provides the same cool protection as a cover. It has a further benefit in that it minimizes leaks caused by heat-induced porosity.

To help prevent theft, paint your yacht's name on all parts of your inflatable with durable, bright-colored hypalon paint and also be sure to record the serial numbers in your log book.

Though I have often used soft dinghies, I have only owned the rigid

FIGURE 11.1

FIGURE 11.2

type, so I guess my preferences are going to be obvious. We had a 6′ 8″ fiberglass Montgomery lapstrake sailing pram for 12 years on our last boat. Mexican kids jumped off a 12-foot high dock into it and debonded all the seats. Another time a trimaran caught its painter and pulled it right into its propellor. This chopped a football sized hole in its bow. I once tied it across the stern of a fishboat in Sri Lanka and another fish boat rammed it, squishing our poor pram into an hourglass shape. All of these disasters were quickly repairable with some fiberglass and resin. If I had had a wooden dinghy, each one of these incidents would have totalled it.

A lapstrake fiberglass dinghy is usually stronger and lighter than a round bilged glass dinghy. The lands or ridges act like longitudinal angle irons adding rigidity which keeps the weight low and strength high. Our first pram weighed 62 pounds. A well designed hard dinghy will make headway to windward in wind chop of two or three feet. I rowed *Seraffyn's* pram a half mile to windward in force eight winds, but I had to stop and bail three times. If *Seraffyn* had been dragging anchor, this ability to row windward could have been vital. On our new 29-foot cutter, we have an 8-foot Fatty Knees lapstrake stem dinghy which weighs 82 pounds. I have rowed this in similar force eight conditions. The sharper bow has proven to be much drier, and cuts through the wind chop more easily. A hard dinghy stored on the cabin top ready to use can be launched in two or three minutes if you have to kedge out an anchor.

Many cruisers who have good rowing dinghies find that unlike their friends with inflatables, for them an outboard motor is a convenience and not vital. So they row more and find that rowing is kind to the ears of neighbors who are seeking the solitude of a quiet cove. From a social point of view, it is easier to start up a conversation with another interesting sailor as you silently row near him. If the discussion continues, it's easy to tread water and hold position with your oars. A noisy, hard-to-maneuver outboard makes this kind of contact almost impossible. A well designed rowing dinghy can be relaxing to use and can provide some of the exercise that we find missing from our life afloat.

Our new dinghy has a sailing rig with a row of reefs in the sail so we can beat home even in strong winds. In Cabo San Lucas last month I ferried 85 gallons of water from the cannery docks a mile away from our anchorage in five trips. The sailing rig made an otherwise boring job into a two hour afternoon treat.

The seat of your pants is more likely to stay dry if you have a hard dinghy (figure 11.3). This is because you sit on thwarts that are well below the gunwales. With most rubber boats, you sit on the side or stern tanks so even wavelets tickle your cheeks. Repairing a damaged glass tender can be quick and relatively easy for the unskilled sailor. It requires no special equipment. A temporary cardboard form covered with wax

FIGURE 11.3

paper can be duct taped inside to accept the wet glass. Two or three hours later when the resin is hard, the boat can be back in service.

If you are commuting from a sandy beach like we have been the last few weeks in La Paz, it is hard to keep sand out of your cruising home unless you keep your dinghy sand free. This is where the fiberglass dinghy shines. It is easier to wipe clean with a damp rag. There are no folds or wrinkles to trap and hold sand. To cap off the advantages of a hard dinghy, let me state that I have never seen one flipped over by wind alone. The only time I have seen one capsize other than through careless boarding was while it was being towed in breaking seas.

The main reason hard dinghies are not sailors' first choice is that it takes time, effort and money just to store one on board where it is least in the way. The place to fit a solid dinghy on a sailboat should ideally be designed right along with the basic deck, cabin and sail plan (figures 11.4–11.8). The importance of a good dinghy on the long-term cruising yacht is overlooked by almost all modern yacht designers and the dinghy is rarely shown on the plans. It is easier to let the owner solve this problem in his own way. Midship cockpit boats rarely have room on the cabin top for a hard dinghy because the sliding hatch is too close to the mainmast. Many aft cockpit yachts have their mainsheet travelor and vang arrangements on the cabin top or their boom is too low, or a dodger gets in the way, so once again there is no room for a dinghy. Some people fit a hard dinghy in davits astern, but this is ruled out if you want a

FIGURE 11.4

self-steering vane. It could also be a problem if you shipped a green sea over the stern. Another spot often chosen is the foredeck. This is okay on a larger boat if it leaves sufficient room on the side decks and between the dinghy and mast to allow you to work the halyards. But changing sails and handling ground tackle is inconvenient with the dinghy always

FIGURE 11.5

FIGURE 11.6

FIGURE 11.7

in the way and could be downright dangerous on a small foredeck. These design problems, combined with having to build special supports and chocks, discourage many cruising sailors.

Once you finally fit your hard dinghy on board, it's highly unlikely that you'll find another brand of tender that fits the same chocks or space without modifications (figure 11.9). This leads to another of the drawbacks of these tenders. Total replacement is difficult in foreign ports. Freighting a replacement from the U.S. or Australia to the Marquesas will be costly because of the size.

The most common complaint about hard dinghies is that they are less stable than inflatables. Inexperienced visitors invariably step on dinghy

FIGURE 11.8

FIGURE 11.9

gunwales. This is okay with an inflatable, but exciting and sometimes very wet with a hard dinghy. For this reason you should choose the largest tender possible, given the limitations of your cruising boat. The size limitation for our tender on *Taleisin* was based on weight, it had to be light enough to allow Lin to pull it up the beach herself. Ours weighs 82 pounds and is just at the limit. If you added the weight of an outboard motor, Lin could not handle it alone.

The solid dinghy is more difficult to lift on board and launch than the

FIGURE 11.10

FIGURE 11.11

inflatable, and it blocks visibility no matter where you store it. It is not as good for skin diving, an efficient fender (figure 11.10) has to be fitted to protect the topsides of the mother ship, and the boat is noisier when it is tied alongside. And finally, hard dinghies eventually require painting to keep them looking their best.

Some of the problems involved with owning a solid dinghy can be solved if you arrange to store it in such a way that it can be lifted off and on with the main halyard and its winch. Even a 100- to 120-pound

FIGURE 11.12

FIGURE 11.13

dinghy can easily be handled by two people this way. Our eight foot tender is light enough to pull quickly on deck and launch by hand, but we have each practiced launching it with the main halyard just in case we need to do it singlehanded (figures 11.11–11.15).

Adding a metal strip to the keel of a hard dinghy makes it easier to maintain, since it eliminates the main wear problem these little work boats have. Positive foam flotation in the seats is important and so are good oars. We use ash for ours because it can be left bare to cut maintenance. We choose 7′6″ oars, ones that would just fit inside the dinghy. We have a high freeboarded tender, one with lower sides could possibly use shorter oars, but it is better to start with the longest oars possible, and cut them off if necessary.

We found an interesting piece of gear in the English yachting magazine, *Practical Boat Owner,* last year, a flotation collar that solves two

FIGURE 11.14

FIGURE 11.15

of the hard dinghy's main faults, stability and fendering. We purchased an Add-A-Buoy and used it for a week in various rowing conditions here in Baja California. We found it added enough stability so I (180 pounds) could literally stand on the gunwale without taking water over the rail. This added buoyancy made it much easier to transfer water and stores from the dinghy to *Taleisin* on the one day when we had a two-foot chop in the harbor.

We also tried this collar for a day of skin diving. The hard dinghy then offered safety since it couldn't easily be punctured by diving gear, yet it was easy for a diver to board because of the stability of the added buoyancy tanks.

But our original idea was to have this collar in our emergency abandon ship kit and that is where we now keep it stored. We hope we never have to use that kit, but if we do, the added buoyancy could make our probably over-loaded sailing tender a more successful lifeboat. The nine-pound collar does increase the overall weight of our tender, it definitely looks a bit odd and it makes rowing to windward slightly more difficult. So at this time we do not use it except for skin diving expeditions. But if you used it with an outboard it could become a permanent fixture to combine the best of both worlds for long-term cruisers.

Two of the sailors we met in La Paz had Fold-A-boats. These hard chined tenders collapsed into a stack of four pieces. They seemed to row quite easily the one afternoon when we paced each other on the short row into shore. The owner of one mentioned that the fold-a-boat company gave a ten year guarantee and that his stowed float on the cabin top of his small trimaran. This, like the Add-A-Buoy is an intriguing idea, one worth investigating, especially for small boats with little deck storage area.

The cruisers of La Paz confirmed our long-term observation that as a general rule, the short-term cruisers, those out for a year or two, tend towards inflatables. The longer term cruisers usually end up with a hard dinghy. This could be because of attrition, rougher service or any other reason. But whichever way you go, there is no perfect solution. What you really want is a tender that's a tractor in the daytime, a tidy stable launch for those times when you happen to be invited aboard the Aga Khan's yacht at cocktail time, a fun sailing boat and an instantly stowable, unobtrusive passenger when you set off across an ocean. This paragon can be achieved on larger yachts where there is lots of room to stow

---

both an inflatable and a solid tender. But for average cruising sailors with 25- to 35-foot cruising homes, any single dinghy we choose will be a compromise.

Addresses:

Add-A-Buoy
  W.F. Walters and Company
  103, The Street
  Bramford, Ipswich IP8 4DY
  England

Fold-A-Boat
  Pacific Marine Supply
  1104 Cannon Street
  San Diego, California

12

In the Extreme Emergency

Emergency safety equipment gets the same treatment as spare parts for sailing gear on board *Taleisin*. We acquire it out of a sense of prudence then store it carefully away with the thought that is really half a prayer . . . if we carry it on board we'll probably never need it, but if we leave it behind we'll jinx ourselves. We had the feeling that we'd covered our bases when we made up our abandon ship kit for our first cruising cutter, *Seraffyn*, then religiously lashed it inside our ready-to-launch dinghy *cum* life boat every time we set off on an ocean crossing. This lead to one of the most disconcerting moments of my sailing life.

We'd been asked by *Sail Magazine* to test and evaluate two brands of portable solar stills being commercially introduced for kits such as ours. We decided the only fair test would also include a Second World War emergency still like we carried in *Seraffyn*'s kit and had purchased through a war surplus supplier for our new cruising home *Taleisin*.

On a sunny March day in Newport Beach, California, in 1984, while we prepared *Taleisin* for sea trials, Larry watched as I launched what the neighbors came to call my fleet of plastic space ships. Within two days the results were obvious. If we had ever had to abandon ship and depend on our war surplus solar still for water, we'd have been dead. The most disconcerting part of this revelation was that if we hadn't been

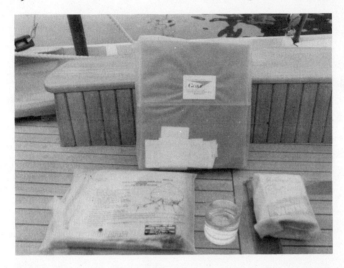

FIGURE 12.1   The solar stills in their packs. That is an 8 ounce old-fashioned glass in the middle to give you an idea of their size.

FIGURE 12.2   The stills launched.

chosen as test personnel we'd never have known we were sailing with an unreliable piece of gear until it was too late. This incident and what we learned as our test progressed gave us a different attitude towards safety equipment, especially that which comes in a "Sealed—don't open until you are forced to use it" package.

FIGURE 12.3   Filling the Airborne still.

Since the instructions for any emergency equipment should be comprehensible to the least mechanically inclined member of the ship's crew, it was decided that I rather than the far more mechanically gifted Larry, would conduct the deployment tests on my own. I launched the Airborne emergency solar still (figure 12.3) first because it is definitely the easiest of the three packages to open. This is an English-made unit used in the European Common Market by Air force units and merchant seaman life raft outfitters. It is distributed in the U.S. by Europacific Marine Inc., 13377 Beach Avenue, Marina Del Rey, California 90292 and is now becoming available in marine stores at prices ranging from $89 to $100. The packaged unit is 10½ by 14 by 1¼ inches and weighs 1¾ pounds. The instructions printed on the plastic container are easy to understand, the container itself could be used as a one pint spare water storage unit.

The inflation procedure was arduous. First I had to inflate an inner-tubelike support float then blow up the teardrop-shaped condensation canopy. This took thirty minutes and every bit of wind in me. I used our dinghy bailer to put salt water in the reservoir/ballast section but

the fill tube is large enough so water could be added using your hand
as a scoop. An orange polypropylene attachment line was well secured
to the still and went completely around its circumference but the slippery line untied itself from the round turn and two half hitches I used
to secure it to the leg of our dock cleat only minutes after I launched
it, fortunately I was able to retrieve the still in the calm waters of
Newport Harbor, but wondered about the devastating affect of the same
problem in a raft adrift at sea. My general impression of the still once
I launched it was that the inflated top looked rather delicate and there
were no patching or repair materials with the unit. I could almost
immediately see condensation droplets inside the canopy.

The Lifeline survival still by Direx Inc., 519 W Lancaster Avenue,
Haverford, Pennsylvania 19041 was a much bulkier unit than the Airborne at 12 by 12 by 2 inches and 4.2 pounds. Its price of $269 to $295
retail seemed steep at first. The Lifeline still (figure 12.4) was easy to
deploy and only took ten minutes of blowing before the upper float
cushion looked like the pictures on the instruction sheet. Since the still
wicks salt water through its velcro closures it becomes virtually self-
tending after its initial launching. A shock cord bridle attached in two
places to the front of the mattress shaped still is secured to your life raft,
in our case a dock, with a plastic snap hook. I would have liked more

FIGURE 12.4   The cushionlike gortex still is self-priming, but opening it as
I am doing here, starts the distillation process working sooner.

than a two point attachment to the raft, but subsequent tugging tests showed this was a strong design. A person in a life raft situation might want to put an extra safety line to the still. Once set afloat the Lifeline still did not inspire immediate confidence like the Airborne still since I could not see the distillation process happening with this unit. But the zipper opening packing container did hold a generous selection of self-sticking repair materials and it was large enough to hold almost a gallon of spare fresh water.

The WWII survival still (figure 12.5) built for the air force came last that afternoon. I have never had to fight so hard to break into any easy-to-open package. The well-illustrated instructions seemed not only easy to use but complete, including a discussion of production and repair. The repair tape was enclosed and the unit in excellent condition even though it was produced sometime between 1944 and 1952. Inflating the still took more time and breath than the Airborne unit. Then water had to be slowly added to an inverse funnel at the top of the beachball-like still. This salt water served both as ballast and as fuel for the distillation process. This filling took patience, even with the dinghy bailer. The attachment line threaded around the whole unit securely and had a strong, carbineer type clip to secure it to the life raft/dock. Unlike the Airborne still which needs saltwater added once each day or the self-tending Lifeline still, the WWII still required refilling every hour.

All three survival stills were solar powered so I started my production

FIGURE 12.5 The air force still was the hardest to refill.

tests at sunrise the next day. Air temperatures ranged from 62 degrees to 82 degrees with a water temperature of 58 degrees. The Airborne still began showing signs of water production within an hour. Salt water from the reservoir ballast tank soaked the black cloth wick stretched by the inner tubelike float. Heat generated by the sun passing through the clear magnifying canopy top caused this salt water to evaporate and soon a film of distilled droplets covered the inside of the canopy and began dribbling down into the trough around the outer parameter of the float then into the ¼-inch drain tube that lead to a trailing water reservoir bag.

The Lifeline still just sat there undulating slightly, a bit of mist forming in the clear top float chamber. The WWII still became misted inside with evaporating saltwater, its top loading reservoir required refilling hourly.

After four hours I pulled the stills next to the dock and found the Airborne reservoir about half full, just over a cup of fresh water had been distilled. I tasted it and found a plastic flavor but no brackishness at all.

There was no water in the reservoir bag floating at the stern of the lifeline still so I pulled it from the water to figure out what was wrong. As I lifted the 2- by 5-foot still, just over a pint of fresh water rushed into the reservoir bag. I tasted this and found it almost free of any flavor, plastic, salt or otherwise. I then called the manufacturer to find where the water came from. Their explanation, which I feel should have been included in the written instructions, is that this still works on the vapor diffusion principle. There is a special film of Gortex material, a vapor-permeable fabric with 90,000 holes per square inch between the saltwater wick and the collector area. Since vapor always seeks the coldest surface, condensing saltwater vapor moves away from the sun heated black cloth, through the waterproof but not vaporproof barrier toward the colder seawater and becomes distilled. Since salt and mineral molecules are larger than vapor molecules, the distilled water is amazingly pure. I contacted the local county health board and found that the water supplied to city taps has twenty times the impurities of that from the Lifeline still and about the same as that from the Airborne. So even water from a polluted bay such as Newport, became safely drinkable once it was distilled in either of these units.

When I tried to find the distillate in the WWII still I came up with a complete zero. After three days of trying during which the Airborne successfully produced about 1 quart of fresh water during 9 hours of sunlight and the Lifeline about 2.3 quarts, Larry and I admitted defeat with the still we once thought would have supported us if an emergency occurred during our cruise on *Seraffyn*. We contacted Steve Callahan a naval architect who had had the misfortune of being forced to spend 76 days adrift in his life raft after losing his singlehanded race boat 800 miles from the Canary Islands. His survival had been completely dependent on the very still we'd had a failure with during our tests. (His book, *Adrift*, tells of this experience.)

Steve confirmed that the WWII surplus still requires constant tending to produce even a minimum of drinkable fresh water. He fortunately had carried three. When his first still failed to produce after several days, he decided to dissect it in hopes he could learn how to make his two remaining stills work. He was successful. His stills produced just over a pint of water a day after that. "But that meant keeping the stills constantly inflated because if the sides collapsed even for a minute, they touched the saltwater permeated drip cloth and my reservoir of fresh water was ruined. The worst problem was that each still had its own personality. To get the best production I had to inflate each one differently and regulate the dripping process to get the very slow drip that worked best." Steve was afraid to launch the stills except during good conditions because as he stated more than once during our discussion, "those stills were all that were keeping mc alive. If I over used them they might not last. If I lost one I was lost." Steve eventually created a surplus of 8 pints of fresh water by conserving and storing it in containers he salvaged from the sea. He kept these for overcast or rough weather days and only consumed amounts in excess of his storage capacity on sunny days. When he was picked up by fishermen about a dozen miles from Marie Galante Island in the southern Caribbean he had survived on sea life and approximately one pint of water a day.

He recommended carrying several of the WWII surplus stills in any abandon ship kit remembering that it took three to sustain him at the very edge of survival. When he heard about the stills we were testing he said his biggest fear was caused by fish being attracted to the trailing water reservoir bag. Both the Airborne and the Lifeline have detachable reservoir bags with shut off caps for the still drain tubes. So it would probably be best to attach the reservoir for a short period every few hours to drain the distillate.

Steve Callahan's survival on only a pint of water a day was considered almost a miracle by the instructors at the San Diego Naval and Air Force Survival Training school. Larry and I spent the afternoon there with two officers who willingly tested any distillation units they could in hopes of improving the chances of downed fliers at sea. "An adult man can survive in 75- to 80-degree air temperatures for 4 to 7 days without water, but he'll start becoming dehydrated after two days," one officer told us. "That means he'll become weak and lethargic. To maintain their ability to react well and actually work, most men need two quarts of water a day. That's why we abandoned the WWII stills long ago. They are too inefficient and don't provide nearly enough water for the space they take up." Since airmen are in radio contact at all times, most rescue efforts are aimed at picking up survivors within 24 hours. So water supplies are provided in the form of a desalter kit, a 4½ by 4½ by 2 inch plastic box containing chemical bricks and a filter bag which will produce 8 pints of drinkable water. These kits have an unlimited shelf life and are often available through navy surplus stores or from Permute Co., 1915 Old Philadelphia Dr., Lancaster, Pennsylvania 17603. I asked the officers what they'd recommend for yachtsmen who might find themselves adrift without the extensive search and rescue network available to service fliers and he told us of a hand-operated reverse osmosis desalter unit capable of producing over 30 gallons of fresh water a day that he felt would be perfect for multiman life rafts (see following section). But for the couple in a small boat his recommendation was desalter kits for immediate use and more than one of the portable stills.

Larry and I continued testing the Airborne and Lifeline stills for another two weeks but discarded the WWII still after three more unsuccessful days. We allowed each unit to spend two nights in contact with the barnacle covered floats at our dock and were surprised to see they sustained no damage if they were free to move on their tether lines. Both distillation units began to develop barnacles after seven days. These barnacles were easy to scrape off. Our best fresh water yield for the Airborne still was 1.2 quarts during 9½ hours of bright sunlight. The Lifeline still produced 2.7 quarts during the same period. The one worrisome difference between the stills was that the distillate in the Airborne settled around the rim of the inner tube and if you tilted the still past 35 degrees of angle, fresh water could run back into the salt reservoir. So this still cannot be used as safe storage for more than one quart of water. The Lifeline fresh water collector, on the other hand, is fully protected from recontamination and can hold about a gallon of fresh water.

Unfortunately, we could not come up with a way to simulate rough weather conditions for our tests. Our conditions were in fact close to ideal, with smooth water, a stable dock to work from and the security of a water hose nearby. The instruction sheets of all three stills suggested bringing the units on board during rough conditions. With this in mind, the Lifeline still has a slight advantage as it is easiest to deflate and can still be used as a storage unit in its deflated condition.

When we finished our tests we tried to flush the two units, dry and repack them for future use. The Lifeline still opens for this purpose and we were able to wash it salt free and dry it in about three days. The Airborne was very difficult to flush and was not fully dry inside after three weeks. Two months later we saw mildew inside this still and do not know if it will affect its reusability. The manufacturer does not state this still is repackable and suggests that in its original package it has a five-year shelf life.

After our testing ended we were left with two major questions. Where do emergency distillation or desalinator units fit in the average sailor's list of safety equipment priorities, and secondly, which unit should offshore sailors carry in a comprehensive survival kit?

There are no all-encompassing answers. If you accept the navy estimate of two quarts per man per day as an absolute necessity, no portable still of reasonable size and cost will fill the demand. Steve Callahan's estimate of a pint a day seems low, yet he has recovered full health in spite of his 76-day ordeal. So we would be willing to accept an average safe minimum of one quart per day per person as the standard for choosing a still to pack in our new abandon ship kit. We would augment this with a desalter kit to take care of the first two days and try to have a five-gallon jug of water tied near the shrouds to be tossed into the lifeboat in an emergency situation. Given the fifty-fifty chance of actually getting the spare jug safely on board the life boat, our evaluation of the three stills we tested would be based on the size of our crew plus costs. The WWII surplus stills can be made to work. But even at their $12 to $15 cost, if you can locate them, they seem a poor choice. With only a fourth of a quart production a day and a 33 percent chance of failure, you would need five stills per person in your kit with a space loss of almost a cubic foot.

The Airborne still in its sealed pack cannot be pre-tested. With its average output of about a quart per day, one still per person would be a minimum with one extra still just in case the first proved to be defective. In otherwords, two stills for the singlehander, three for the couple. Cost-wise and space-wise this still makes sense for small crews. The reusable, pre-testable Lifeline still with its 2.6 litre production average would be our choice for crews above two. Since it can be used right on deck then cleaned and repacked, it could be a back up water supply if your main water tanks failed or your shipboard water supply became contaminated. Because we could pre-test this unit we would carry only one for two people, two for four crew.

The priority position is more difficult to evaluate. For people on two-week cruises within their home waters, these stills probably belong low on any list. For people voyaging in heavy rainfall areas and inland seas such as the Puget Sound or New Zealand, these units are not essential. But for anyone cruising in areas with deserted islands and limited rainfall such as Baja California or the Bahamas, these units belong right next to their EPIRB. When you begin to cross oceans and sail away from the beaten path, we feel an emergency distillation unit should be placed above an EPIRB on your list, because in effect these stills are the back up for that transmitter. If it fails to bring help, you can help yourself.

Abandoning ship, being stranded on a deserted island, being twenty days from land with a contaminated water supply—its hard to imagine these scenarios as part of an offshore sailor's life. Yet in the past decade we've personally spoken to the Robinsons who were adrift for 47 days, Steve Callahan who survived for 76 days. We've read the Bailey's account of 117 days adrift and we were in the Balearics while a French couple drifted for 12 days in a life raft just 100 miles north of us. Had we been in the same position on *Seraffyn* our preparations might have only prolonged the agony when we found our WWII still was inoperative and inadequate. That knowledge gained from the tests at our dock was a real shocker. It showed us once again that the contents of a survival safety kit have to be carefully considered by any prudent sailor. And some sort of water producing system belongs at the heart of this kit.

MECHANICAL EMERGENCY DESALINATORS

Reverse osmosis desalinators have been promoted as the breakthrough water maker for the past eight to ten years. Unfortunately these units, which work by forcing salt water through a series of semi-permeable membranes, tend to be much bulkier than the waste heat evaporators used as water makers on sportfishing boats and larger ships for the past three decades. Furthermore, the membranes and filters in these units need frequent changing which raises their maintenance costs above those of the evaporator desalinators. But, as usually happens, time, testing and market acceptance has now made reverse osmosis units more competitive and smaller. The membranes have been improved and a spin-off of this development has been the manual water maker tested at the North Island Naval Survival School in San Diego, California.

This completely portable, hand-operated desalter is made by Recovery Engineering, Inc., 1204 Chestnut Avenue, Minneapolis, Minnesota, 55403. It is a compact 26.5 by 4 by 6 inches, weighs 11.6 pounds and has an output of 1.5 gallons of fresh water per hour if you pump at a rate of 30 strokes per minute (figure 12.6). That means 12 minutes of pumping would provide the minimum daily survival requirement of a

FIGURE 12.6   The reverse osmosis hand-operated unit for large life rafts.

quart of water for one man. The officers we spoke with said the pumping action was extremely simple and light work. The unit seemed well built of stainless steel and heavy duty plastics and withstood over 300 hours of their testing with no sign of deterioration. The manufacturer feels the membrane on the R.O. unit will last 3,000 hours and suggests using this system to augment shipboard supplies on smaller boats with the desalter stored next to the life raft when not in use. (In 1986 the United States Navy began equipping their 25-man life rafts with the Recovery Engineering WL-SB RO unit.) The major disadvantage is the cost, $1,825 retail at the present time. For vessels with ten-man life rafts, this cost would be definitely justified. For the small-boat sailor who wished to cruise in remote places where water supplies were limited, the R. O. pump could possibly be a good supplement for his regular tankage.

In the fall of 1984 Recovery Industries introduced a miniaturized version of their manual desalinator. It weighs less than four pounds and takes up about the same space as an average college hardcover textbook, yet is capable of producing up to six gallons of drinking water during a 24-hour period. We tried one of these Recovery Survivors in San Diego the day before we left for Mexico and watched in amazement as fresh water began to drip into our collector within about 90 seconds. The pumping action was easy, there was no set up time, and within 13 minutes the desalter produced a cup of water that was slightly more brackish than that we distilled with the solar stills but definitely as drinkable as Newport Beach municiple water.

John Bowyer, controller of the originators of the Survivor, explained that the patented energy recovery pumps inside the sturdy appearing unit magically increase your pumping pressure until it reaches the 800 pounds pressure necessary to force salt water through the membrane. This technology doesn't come cheaply. The unit presently sells for $500. But for a four- to six-man life raft this makes it a better buy than either of the solar stills, especially since it is reusable and testable. This unit has been tested up to 2,000 gallons of production with the same membrane. The membrane can then be replaced. It also comes complete with a bottle of bacteria inhibitor which means you can test the unit occasionally, then clean it and store it away again.

In May of 1986, Recovery Engineering announced plans to introduce a new Survivor model within a year that will be under five pounds weight and produce up to 18 gallons of water a day, yet sell for less than $350. We have not seen this unit, but it could prove to be the best possible solution for any cruising emergency kit planned for crews of three or more.

13

Outfitting *Taleisin**

When Larry and I made the final commitment to build a new boat, we also made some promises to ourselves. This time we'd be realistic. Instead of hoping to build a boat in a year or two like we thought we could when our first boat was just a keel timber lying next to a loft floor, we'd plan on three and one-half or four years, because in the end that's the time it took to build *Seraffyn*. † If we didn't feel pressured, we hoped we'd enjoy the experience of boat building as much as we'd enjoyed cruising. Now that launching is less than four months away we can look back on three years that were sometimes tedious, sometimes frustrating, usually interesting, occasionally exciting, but all in all just hard work that we knew would be worth the effort once we launched a boat that was uniquely ours, free and clear of payments. Yet all during those months when our every effort and every dollar was aimed toward one goal, there were moments of extraordinary fun, times when we'd feel like kids on Christmas morning. Each time we'd make a final decision on some fitting, some piece of gear for the boat, we'd save our money, place our

*This chapter was written in 1983 for *Cruising World Magazine,* just before we were ready to launch our new cruising home. Rather than change the mood, a mood I think appeals and applies to anyone who has ever built or finished their own boat, I have left it as it was originally written and only updated information, prices, and addresses where necessary.

†We had approximately 4,200 hours of labor in *Seraffyn* who displaced 11,000 pounds, and figured we'd need approximately 6,800 to 7,200 hours to complete *Taleisin* at 17,700 pounds displacement. The average working man spends 2,000 hours a year at his job (50 weeks times 40 hours).

order then wait impatiently for the big brown UPS truck to rumble up our long gravel driveway. Then, when we'd unpacked our newest treasure we'd rush inside the frame work of our future home and play "pretend."

We ordered our storm anchor before the first frames were bolted in place above *Taleisin*'s teak keel. We'd read about the three piece fisherman type anchors Nat Herreshoff had designed years before. These anchors came apart into simply shaped pieces that were easy to stow, easy to carry. That meant we could have an oversized storm anchor for that once-in-five-years situation when all hell breaks loose, yet we could store it away below the cabin sole in a space we'd rarely use for anything else. Unfortunately, no one makes the exact Herreshoff anchor any more. But Paul Luke Company in Maine makes a very good copy.* So we ordered a 65-pounder and waited for it to arrive. We got a good laugh when a semi-truck rolled to a stop at the bottom of our driveway and a burly six-foot-four-inch driver yelled, "What the hell do you want with an anchor out here in the desert?" When he unloaded the assembled anchor I stopped laughing. It looked huge. But as Larry had promised, once it was disassembled, each part weighed less than 30 pounds. I practiced putting it together and soon felt confident I could assemble it on the foredeck then hoist it overboard with a halyard even if I was caught on board alone in a tight situation. That anchor worked as a door stop for two years and just two weeks ago Larry built a simple holder in the bilge aft of the galley. We'll probably use that anchor less than once a year as we cruise, but I'll never resent the space it takes

We had five rounds of planking on the boat when our galley stove arrived. There had been no question about what type of fuel we'd use for cooking. Butane was the sensible choice for us since I love to cook and we'd found butane or propane, which can be used interchangeably to be relatively easy to get everywhere we sailed on *Seraffyn*, clean to use, and surprisingly cheap. Our biggest question was, should we do as we had on *Seraffyn* and save money by using a propane stove built for the motor home trade, or should we invest in a stove built especially for salt water sailors? The cost difference was substantial. Very nice looking trailer stoves with three burners, an oven and broiler could be had for under $300. Stainless steel marine stoves by Kenyon, Dickenson, Ship-

---

*See end of article for source of items marked with asterisks.

mate or Gas Systems started at $800. We thought it over for a long time and remembered the hours we'd spent attacking rust on *Seraffyn*'s stove, replacing the oven bottom with sheet stainless steel when it corroded away, buying a new top for it in Singapore. If we added up the money we'd spent on that stove all during twelve years of cruising, it probably would have topped the cost of a true marine stove. Our final choice was the Dickenson Mariner built in New Zealand by Marine Stainless Fittings Ltd.,* because of five features: a magic click mechanism (piezolighter) on each burner lights the stove without matches or a pilot light; the oven door has a spring latch that clicks it shut automatically; instead of individual pot holders over each burner, the whole top is covered with a grate so pots can be shifted anywhere you want them, there are two burners in the oven, one top, one bottom. This lets you have radiant heat, a broiler, an oven or both at the same time. A movable shield lets you choose how much of the oven you wish to use for each purpose. Finally, every burner has a heat sensitive shut-off valve so no gas leaks into the boat if a pot overflows and puts out the flame. The two disadvantages of this stove were its price and its finish. We justified the high cost by reminding ourselves that no other item on the boat is used six or seven times a day, 365 days a year. The glaring, polished stainless steel finish may not look so bright once it is hidden beside the mast, but if it does bother us we can either rub it with sandpaper for a mat finish, or remove the sides and have them porcelianized in a color to blend with the varnished wood around the galley.

It wasn't until *Taleisin* was planked and her deck framed that we gave up trying to find someone to custom-build an aluminum propane tank to fit into the deck box we planned between the mast and cabin front. *Seraffyn* had had a spray galvanized steel, 20-pound capacity, propane tank with a level gauge custom fitted to the same type of deck box. It worked well but Larry had to lift the tank because even empty it weighed 32 pounds and full that escalated to 52. We'd also had to re-coat the tank every three years to keep rust off our teak decks. So when we saw aluminum propane cylinders arrive on the boating market we reasoned we'd just pay the tank manufacturer a bit more and get a custom fitted aluminum tank for *Taleisin*. Unfortunately, the engineers at three tank companies explained that forming steel and forming aluminum is quite different. Where a custom steel tank would cost an extra $50, no one would make a custom aluminum tank. We agonized over that problem for almost two years until one of us said, "Why do we always do things the hardest way. Why can't we use something standard for once." We spent a whole evening staring at the space where a deck box would someday sit. Then we began trying the measurements from standard aluminum tanks. Slowly, like a puzzle falling into place, our thinking changed and we found a relatively inexpensive solution. Three of the ten-pound aluminum tanks built by Worthington would fit into our deck box, two laying on their sides, one standing up ready for use. Each tank weighs less than eight pounds empty, 18 full. We'd get 50 percent more capacity, or the ability to cook in the cooler climates where we like to cruise for four months instead of three between refills. Best of all, the tanks would be easy for either of us to carry ashore. The manufacturer, Worthington Tank Company, was most willing to sell direct at prices far lower than trailer or marine supply houses.*

We let our sailing friends know about some of the special items we were looking for. So when one of them called to tell us he'd found the parachute sea anchor we wanted, we were pleased as can be. We'd used one of those heavy duty, surplus army ordinance drop parachutes with a six foot diameter on *Seraffyn.* (Stretched out, this parachute actually has a diameter of 8 feet, but the legal size is determined when the parachute is measured in a completely relaxed state.) This particular type of parachute is made of a coarse, open weave, white nylon fabric with edge reinforcing of green webbing. The fishermen on the west coast use these parachutes as sea anchors for boats up to ten tons or forty feet. So we ordered one for *Taleisin.* After Len bought us our parachute sea anchor, we found another source for these wonderfully strong, rot proof, shock absorbing, easy to store substitutes for the old canvas and iron hoop cones sailors like Voss and Slocum had to use.*

We had one very pleasant surprise all during the past few years. When we'd built *Seraffyn,* fiberglass boats were the up and coming thing along with stainless steel and aluminum fittings. So we'd had to search long and hard to find some of the bronze fittings we wanted. In most cases we resorted to casting our own. But during the twelve years we've been out cruising, a quiet revolution seemed to take place, guided by magazines like *Woodenboat* and *Cruising World.* Now dozens of companies were again making nice bronze fittings. The Southcoast bronze stropped blocks that we'd used so successfully on *Seraffyn* are now made by another company but they are still just as nicely machined and the prices for handsome, traditional looking gear that won't bang up woodwork or scratch the mast, are surprisingly low. We have made one compromise on this new boat. On *Seraffyn* we used all Southcoast blocks except for the mainsheet arrangement. There we used three single blocks on the taffrail and a double on the boom which gave us a four-part purchase, double ended mainsheet arrangement. Each of these blocks was an original Merriman lignum vitea block with ten coats of varnish. Each block had been a gift from one old friend or another. All were at least forty years old when we launched *Seraffyn*. Since *Taleisin* needs a six-part purchase on her five foot longer boom, we have decided to use four single blocks on the taffrail, three on the boom. The last lignum vitea, bronze stropped Merriman blocks now reside as collectors items on mantels or on yacht club trophies. So we'll use Southcoast blocks and some day we'll carve, then varnish some lignum vitea to replace the easy-to-care-for neoprene shells on these taffrail blocks.*

It wasn't until *Taleisin* was fully planked with our deck framing in place that we were finally able to figure out our interior. We knew we wanted a heating stove somewhere in the main cabin, but what size, and what brand were complete mysteries. We knew nothing about heating stoves from direct experience other than in homes we have rented ashore. But after crossing the North Pacific in *Seraffyn* and suffering through 30 days of dense fog and 47-degree temperatures with only our propane oven and oil lamps to warm us, we've decided a heating stove is essential. Our first idea was to have an oil burning stove such as the fishermen in the Baltic use. But as we cruised through the waters of British Columbia, we asked every sailor we met about these stoves and learned that oil burners have some real disadvantages on board yachts. It seems that oily black soot is produced in large quantity when these stoves are turned to their lowest settings. Its a case of incomplete combustion. On fishing boats this is rarely a problem because larger sized windows and cabins require more heat so the stoves can be turned on high. But in a 30- to 35-footer, even the lowest settings are usually too high. The only solution to this low setting problem is to add an electric blower or fan. That is a complication we cannot afford since we carry no engine, and no batteries. This oily soot would drive us crazy. We saw northern sailboats with black marks on their sails, decks, cabin tops, even on bed clothes that were laid out to air. So we cut our choice of cabin heaters by deciding we'd rather put up with the ash produced by burning charcoal or wood. This left us with four different stoves to choose from. We mocked up the main salon furnishings with old pine planks, bits of plywood and cardboard cut outs. Only one stove fit the space we'd designated. Fortunately (and a rarity for us) we'd ended up with the least expensive wood burning stove on the market, a Fatsco Midget (this is a larger version of the famous Tiny Tot). The body, heatshield and flue are made of stainless steel; the other parts are cast iron.* The cost including damper, shield and flue plus freight is less than $150. Unfortunately for us, the proprietor of the Fatsco company is a real independent type and almost drove us crazy with his insistence that we fill out order forms exactly to his specs, and his refusal to take our order over the telephone and ship COD. But the stove arrived just as *Taleisin*'s teak deck was finished and it fits perfectly in a corner near the head area. Now we are busy researching the pros and cons of differently shaped stove pipe heads. (The quest for a heating stove didn't finish here.) When we were launching *Taleisin,* Larry's father arrived with an English-made Valor* kerosene heater he had used inside his 26-foot boat during a long Canadian winter. It had a round wick and was built so that air vented through the center of the wick produced a hot, clear burning blue flame. When we computed the volume of wood we have to carry to warm the boat on a 40-day passage, then compared it to the 12 gallons of kerosene this heater would require, our plans took on a new twist. Why not combine both stoves. The vented wood stove would carry off the moisture produced by burning kerosene, it would be safer since carbon monoxide wouldn't vent into the cabin. The heavy metal body and long stainless flue would radiate heat into the cabin. Best of all, we could raise or lower the wick to control the heat, something we couldn't do easily with a solid fuel coal or wood stove. So with about 50 hours of work we ended up with a fine compromise, the good looking Fatsco Stove and its internal Valor kerosene burner. We are still looking for the right smoke head. Ours creates down drafts in winds of 35 knots or more.

One piece of gear we especially liked on *Seraffyn* had been her bottom action sheet winches. They were Merriman No. 3 winches and we knew they were not only out of production, but far smaller than we needed for our new boat. We wrote an article in *Cruising World* and *Practical Boat Owner* magazines asking readers to help us start a campaign to get someone producing a good range of bottom action winches including larger ones with two speeds. The response was great. Over 120 people

FIGURE 13.1 The
Murray MW8,
two-speed winch.

wrote in and told us of several bottom action winches we might like. Chris Bousaid, racer, sailmaker, Kiwi, working for Hoods, wrote of the winch he'd used in his race boats, a Murray MW8 with a direct-action bottom handle for moderate conditions and a worm drive side winding handle for heavy weather or micrometerlike fine tuning. This winch also had a top cleat which made it semi-self-tailing and the worm drive handle worked both ways, clockwise and counter-clockwise so you could wind out an override. We wrote to New Zealand and when their brochure arrived found they had five sizes of winches in bronze. Our final order included two of the two-speed larger size for sheets, three medium MW5's for halyards and a tiny MW1 for the bottom of the boom where it helps us outhaul the clew reefing pennant. These winches gave us the speed and convenience of handles that were always in place, ready to use—no hunting, no lost handles.

(After 3 years of use we'd give the Murray bottom action halyard and boom winch 100-A-1 ratings—couldn't be better for the job. The sheet winches get 95 percent approval. The top cleat is superb, the override wind out has kept a few sail sheeting errors (overrides) from becoming incidents. Our only complaints are that the 40-to-1 power speed of the worn dive is a little slower than we'd like, and the two separate handles sometimes get in the way. Guests who have never seen winches like these sometimes find them hard to use at first.)

There has been no question in our minds about the lighting system for *Taleisin*. Kerosene running lights and interior lamps worked well on

Seraffyn for eleven years, kerosene lamps work well in the old isolated stone house we are living in as we build *Taleisin.* So kerosene it will be. Once again, as we've done over the past fifteen years of our life, we'll make filling our oil lamps simple by having a gravity feed tank with an easy-to-use spigot in a convenient place. *Taleisin's* kerosene tank is a ten-gallon stainless steel fuel tank made for a Saab diesel engine. We picked it up at a marine swap meet long before we put the decks in place. The round tank nestles neatly into the bow over the chain locker where it will gravity feed on either tack. A ⅜-inch copper tube leads from the shut-off valve under the tank, along the bilge stringer and back to a tap next to the bathtub and companionway ladder. The fill for the tank is through a deck plate.

We used Perko brand oil lamps on *Seraffyn* and found they gave a nice light. But after observing all of the different lamps we have in our old stone house, we learned that the wider the wick, the whiter the light. So we tried several brands of marine oil lamps including two round wicked ones. The round wicks varied; some gave good light, others didn't. We ruled them out because they required extreme care in trimming to prevent sooting. In the end our choice was a set of lamps from Holland.* The flat wick is a full inch wide, the glass chimneys screw in place and the whole top hinges so you can light the lamp without taking the chimney off. This just might cut down our breakage rate. But just in case, we invested in three dozen spare chimneys. These lamps had one flaw: The lower part of the kerosene bowl is fitted to the upper and crimped in place, then sealed with an epoxy substance. This joint leaked on four of our five new lamps. Larry ran a bead of solder around the joint and solved the problem.

One of the nicest features on *Taleisin,* and one of the big reasons we wanted a larger boat, was the work shop area. We planned for a real solid work bench and vice under the cockpit hatch. This area then solved our tool storage problems. On *Seraffyn,* we'd stored tools under a settee. This was the only space we had for what Larry wanted to carry. We tried all sorts of protective methods, but the only tools that stayed rust free were the ones that could fit inside the only plastic tool box we had room for. Soon after we laid *Taleisin's* keel, we began looking for the company who'd made that tool box. We didn't locate them until Taleisin's hull was fully planked and it wasn't until we'd built the work bench that we figured out which of their selection of boxes to order. We finally settled on a large, water-resistant tool chest with eight different drawers to hold screws, bolts, nuts and small hand tools, plus eight assorted sizes of tool boxes with trays for other tools.* Each box will hold a specialized type of equipment, rigging tools in one, caulking tools in a second, mechanics tools in a third, electric drill, sander in their own separate storage box. Any tools that can rust will be misted with WD 40 after we lay them in the box. The boxes are rain proof so I can leave them on deck and the tools will stay protected. Even better, any rust, oil or grease will stay in the box with the tools. When its time for Larry to earn cruising dollars with his boat building skills, he'll simply have to choose the right box of tools and take it ashore with him.

That's the way it's gone all during the times when boat building seemed the slowest possible way to ever reach our goal of cruising again. Those carefully planned purchases kept us feeling like we were making progress. Victorian-style ironstone dishes perked me up as I applied yet another of the five coats of varnish to the inside of *Taleisin*'s teak planking. A huge 2-inch capacity, all bronze, hand-operated, gallon-a-stroke Edson bilge pump showed up at a bargain price at a local swap meet when Larry's knees were sore from caulking and paying the decks. He used it as an excuse to break the routine and before the deck was finished he'd installed the bilge pump platform which sat in lonely splendor for five months until the interior cabinetry joined it.

Now the launching date is less than four months away and it's harder than ever to remember that we promised to give ourselves plenty of time to enjoy building this boat. We want her in the water now yet know that any project we leave unfinished will be twice as hard to do if we leave behind the power tools and convenience of our country boatyard. Almost all of the gear we need for *Taleisin* is sitting in the gold room waiting to be placed in its assigned spot and we are hurrying impatiently toward the biggest Christmas morning of all, the day our three and a half years of work settles into the water and we get a chance to use all of our new toys.

*1. Luke three-piece anchors
   Paul Luke Inc.
   East Boothbay, Maine 04544 USA

2. Mariner stove
   Dickinson Stoves
   4611 11th Avenue
   Seattle, Washington 98107 USA

   Marine Stainless Fittings Ltd.
   9 Sir Williams Ave,
   East Tamaki, Auckland
   New Zealand

3. Aluminum propane cylinders
   Worthington Propane Tanks
   Marine Division
   1085 Dearborn,
   Columbus, Ohio 43085 USA

4. Parachute sea-anchors
   Fiorentinos Marine Service
   311 22nd St.
   San Pedro, California USA

   Para-anchors International
   P.O. Box 19
   Summerland, California 93067 USA

5. Blocks
   Racelite-Southcoast Corp
   16516 Broadway
   Maple Heights, Ohio 44137 USA

6. Wood burning stove
   Fatsco
   Benton Harbor, Michigan 49022 USA

  Oil heaters
   Valor Engineering Ltd.
   Erdington, Birmingham 24,
   England

7. Murray winches
   South Pacific Associates
   3827 Stone Way Naval
   Seattle, Washington 98103 USA

Cleveco Murray-Sealine Marine
Ltd. PO Box 37131
Parnell, Auckland,
New Zealand

8. Holland oil lamps
   T.D. Marine
   PO Box 937
   Redwood City, California 94064 USA

9. Tool boxes
   Flambeau Products, various marine hardware stores

14
Cruising Wheels

When we first set off cruising on *Seraffyn*, we were thrilled to eliminate the complications of shore life. To be without a motorized vehicle and its maintenance problems seemed like a special kind of freedom. Like most Americans, especially those on the West Coast, we'd forgotten what it was like to walk, to use buses or hire taxis. So everyday chores like grocery shopping or setting off to mail letters became mini-adventures as we took time to notice the world at this newer, more sedate pace.

We cruised for seven years without having any great desire to own a vehicle except for three times when we settled in to work at boat repairs for more than a few months at a time on the East Coast and on England's southern coast. Each time we were able to buy $200 clunkers that served as rolling tool boxes and got us out into the countryside on weekends.

Then when we reached the Balearic Islands of Spain we realized we'd soon be leaving Europe and we'd miss seeing the Swiss Alps, the French canals and rivers. That started us thinking about touring inland and lead to one of the highlights of our cruising life, an eight-week inland tour on a motorcycle. We knew nothing about these two wheeled wonders but asked every rider we met a hundred questions and with very good fortune were able to buy an excellent machine, a two-year-old Ducati 350 single cylinder, long stroke cycle that carried the two of us and our camping gear over 6,000 kilometers of European country roads, through the Pyrénées and up the steep roads of Switzerland. We were able to sell the motorcycle for the same price we paid so our adventure cost us little more than life on board *Seraffyn* normally did. That set us thinking about plans that were just starting to happen, plans for the next boat. "What if we carried a motorcycle in the lazzerette area? We could hoist it out with our boom-topping lift. Just think of the freedom we'd have."

We shared this idea with half a dozen cruising friends we met as we sailed east toward Malta and each one put more of a damper on it. One showed us the moped he stored on deck. The year-old machine was a mass of rust in spite of its canvas spray cover. "We'll keep ours below decks," we replied. Another said, "Then you'll have the danger of gasoline inside the boat." "We'll drain the tank before we store it away," we said. "What about registration problems," a third friend asked as he told us of the hassles he'd had when he tried to land his British-bought motorcycle in a Spanish village. "We'll only use it where the authorities don't care," we answered. But we ran out of answers when a friend showed us a letter from a cruising family in Indonesia. "J--- is dead. We took our motorcycle ashore three hours after we arrived in Bali. He went off to shop and was hit by a bus."

We remembered countless times when we'd come into a town or city after a voyage and walked ashore feeling sure of ourselves, pleased to be in the safety of a port and then had almost been hit by a passing car because we'd forgotten the faster pace of life on shore. This letter was a firm reminder that a carefully planned tour on a motorcycle is different from popping ashore in dozens of new, unknown countries where traffic laws and customs may be completely alien. When you get off a sailing boat your senses seem to be slowed down and the quick thought needed to maneuver at 30 or 40 miles an hour takes time to resurface. So our motorcycle dream faded as our new boat dream grew.

Then, as we decided to head for home, and our cruising life style changed to include more ocean voyaging and less exploring among anchorage filled island groups, we found we had less time for those forays ashore that we enjoyed so much. During the last year and a half of our travels, we spent far more of our time in harbors with towns or cities along their shores than we had during the first nine years. As we moved at a pace dictated by typhoon seasons, we had to stock the boat, refit and shop for stores for the 16,000 miles of ocean that lay between Malta and California. That's when we wished we had some sort of simple transportation to hasten those trips to the port captain's office or across town to the only shop with oil lamp parts.

We'd met a Canadian couple, the Bilsbarrows, who carried two high quality bicycles on board their 34-footer. As we cruised along Minorca, we'd enter a new port and see them bound off for a picnic and listen jealously as they described sights just two or three miles beyond the range of our walking forays. So our thoughts turned to this slower, safer mode of transportation, one that definitely seemed in keeping with our unhassled life style.

When we reached Penang in Malaysia we found our legs got tired after only a mile or two of walking. They'd grown weak because we'd spent so much time at sea during the four months it took us to sail down the Red Sea and across the Indian Ocean. So when an Australian couple we met on shore suggested we rent bicycles for a day trip around to the back of the island, I was a bit reluctant. Not only were my legs feeling weak but my bicycle skills had last been used when I was about 15 and they were more than a bit rusty. That day held a great surprise. Not only was I able to pedal almost 24 miles, but my legs seemed to grow in strength from the exercise. We reached some of the loveliest parts of the island, far from tourist crowds. Villagers we passed seemed to have time to stop and chat. Best of all we learned one of the special treats of bicycling. In most countries it is fully permissible to take a bicycle on the local buses and trains. So if you plan carefully, you can ride a bus to the highest elevation you wish to visit, then leisurely pedal, mostly downhill, seeing the sights, exploring the tiny by-ways and stopping for a cool drink along the way.

As we crossed the North Pacific on *Seraffyn* and whiled the time away by designing and redesigning *Taleisin*'s future interior, one area of the lazzarette always remained open, labeled "bicycles."

Our first solution to the problem of carrying bicycles below decks were they could remain relatively free of salt spray was to look at folding bicycles. They'd be easier to carry ashore because of their more compact size, we'd be more willing to bring them back to the boat in the dinghy each night and busing or hitchhiking up mountains would present less of a problem, we reasoned. So while we lived in Southern California and built *Taleisin* we explored the world of folding bicycles.

A visit to the bicycle dealers show case, a trade show where bicycle manufacturers try to lure dealers into carrying their goods, was an eye-opener. We learned that folding bicycles are extremely common in countries like Japan or Italy where even executives carry a bicycle on to the commuter train from home, then unfold it to cover the last mile or so to their office. But Americans are not quite so attuned to bicycles and the only market for these handy machines is in the limited marine and personal aircraft field. Our research turned up only about a dozen different choices ranging from the all aluminum Bikerton which bills itself as the world's first truly portable bicycle, to the husky Workman, an old American standard that can be motorized. Few of the bicycles can be bought from your corner shop, but we have included a list of the main distributors who, we have been told, in each case will give you information about where to see these different models.

The Bickerton was the lightest of the folding bicycles we looked at, it is cleverly designed. A few simple motions collapsed the 20-pound machine into a carry bag which measured 20 by 30 by 9 inches for the single speed model. The alloy construction promised to be easy to maintain. The three problems we noted after a ride around the limited space in the aisle of the show were, the small wheel diameter (the front wheel is 14 inches, the back 16 inches) which made the Bickerton seem unstable to our inexperienced senses, the off-standard parts which would be hard to duplicate away from cycle shops, and the high price. At $385 for one bicycle we'd feel terrible if one was accidentally lost or stolen.

The Japanese-built Bridgestone was by far the easiest to fold. Pull a lever and the bicycle collapses until it is a compact 45 by 18 by 10 inches. It weighs about 25 pounds. These folding bicycles are a big seller in Japan where over 100,000 people use them for commuting then store them away inside tiny homes at night. Unfortunately the 12-inch wheels make this bicycle a definite second choice for the dirt and gravel roads which make up a large percentage of the places cruising sailors are likely to want to ride.

Several companies make folding bicycles using steel frames and wheels that range from 16 inches to 22 inches. They include Di Blasi, Peugeot, Univega, Husky, Sekai and Workman. The complete bicycles weigh between 30 and 35 pounds and all use standard hubs, wheels and parts. This could definitely be an advantage when you are cruising since replacement parts in far-off places would probably be limited or second-hand. According to two dealers I spoke with, the most commonly used bicycles in less developed places are balloon tired, steel framed and made in Japan, Taiwan or Italy, so the bicycles with steel frames listed in this paragraph would probably be the easiest to find parts for.

The folded size of all these bicycles except the Di Blasi is about 34 by 30 by 10 inches. The Di Blasi folds to 35 by 24 by 10 inches. All have a safety latch design on the folding hinge to meet specs put out by the French and Italian governments.

For those cruising sailors who want a bit of both worlds, two of these folding bicycles come with optional small motors. The Di Blasi scooter bike can be pedal assisted and fold quite compactly. The Bumble Bike company takes a Workman bicycle and fits a tiny 1.3 or 2 horsepower motor onto the frame behind the seat. The motor weighs seven pounds and can power along at between 25 and 30 miles per hour on level ground. If you want a non-motorized bicycle you can unbolt the Bumble bike motor with about 20 minutes work. We tried one of these and decided the motor might be lots of fun for errands in town but would take away from the exercise we need. It also adds the problem of storing gasoline below decks and again adds speed to the equation of riding along streets where people may drive on a different side or use different customs.

After thoroughly confusing ourselves by looking at too many different folding bicycles, we came to the conclusion that we'd keep looking for an all alloy and stainless bicycle with 20 inch or larger wheels. But if two were not available before we set sail we would locate and compare the Univega and Peugeot folding bicycles then decide based on ease of folding, weight and ride.

Then we called Mel Pinto of Fairfax, Virginia, a major cycle importer and rider, to ask him for maintenance tips on bicycles that face the rigors of life in a saltwater atmosphere. He added to our confusion by saying, "If you are a serious bicycle rider why not get a good lightweight, full-sized touring bicycle with quick release hubs? They weigh between 18 and 25 pounds and fit into carry bags that are 48 by 26 by 10 inches. You can break them down in three or four minutes and have the pleasure of a real bike under you." When we asked about prices and brands he told us, "You can ask any reputable dealer to show you half a dozen different models. For about $400 you can get one with alloy rims, hubs, cranks, handlebars and kick stand plus a plastic seat. That should cut maintenance problems down."

We considered this for a while and had to admit that we're not real cyclists, just "day trippers." Our main concern is having two bicycles that are easy to take in the dinghy and store on deck at night so theft is less of a concern when we lie at anchor. A simple folding bicycle seemed a better choice for us.

Mel's maintenance tips were straight forward and easy for any sailor. "Hose the bicycle down whenever you can, clean it using WD 40 to cut the grease then oil the chain. Chains are the first thing to corrode and the easiest to watch. Grease the cables with a waterproof grease, not oil. The oil will dry up, grease stays put. Then use the bicycle. The more you use it the less it will oxidize." He agreed that a canvas or dacron carry bag would keep the bicycle in good condition and storage below decks was a must for long life.

A month after *Taleisin* was launched, we made our decision. We purchased two Peugeot folding bicycles. After playing with them for a few days, we delivered one to the local canvas shop. The canvas people made us two 10-inch thick, 26-inch long oval-shaped bags (figure 14.1) of oil resistant plastic sail cover cloth on the inside and a dacron twill on the outside quilted over one-inch foam. Plastic zippers open the bag 80 percent of the way around its top. Carry handles help us lift the bagged bikes out of the lazzerette hatch and into the dinghy.

By the time we added the cost of the bags, spare tires and tubes, nylon saddle bags, locks and an air pump, we had over $700 invested in two bicycles. Being ever the cost accountant, I wondered if they'd pay for themselves.

FIGURE 14.1

The answer is a resounding yes. Because of their heavyweight construction and 22-inch wheels, they can carry an astounding load. Fifty pounds of ice, a bag of groceries plus two one gallon boxes of wine are well within their payload. Once we had those bikes, our truck only got used about once a week as we did our sea-trails.

When we set sail, the bicycles came out almost everytime we decided to stay in port for more than four days. In Moorea we used them to make our twentieth anniversary a memorable event as we circled the island, stopping at every artists studio and staying at a romantic, beachfront hotel for the night. In Auckland we used them constantly. Over the past two years we figure we've saved half their cost by eliminating all but the occasional use of taxis.

When you are choosing the right bike for you and your cruising boat, look for the largest possible folding bike that will fit into your storage spot. Try not to store the bike on deck. After three years our bikes look just slightly used, slightly rusty on a few nonessential parts. The bikes owned by friends who store them on deck need replacement after less

FIGURE 14.2 Lin on her folding bike in Papeete. That's 20 litres (5 gallons) of kerosene on the back rack.

than three years and their tires need replacement yearly. Our tires are just now ready for replacement.

Although we thought the weight savings of a light frame seemed desirable, the extra eight pounds we have to carry are more than paid for by the rigidity of the heavier steel frame. These boat bikes are rarely used by people who are after speed, the main gain with light weight. All of us are after cargo-carrying capacity. So look for a bike that can be fitted with stout fore and aft luggage racks.

Spend the money to put reflectors on both wheels, fore and aft. Fit a generator and fore and aft lights. All of these extras are standard on the Peugeot, so higher cost compared to bicycles like the Univega and Huffy, are justified.

Finally, if you are getting a bicycle with gears, such as ours have, look for a derailleur type main hub instead of a Sturmey-Archer type of gearing. The derailleur is an open arrangement that can be flushed with fresh water and easily cleaned if the bicycle does accidentally fall overboard. The Sturmey-Archer gear requires special tools and care if it is submerged in salt water.

Bikes and cruising seem to fit together better than we ever imagined they would. Right now we are wintering in a cottage on the beach in northern New Zealand. To reach the village one mile above us, we have to push our bikes up a steep hill. And every time we glide down the hill with fresh milk, groceries and the newspaper, Larry looks smug as he says, "These wheels are the best investment we ever made. Not only do they make us more mobile, but they add to our fun and help keep us fit too!"

DISTRIBUTORS FOR BICYCLES MENTIONED IN CHAPTER 14

Peugeot USA, 555 Gotham Parkway, Carlstadt, New Jersey 07072, (201) 460-7000; 22-inch wheel approx. $250–$300

Univega Cycle Co., 899 Cowles St. Long Beach, California 90813, (213) 437-6478; approx. $190

Husky, P.O. Box 1204 Dayton, Ohio, (513) 866-6251; approx. $200

Sekai, 626 Alaska Street, Seattle Washington 98108, (206) 682-2730; approx. $220

Di Blasi, Marine agency, 2888 Bayshore Dr. Newport Beach, California 92663; approx. $345 (three speed) motorized cost $895

Workman Cycles, 94-15 100th Street Ozone Park, New York 11416, (212) 322-2000; approx. $139

Bumble Bike, P.O. Box 1116 Havana, Florida 32333, (904) 385-8208; approx. $299 with 1.3 horsepower motor.

Taking Care of Your Boat as You Cruise

Art Clarke, a friend and boat-building mentor, once told us, "If you take good care of that boat, she'll take good care of you." We came to understand the depths of his insight as we cruised on *Seraffyn*. Each bit of preventative maintenance we did saved later work, probably kept us safer, and definitely helped us enjoy the boat more as she carried us through 45,000 miles or more of breakdown-free cruising. The section that follows will give you an idea of some of the multitude of maintenance considerations you will have for even the simplest type of cruising boat.

The last chapter is intended as a guide to yacht fastenings. It might help you plan the list of spare parts you need when you set off on your voyage.

15

Take the Emergency Out of Steering Failures

It happened to Horatio Hornblower, Alexander Kent inflicted it upon his hero, in fact it seems to occur in all of my favorite sailing ship stories. A ship loses its steering and flies into the wind all standing, sails thunder and threaten to rip, yards sweep sailors off into the blue and the enemy begins to gain. Then the hero reaches in to save the day. I turn the pages anxious to hear how he regains control of the ship.

I guess I feel comfortable with this novelist's ploy because of all the emergency situations we've read about, loss of steering is the one we've actually encountered, not once but several times on boats we've either delivered or crewed on. But since the ships we sail on are fore and aft rigged and far smaller than the ones in adventure novels, down grading steering losses from an emergency to an inconvenience can be accomplished by mortal men, not heroes. All you need to do is react calmly and if all attempts at jury rigging fail, know how to sail your boat without a rudder.

If you are sailing in any winds over eight knots when your tiller breaks, a steering cable breaks, or in the worse case, your rudder literally falls off, your story will have one thing in common with the adventure novel, your boat will round into the wind. If you are running before the wind, your boat may jibe before it rounds into the wind. But in either case, that's where you'll end up, head to wind, sails flogging and slatting. Then your boat will begin drifting astern, shoved by wind or tide. This is the moment when a calm, careful analysis of your position can save the day.

Before you try to find out what your technical problem is, decide if you have enough searoom to drift temporarily. If not, let your anchor go and set it to keep you from drifting into other boats or onto a breakwater. Larry and I were short tacking out of the mooring area in Gibraltar several years ago when *Seraffyn*'s tiller snapped in half. We'd known the tiller was beginning to develop a crack and meant to replace it before we cruised deeper into the Mediterranean that spring. But we decided to take the weekend off from the boat work that was refilling our cruising kitty and sail to Morocco, 18 miles across the straits. Larry had a surprised look on his face when he saw the splintered tiller end in his hand. He looked around at the anchored boats we were drifting towards and called, "better set the hook." I unclutched the windlass and seconds later *Seraffyn* lay calmly anchored in a spot we normally wouldn't have chosen, but we'd avoided hitting any boats and now had time to calm down and survey the situation. Our story had a pleasant ending. We used four stainless steel hose clamps and two pieces of scrap wood from Larry's secret stash and fished the tiller so we could set sail again within twenty minutes (figure 15.1).

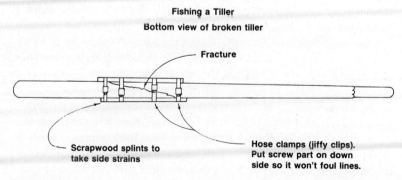

Fishing a Tiller
Bottom view of broken tiller

Fracture

Scrapwood splints to
take side strains

Hose clamps (jiffy clips).
Put screw part on down
side so it won't foul lines.

FIGURE 15.1

You can anchor to sort out emergencies like this in amazingly deep water. We have laid to a 12 pound Danforth type anchor on 600 feet of line in 220 feet of water in the South China sea while a 3-knot current rushed past us. Another time we set 300 feet of nylon and 30 feet of chain in 115 feet of water in spite of 35-knot winds and a 3-foot chop in the approaches to Nuku'alofa, Tonga, to solve a navigational mix-up. If you have shallow enough water, think about anchoring first, it will give you time to plan your next move.

If you lose your steering in a tighter situation, one where there is no room to anchor before a collision becomes imminent, get out some fenders and mooring lines and prepare to tie up alongside the first boat or pier you can reach. Then if you have time, drop your sails. Flogging sails are a nuisance but are definitely second priority. The first is to avoid damaging other people's boats or your own.

Most likely you will be out in open water when you find your steering has failed. In this case there is room to drift while you think, but it may still pay to preserve all of the searoom you can. So heave to. To do this, sheet your mainsail or mizzin flat amidships and drop your other sails. This should stop your forward motion and cause your boat to lie quite comfortably with its bow 50 or 60 degrees from the wind. (See *Seraffyn's Oriental Adventure* for a complete appendix on heaving to). Once your boat is quieted down and in a hove-to position you will have the time and calm you need to find out what has happened to your steering. If your tiller has broken, the cure is usually simple, a boat hook, a flag staff or spinnaker pole can serve as a temporary substitute. But if your rudder head has broken off, your problem is a bit more difficult. You can be prepared for this by drilling a hole through the trailing edge of your rudder before you launch your boat (figure 15.2). If you have this hole you can rig temporary steering cables. Pass a line through the hole, tie a figure-eight stopper knot on each side of the rudder, then lead the lines forward and onto the deck through a set of snatch blocks. This will give you steering control lines that will let you set sail once again.

On a boat with an inboard rudder, rigging these emergency steering cables will be a bit more difficult because you'll have to go overboard to do so. But they will still work so it pays to have the emergency steering cable hole drilled before you set off on a cruise. To get the emergency cables working on a boat with an inboard rudder, you might have to jury rig a long steering arm to keep your lines clear of the hull. Your spinnaker

Emergency Rudder Hole Positions

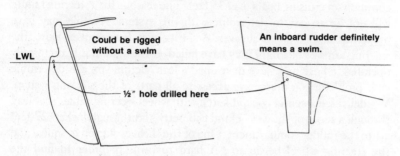

FIGURE 15.2

or whisker pole will do the job if you lash it across the deck and attach a block at each end, then lead the steering lines from the rudder through the blocks at either end of the pole and back on deck to a comfortable position where you can once again steer toward port (figure 15.3).

Rigging an Outboard Fairlead for Emergency Steering

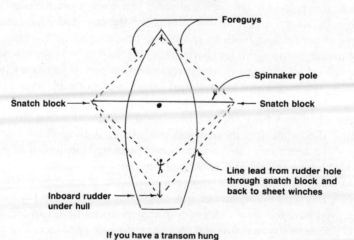

FIGURE 15.3

Wheel steering with its added complications has now become quite common on cruising boats over 35 feet. The reasons for a steering failure will not be as easy to determine with this system. A cable may have broken or slipped off its sheaves. A sheave may have broken loose, the steering arms or quadrant may have failed. If the system is hydraulically operated, a hose may have developed a leak. Before you can determine your problem, you must have access to all parts of the steering system. We delivered a center cockpit ketch with wheel steering cables that lead through a series of sheaves behind cabinetry and through lockers 22-feet aft to the rudder compartment. One of the sheaves started to squeal and the steering wheel began to get hard to turn. In order to find the problem we had to spend five hours carefully removing joinery work and trim. We were glad we'd done it when we found one steering cable sheave had pulled the lag bolts loose from their mounting. A small access door would have made this repair job easy.

Our repair was a simple one—we just through bolted the sheave base, drilling holes through a nearby frame. But what did concern us was that the complexity and length of the steering cable system would have made it almost a two or three day job to re-thread a new cable if the old one had chafed through. We did mention this to the owner when we turned the boat over to him. His comment was, "I have never heard of steering cables breaking." Unfortunately, this is not the case. Larry has earned some of our cruising funds by splicing up new steering cables, often in the middle of the night, for charter boats that had to be underway with the tide or risk missing a charter party in another port. If you have wheel steering make sure you can rethread cables in a reasonable amount of time.

An emergency tiller can save the day on a boat with wheel steering. But if the failure is a sheared rudder shaft, or if there is no way to connect a temporary tiller, an emergency steering hole, drilled in your rudder before you set sail, could bail you out.

Whichever type of steering system you have, if a complete failure occurs and you have no way of attaching steering lines or, in the worse case, you have lost your rudder completely, you still have two avenues of action open to you before you consider calling for assistance. The first is to rig a substitute rudder.

The most ingenious substitute we have ever heard of was rigged by

Winston Bushnell when his boat *Dove* rolled over in the Argulas current off South Africa (figure 15.4). His rudder and most of his rig disappeared in the accident. But Winston and his family reached port seven or eight days later under jury rig. To steer the boat, he took about 660 feet of his spare lines and lashed them into a bundle six-feet long. He trailed this bundle about thirty feet aft of the boat and steered the tail by using two lines lead from its aftermost end to the quarters of his 31-footer. Winston's steering loss is a pretty extreme example, but his solution does illustrate the simplicity of arranging temporary steering. Lash ups with bunk boards or a long oar would work. If you have an independent windvane self-steering mechanism with its own rudder hung on the transom, it could be used as a substitute for the boat's main rudder. But

Dove's Steering Tail

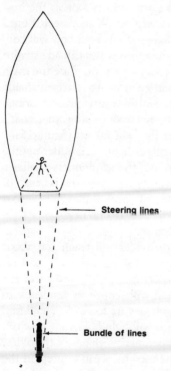

Steering lines

Bundle of lines

FIGURE 15.4

if all attempts to rig a substitute fail or if you only have a few miles to go before you reach port, it may be best to learn about the second replacement for your own steering system.

A sailboat is an amazingly simple machine. If it is sloop, cutter or ketch rigged, it has a balance point somewhere just aft of the main mast. If you practice you will find you can use your sails to steer your ship to port. This is not the case with a cat boat and unless the mast can be raked easily and conveniently, you will find it almost impossible to steer using just your sails. Next time you go out for a sail, find some open water and remove your tiller then wait for the boat to head into the wind. When it stops making headway, let your mainsheet right out and, if you are lying head to wind, take the clew of your jib and back it, i.e., pull it to port until the wind is on the wrong side of the sail, trying to push the boat backwards instead of forward (figure 15.5). The pressures on the jib will pull the bow of your boat to starboard. As soon as the bow starts to swing away from the wind, let go of your jib and sheet it until it is in the going-to-windward position (figure 15.6). Your bow will continue to swing until you sheet in your mainsail. Now you can adjust your main until you see your bow begin to head into the wind. Ease the main sheet a few inches and your boat should settle down on a relatively steady course. Once you are underway, you can control course changes caused by wind shifts or waves by sheeting in the mainsail to bring your boat's bow up toward the wind, easing it to let the boat fall off (figure 15.7).

If your boat has a tendency toward weather helm, i.e., under normal sailing conditions she wants to round up into the wind unless you keep the tiller four or five inches to windward when you are beating or reaching, you'll probably have to do one of three things; allow your mainsail to luff a bit, reef the mainsail, or sheet the jib in snugger than you normally would to maintain your course.

Practicing to steer without using your rudder will teach you about both sail balance and sail trim. If you have a full cut mainsail and your boat tries rounding into the wind no matter how tightly you sheet the jib, putting a flattening reef into the sail will reduce its tendency to create weather helm. If your jib sheeting angles are too wide, you'll find that releading the sheets closer amidships will help hold your bow off.

If your boat has a cutter rig, you can experiment with one of the oldest forms of self-steering we've heard of, one used by ocean cruisers in the 1940s, a system that works even dead downwind. Set your jib and

Ease the mainsail completely, back the jib to pull
the head of your boat away from the wind.

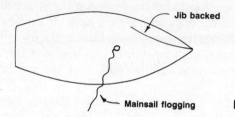

FIGURE 15.5

Now sheet the jib into the proper going to windward position and slowly begin pulling in (sheeting
in) the mainsail.

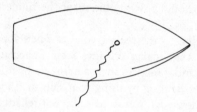

FIGURE 15.6

Forces on Your Sails

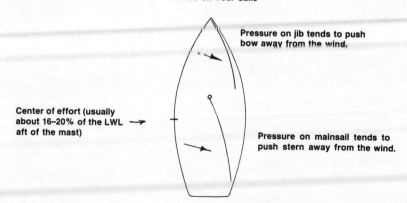

Pressure on jib tends to push
bow away from the wind.

Center of effort (usually
about 16–20% of the LWL
aft of the mast)

Pressure on mainsail tends to
push stern away from the wind.

FIGURE 15.7

mainsail as you normally would, then sheet your staysail either slightly
to windward or dead amidships. As your boat tries to round up, the
staysail will exert extra pressure forward of the pivot point of your hull
and the bow will fall off until the mainsail is pulling again. If the bow
falls too far away from the wind, the mainsail will blanket the jib and
gain more power until it begins to push the stern of your boat away from
the wind. You'll find your course is slightly erratic, but you will be
steering without a rudder.

Your practice sessions will be a close approximation of the way your
boat will feel if it does actually lose its rudder. Lyle Hess, designer of
both *Seraffyn* and our new boat, *Taleisin* said, "The average designer
only considers 25 percent of the area of a rudder when he is calculating
a boat's center of effort to determine the sail plan." He explained the
reasons for this and assured us that the average sailor would find his
boat's center of balance changed by only a slight amount if the rudder
fell off.

There is nothing quite so rewarding as the feeling you get when you
solve your own problems. That's what makes cruising such a special
sport. A bit of preparation beforehand, practice, such a man-overboard
drills, sailing without an engine and steering by using your sails instead
of your rudder will give you the knowledge you need to be self-reliant.
Knowing how to heave to and assess the problem so you have time to
decide on your course of action will put you in the position to use the
skills you acquired while you practiced to become a competent offshore
voyager.

16

Cruising Canvas Care

Sails go through hell on a long cruise. It is difficult to wash, dry or fold them. They are set for days at a time, through hundreds of hours of harsh sunlight, subjected to constant strains. But the worst sail-destroying elements can be eliminated or reduced. We had to learn the hard way but now we know how to save ourselves a lot of chafing of the brain by practicing prevention instead of cure. We now work to control hardening of the dacron and excessive wear of sail stitching by watching sail set, handling our sails with an eye to reducing wear and by ordering durable cloth and construction from our long-suffering sailmaker.

Work hardening of dacron is a somewhat unpublished fact. Bending a piece of sheet metal back and forth causes it to crease, continued bending causes weakening and eventually the metal fractures. The same sequence develops when dacron sail cloth is bent or flogged repeatedly. This concentration of bending at the creases weakens the fibres and causes prematurely weakened sails (figure 16.1).

Flogging leeches are a common cause of this type of cloth failure. This breakdown usually occurs just forward of the tabling and clew patches. The leech, clew and head are the most highly stressed parts of a sail. When they start to wear or weaken, your sail is likely to fail. So if the

Plan View

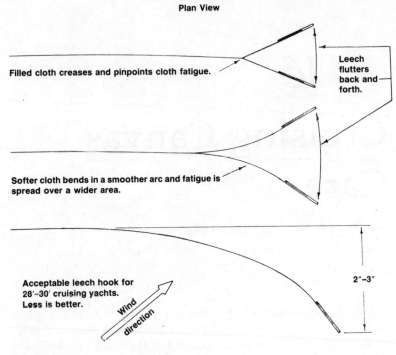

Filled cloth creases and pinpoints cloth fatigue.

Leech flutters back and forth.

Softer cloth bends in a smoother arc and fatigue is spread over a wider area.

Acceptable leech hook for 28'-30' cruising yachts. Less is better.

Wind direction

2"-3"

FIGURE 16.1

leech or foot of your sail starts to flutter or flog the leech line should be slowly tightened until it is just snug enough to stop the movement. A twenty-four-hour beat to windward with a flogging leech can take six to eight months of life out of a dacron sail. I feel all sails should be fitted with leech lines.

Letting your jib luff continuously in strong breezes, even just a slight luff, can cause not only cloth fatigue but ruin your jib hanks by rubbing them against the headstay which wears grooves in the softer hank metal. A cruising solution is to sheet the jib in an extra few degrees to stop any luff movement. To further combat work hardening when tacking ship, we back the jib until the main sail starts to fill on the other tack. This shortens the jib slatting time and keeps chafing against shrouds to a minimum.

Your sails should be built to handle continuous passage use. The first thing to specify is pliable soft dacron. Look and feel cloth samples before you sign the order for a new sail. (Soft 8-ounce dacron should feel about as stiff as new Levi work jeans.) Pliable cloth is the cruisers best choice because it is easier to fold, bag, furl and reef. The flexible cloth work hardens less than stabilized (filled, tempered) dacron. Soft cloth is a little stretchier than filled dacron. This is both an advantage and a slight disadvantage. A flexible cloth is a durable cloth because it absorbs strains like a nylon anchor rode, stretching instead of breaking. The performance difference between hard and soft finished cloth is so little most people would only notice it if they were racing one-design boats to windward.

Passagemakers' sails last longer without battens. A sailmaker here in New Zealand, Haven Collins, stated, "Eliminating battens can increase your sail's life by up to fifty percent." The battens crease and bend the cloth just forward of the pocket. This persistent chafe and flexing causes the material to work harden, then tear. (For more on battenless mainsails see *Self-Sufficient Sailor.*) Other specifications to give your sailmaker so you get cruise-durable sails are large multi-layer patches at clew and head. Tack patches take far less load so they can be two-thirds the size of clew patches. *Taleisin*'s 290-square-foot mainsail (our working sails were built by Jim Marshall of North Sails), is as perfect a cruising main as I have seen. The four clew patches (three for the reefs), overlap the lower panel seams. This extra cloth reinforces the weakest links on the mainsail, the seam stitching. (Tom Linskey, a California sailmaker, adds a triangular patch over each seam at the leech to strengthen all seams not covered by clew patches.) All seams are triple stitched with dark blue thread (dark colors tend to resist ultraviolet caused deterioration better than light colors.) The full-length leech line in our mainsail has so far not been needed to stop flogging or flutter. This sail is living proof that a battenless main built of soft but stable cloth can be designed to set without a hooked leech. A badly hooked leech acts just like an air brake as you sail. This is a considerable performance defect on a racing boat, on a cruising boat it is not quite as important, but why should you give up potential speed. If your sailmaker can cut a jib without a hook, he can do the same for you on a long-life cruising main.

I prefer high-cut jibs for cruising for various reasons. They provide all around visibility, which is a *great* safety factor; they also last longer; the high clew does not scoop up waves and stress the foot of the sail (this

wave scooping can easily blow a sail out). The high-cut foot is also less
likely to chafe against the pulpit. If you have a high-cut jib and it still
hits the pulpit, it pays to lift the tack with a pennant to clear the sail.
(U-shape pulpits are more likely to foul a jib than those with more
rounded top rails.) Fine tuning leech line adjustments are difficult to
make on high-clewed jibs, so these jibs are often left to flutter their life
away. When you order a new high-cut jib, ask to have the leech line lead
to the tack area along with the foot line for easy adjustment.

Work hardening and chafe can be minimized by using your nonwork-
ing sails sooner and more often. The trysail can be a convenient sail to
set if it has its own track led down to the deck or cabin top. In an area
known for strong winds, it can be left bagged right on its track. Instead
of putting deep reefs in the mainsail, you can instead easily hoist the
trisail. A trisail is normally used very little and will far outlast the boat
or its owner, so the bit of extra use makes financial sense if you use it
more and take the wear and strain of boisterous sailing off your mainsail,
the one sail that rarely gets a rest. This method of substituting sails to
reduce wear and chafe can also be used in light winds. When the main
or genoa starts to slat, drop them and hoist the nylon. A nylon drifter
is built of soft, pliable stretchy material which absorbs work hardening
much better than dacron. It is also light in weight, yard for yard, and
will not crash and slat like dacron. A nylon spinnaker can also be used
without the main in light winds, but keep an eye out for line squalls.
Spinnakers are hard to get down unless you have the main set to act as
a wind block to blanket the spinnaker as you lower it.

The old bug bear, chafe, can be further controlled by using plastic
hose coverings on all port and starboard shrouds to give a smooth surface
for sails and sheets to lay against. Clear plastic lasts about six years before
it gets brittle from ultraviolet rays. We replace the brittle bits with the
split white colored plastic shroud covers such as are sold in most marine
stores. We use these covers for three or four years and then its time to
replace the ten-year-old shrouds with new wire and chafe preventing
hose. Use the smallest diameter hose that will comfortably slide over the
wire—you'll usually find this is about a sixteenth of an inch larger inside
diameter than the wire. This hose-covered wire causes less windage than
traditional baggy wrinkle so you have less rig resistance when you are
beating off a lee shore or anchored in a hurricane hole.

The ends of spreaders can be cheaply and easily chafe guarded with white synthetic shag carpet sewn so the edges of the carpet are stitched above and below the spreader. We have tried several other methods and so far this is the longest lasting, cleanest one (figure 16.2).

Regular use of a boom vang preventer will cut mainsail chafe. On smaller yachts, those under about 35 feet, you can simply use a three or four part nylon line made up with blocks into a tackle which you attach to the boom one third of its length from the mast (figure 16.3). The other end of the tackle is attached to the toe rail or a pad eye just forward of the upper shroud. This should work out to a lead that is about 30 to 45 degrees off vertical. This holds (prevents) the boom forward and vangs it down at the same time so the boom doesn't pump up and down, rubbing and chafing the mainsail against the shrouds. For convenience you can lead the tail of the vang tackle aft to a jam cleat near the cockpit. On larger boats it is easier to break the boom, especially if you dip it in the water as you roll, so use both a vang and a separate preventer lead from the end of the boom forward.

There is a fundamental, almost religious difference between cruising and racing sailors that can be seen in the way they furl and bag sails. The racing crew (there are usually at least three or four of them) flakes the jib down on deck after a change and carefully rolls it up so it is creased or bent as little as possible. The cruising sailor on the other hand, is alone and maybe a bit bushed. All he wants to do with the wet, miserable headsail is to jam it in the bag, secure it and get ready to

FIGURE 16.2

FIGURE 16.3

change watch at 0300 on the dot. This cramming is definitely not good
for sails, especially the highly filled variety, as it contributes to the same
work hardening we are trying to avoid. A compromise can be made.
After the jib is dropped on deck, leave it hanked onto the headstay (a
racing man would never sail bald headed like this even for a few minutes)
flake the luff rope of the still attached sail back and forth in port and
starboard loops. Tie the head of the sail down so it won't fly up the
headstay on its own (a jib downhaul will do this for you if you have one).
Go aft to the clew and coil up the sheets, grab a hold of the sail about
two feet up the leech and pull firmly aft. This should cause the sail to
fold and line up more or less with the loops you folded at the bolt rope.
Continue working up the leech and flaking the sail in this manner until
you are at the headstay again. Take the sail gasket off the head and tie

it snuggly around the whole luff of the sail. Go back to the clew and fold the coiled sheets into the flaked sail and roll the sail up toward the headstay. Then if it is a large, heavy sail use another gasket to hold the roll together. Unhank the rolled sail from the headstay and bag it.

It is tough to convince a sailmaker to make you sailbags that are large enough for cruising (I haven't succeeded yet). You need a bag that is at least four times the size of the neatly rolled sail. Stuffing a sail into a bag smaller than this not only crushes it down to a small ball but also folds the material harshly, leaving semi-permanent creases. These creases are places for cloth fatigue to get its start. So demand a large bag for those moments when you don't have time to fold your sail and you just want to stuff it and forget it. (I am trying to fold my sails more often, honestly I really am.)

Washing the abrasive salt crystals out of sails is hard to do when you are anchored most of the time, so don't miss taking advantage of a rain shower to de-salt them. The sails can be spread around on deck and shifted during the downpour to rinse them all over. Leave them to dry right on deck. Tie the sails down so they do not blow away. Turn them over to make sure all areas dry well. The on-deck method of drying is a bit more work but it is vastly superior to the very common method of hoisting sails in a breeze and letting them flog. This flogging, as I said before, is the worst enemy of your sails. Naturally, sailing in the rain is the easiest and fastest way to wash sails, especially if the sun comes out to dry them just before you reach your destination (figure 16.4).

If you get stains on your sails you should only scrub them with a soft brush and mild soap. This will minimize stitching wear. Machines that are large enough to wash your sails without over-creasing (work hardening) the fabric, are hard to find even in sophisticated yachting areas.

Storing the sails you use frequently while you are cruising is usually not a problem. Regular use airs and dries them, but storing wet sails you use less regularly below decks against metal fittings can cause problems. We stowed our salt-soaked drifter against the stainless steel water tank in *Taleisin.* This caused the metal to rust and stain the bag, narrowly missing the sail inside. So now I try to leave any wet sails on deck until I can rinse and dry them properly.

Galvanized or stainless steel luff wires which get soaked with salt water, rust in a short time. Our solution to this is the low stretch, kevlar-cored luff rope our sailmaker talked us into using for our free-

FIGURE 16.4

standing nylon drifter. The kevlar rope stows easier than a wire and solves the rust staining problem.

If you leave your boat for six months to fly home, you should try to stow all of your sails below, dry and salt free if possible. Store the sails loosely in their bags along with 15 to 20 sheets of crumpled newspaper, if there is any chance of rodents getting into your boat. Mice much prefer to make nests with soft newspaper than tough dacron sails.

The prevention of sail aging and wear problems is much more satisfactory and ultimately easier than doing the repairs necessary to cure the problem when you are thousands of miles away from the nearest sailmaker. Proper care and strong stable construction of passagemaking sails could lengthen their useful life up to fifty percent.

17

Bare Wood—The Salty Scrubbed Look

Scrubbed wood is as timeless and practical in the sailing world as faded denim is in the garment industry. Bare wood has been used for high wear surfaces on board ships for centuries. It is an ideal non-skid surface for cockpit gratings, decks and toe rails. Choosing the proper woods and using them correctly can cut your maintenance time yet keep your boat looking smart. But improper care can prematurely erode unfinished wood and cause it to look scruffy. This will lower your yachts value.

There are several reasons why scrubbed wood makes sense. The most important is safety. Barewood makes an excellent, permanent, easy-to-clean non-skid surface for cabin soles, companionway ladder treads, cockpit gratings. It is the all-time favorite for safe decks. Some people would even call scrubbed teak the Rolls-Royce of decking finishes. Cruise liners sport romantic teak decks and many state-of-the-art racing yachts have found that a thin teak overlay pays for its weight since a sure-footed foredeck crew can change sails quicker and jump ahead of the competition.

Scrubbed wood minimizes routine boat maintenance jobs such as oiling, sanding, painting and varnishing. Most small pieces of wood above decks such as handrails, cabin trim and wooden cleats can safely be left natural if you choose the proper wood (see accompanying chart). High wear areas like the top edge of varnished cockpit coamings can be capped with bare wood to minimize varnish touch up. Minor bruises or dents in bare wood caused by dropped snapshackles or carelessly handled anchor chain will quite often swell back up and become flush again if you wash the wood surface with salt water on a regular basis. It is one of the few deck surfaces that does not chip or crack with minor abuse, and the only one that sometimes heals itself.

Some bare items on board can be completely ignored for years at a time. The teak boom gallows cross piece on *Seraffyn* was scrubbed only once in eleven years, yet looked fine.

Utilizing scrubbed wood wherever possible on your boat will save you material costs; no sandpaper, paint or varnish to buy. Some of the items you need for your boat can be bought unfinished and left that way to further save money, things such as ash boat hooks and oars. Newly installed teak or ash rail caps can be left bare to give you more free time to earn freedom chips (dollars) to finance your cruising, time to enjoy things like skin diving, sailing and serious research into local wines.

So the next question is, where can I best use scrubbed wood? Basically, wherever you use small dimension pieces of wood on deck and wherever you require non-skid surfaces.

Cabin trim up to ⅞ by 1⅛ inches, hand rails up to 1 by 3 inches, a rail cap of up to ¾ by 1¾ inches, all of these wood parts are small dimension and if the wood you use to build them has been kiln dried or reasonably well seasoned, it should weather well with only slight hairline checking. Even this slight checking can be minimized if your bare wood is washed regularly with salt water.

Direct sunlight is what dries wood out and causes it to split. Since there is little direct, continuous sunlight striking below deck surfaces, you can safely leave large dimension boards bare, especially in places where you require non-skid surfaces, or for areas which receive heavy use. Our teak floor boards are 1 by 5 by 28 inches, the bare ash sink counter is ⅞ by 12 by 24 inches, the wet weather locker, and watch seat lid is glued up teak ⅞ by 22 by 24 inches.

If you don't trust the seasoning of your new wood but still want to

FIGURE 17.1 *Taleisin*'s bare teak companionway boards, compass mount, and trim.

leave it bare, try oiling it every three months for a year, then scrub it. The oil slows any dramatic decrease or increase in the moisture content of the wood and give it time to stabilize (season) slowly.

There are certain wood parts on your boat that should always be protected with oil, paint or varnish. They include the mast, bowsprit, boomkin, glued up skylights, cabin tables and cabinsides—all parts which are large dimension pieces of timber. I would also put a protective finish on any wood that could get stained by oily machinery.

One of the most handsome, labor saving additions to any boat is a bare teak cap fastened to the top of a varnished toe rail (figure 17.2). It will take the wear of mooring lines and deck shoes, two things that grind salt crystals into varnish and make it a constant chore to maintain. By keeping the sides of the toe rail varnished you still keep the elegant yacht look people admire.

If your toe rail is 1½ by 1⅞ inches or smaller you could leave both cap and rail bare. This is purely an esthetic decision. If the rest of your yacht is painted or gel-coated, eliminating all of the varnish could be inappropriate. Bear in mind that vertical surfaces hold paint and varnish

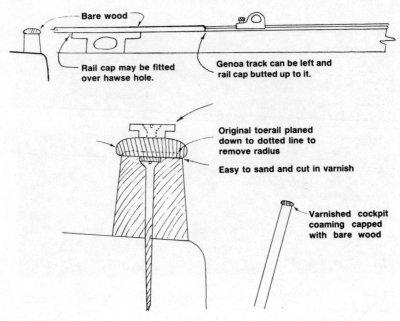

FIGURE 17.2

better than horizontal surfaces. Vertical surfaces get less chafe or direct sunlight. On *Taleisin* we concentrated on eliminating horizontal varnish surfaces and choose to give a bright finish to our cabin sides and spars for a good looking contrast to all of the unfinished teak we have on deck.

Figure 17.3 shows another type of rail which can be made using bare wood. This simple bulwark rail can be made of narrow wood strakes. It works well for wood, glass or steel yachts. It is especially practical on steel yachts as it has a minimum of steel surface encapsulated under the wood, the place where corrosion is usually a problem. Hal Roth added this type of rail to his 35-foot production glass sloop *Whisper*. This scrubbed wood bulwark adds security and a look of elegance with little or no extra maintenance work.

Varnished handrails and cabin trim (eyebrows) can be serious time consumers and are extremely hard to keep well finished because moisture is always creeping in under the varnish at the jointing surface of wood to cabin. These small parts are very tedious to sand and mask for the

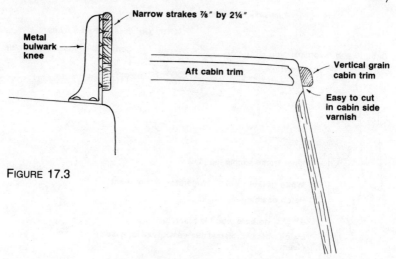

Metal bulwark knee

Narrow strakes ⅞″ by 2¼″

Aft cabin trim

Vertical grain cabin trim

Easy to cut in cabin side varnish

FIGURE 17.3

FIGURE 17.4

necessary build up of several coats of varnish or paint. If these parts are teak I would definitely leave them bare (figure 17.4). If they were good quality, stable Honduras mahogany, they could also be left scrubbed. I would draw the line at Philippine mahogany, which, because of its more open grain, should be protected.

Taleisin's teak forehatch is made of small dimension teak pieces (Figures 17.5–17.8). This hatch has been left bare and has proved ideal during the past two and a half years of voyaging. It requires zero maintenance and has an excellent non-skid finish. It takes the hard wear of foredeck use very nicely. In contrast, we had a varnished mahogany forehatch on *Seraffyn* and it required constant work just to keep it looking tidy.

One bare wood item we have been experimenting with through the years is our spinnaker pole. We have had mixed results here. Our first pole on Seraffyn was a solid piece of spruce. It was 16-feet long, rounded to a 2⅞ inches in diameter which tappered to 1¾ inches at the ends. It worked fine on the jib but was a bit limber and bendy when we used it with our large spinnaker on a reach. Nevertheless, it lasted for eight years with only slight surface checking on the flat grain. The first year we had it we oiled the pole with teak oil. We let it go natural after that.

Taleisin's Forehatch

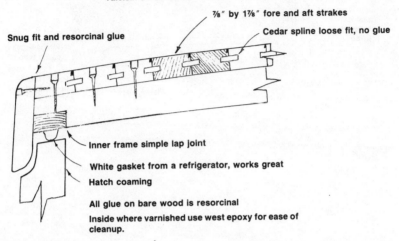

Snug fit and resorcinal glue

⅞" by 1⅞" fore and aft strakes

Cedar spline loose fit, no glue

Inner frame simple lap joint

White gasket from a refrigerator, works great

Hatch coaming

All glue on bare wood is resorcinal

Inside where varnished use west epoxy for ease of cleanup.

FIGURE 17.5

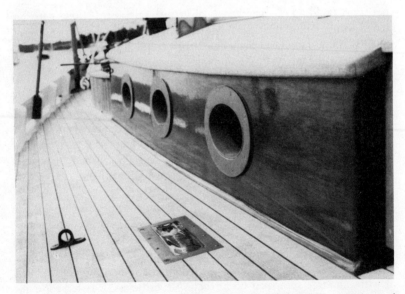

FIGURE 17.6   The varnished cabinside contrasts with the bare decks and cabin trim.

FIGURE 17.7 The skylight hatch trim can be removed to make varnish work simpler.

FIGURE 17.8

Taking Care of Your Boat as You Cruise

On the outboard end, where it banged against the forestay, we protected the pole with three feet of brass half oval. After seven years the screws that fastened the half oval, caused small cracks to develop at 90 degrees to the grain. These cracks may have been caused by leaving the pole bare. Because the screw holes were not sealed with paint or varnish they may have been more prone to shrinking and swelling. So now we cover the chafe-prone areas on our poles with leather that we stick in place with contact cement, then herringbone stitch. We also use this method to secure the leather on our bare ash oars since it eliminates the weak spot caused by nailing leathers in place.

For our second pole on *Seraffyn* we built a stiffer one of hollow bare ash, 3½ inches in diameter with a ½ inch wall thickness. This pole was glued with resorcinal glue. When we sold the boat five years later, there was some slight but acceptable checking on the flat grain areas and some minor, surface glue line separation. I guess the bare pole would have needed replacing after ten years of service, but I felt that was a fair trade because it didn't need any maintenance. I think we gave it a half hour scrub a couple of times in five years.

On *Taleisin* we decided to use a hollow, bare spruce pole 19 feet 8 inches long by 4 inches in diameter by ⅝ inch wall thickness. We built it like a barrel, with eight staves to get edge grain all the way around. The finished pole is as light as an average untapered aluminum pole of the same diameter. So far, so good.

Although we have used brass half oval or leather for most of our chafe-preventing needs in other parts of the boat, this is another place where bare wood can save the day. I have seen spinnaker poles and booms protected with strips of hardwood, preferably teak, fastened to high chafe areas on friends' boats (figure 17.9).

A well-built, scrubbed teak deck can be maintained with a minimum of elbow grease. I have lived with scrubbed decks for almost 30 years and learned some key construction points that make them practical, long wearing and watertight. The most important detail to remember when you are selecting wood for a scrubbed deck is to get all vertical grain (rift sawn, edge grain) for the strakes. A deck is just like the wood flooring or stair treads in a home; for longer, more even wear and a consistant appearance, vertical grain is the only way to go (figure 17.10).

A bare wood deck laid over plywood or over a glass sandwich should be bonded in mastic or glued to the sub-deck for waterproofing. If you

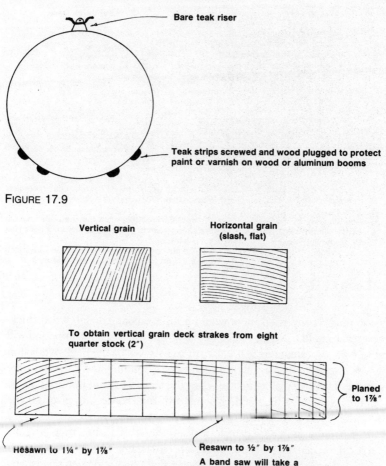

FIGURE 17.9

Bare teak riser

Teak strips screwed and wood plugged to protect
paint or varnish on wood or aluminum booms

Vertical grain

Horizontal grain
(slash, flat)

To obtain vertical grain deck strakes from eight
quarter stock (2″)

Planed
to 1⅞″

Resawn to 1¼″ by 1⅞″

Resawn to ½″ by 1⅞″

A band saw will take a
smaller sawcut and save
valuable timber.

FIGURE 17.10

glue or bond, then plug a teak overlay deck as shown in figure 17.11, a ⅜-inch to ½-inch thickness will last up to 25 years with proper care. The key is the deep seams and wood plugs. We have seen countless overlay decks in terrible condition because the strakes were not bonded down, but instead were held only by the screws. This meant that when the deck wore, the screws could not be counter sunk deeper to fit a new

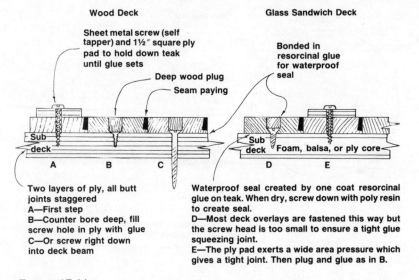

Wood Deck

Glass Sandwich Deck

Sheet metal screw (self tapper) and 1½" square ply pad to hold down teak until glue sets

Deep wood plug

Seam paying

Bonded in resorcinal glue for waterproof seal

Sub-deck

Sub-deck Foam, balsa, or ply core

A   B   C   D   E

Two layers of ply, all butt joints staggered
A—First step
B—Counter bore deep, fill screw hole in ply with glue
C—Or screw right down into deck beam

Waterproof seal created by one coat resorcinal glue on teak. When dry, screw down with poly resin to create seal.
D—Most deck overlays are fastened this way but the screw head is too small to ensure a tight glue squeezing joint.
E—The ply pad exerts a wide area pressure which gives a tight joint. Then plug and glue as in B.

FIGURE 17.11

wood plug. If you tried there would not have been enough wood thickness left to hold the deck strake in place. The black seam compound will not create a permanent seal between the strakes of the deck overlay on its own because the oil in the wood resists bonding and the seams are subjected to powerful shrinkage when the strakes dry out in the sun. The wood overlay must be glued or bonded to the sub-deck to give you the best chance of a long-term waterproof deck.

I personally prefer solid teak decks, although I realize they are only practical on a custom-built, moderate to heavy displacement yacht. Since you can start right out with deep wood plugs and deep seams, you can get long wearing decks. If a leak does occur, it is obvious where it is and the seams that leak can be simply recaulked with cotton and re-payed with seam compound. Unless great care is taken when an overlayed deck is built, water can get between the teak and sub-deck then travel along to drip into the boat at a completely different spot. So the origin of the leak is sometimes next to impossible to locate.

A solid wood deck should be at least 1¼-inches thick to prevent movement which can cause it to leak. (We used 1¼ inch on *Seraffyn* and lost about an ⅛ inch to wear from 11 years of living and cruising on board. So *Taleisin* has 1½ inch teak on her solid deck.) Cotton caulking is an absolute necessity on a single layer deck. When water seeps down past the paying compound to the cotton, it swells and seals the seam. Horizontal tierods incorporated into the deck framing system, work in conjunction with the cotton to insure a drip proof deck. They keep the deck framing from opening up due to cotton swellage (figure 17.12).

We have used 3M 101 as a seam paying compound on top of the cotton with excellent results. We know that eliminating the cotton sounds attractive to people lured by the name caulking compound on other brandname tubes, but we have seen constant expensive and frustrating failures when this method was tried. These products do not stick well enough to teak seams nor do they swell up, as cotton does, to guarantee a watertight deck.

The maintenance of scrubbed wood requires no special materials. You can buy the supplies you need at the corner grocer's instead of at an expensive chandlery. Liquid dishsoap, plastic pot scrubbers and salt water will be almost all you need to maintain your wood. The one piece of gear you don't need is a stiff bristle brush. This is the *worst enemy* of bare wood. A brush scratches out the softer summer grain found on most wood and leaves the harder annual rings standing proud. These ridges look bad and reduce the non-skid qualities of the wood. The valleys between them trap dirt so you have to scrub them more often and only a brush will get the dirt out of the now deepening valleys. So to remove the ridges, periodic sanding becomes necessary. This reduces wood thickness at an astounding rate. It is possible to loose ¼ inch of wood in three or four years of regular brushing, sanding, brushing. This is the equivalent of 22 to 25 years of wear on a deck that is scrubbed more gently.* Besides the premature aging and extra labor of sanding a deck cleaned with a bristle brush, there is the time lost replacing wood plugs and rubber seam compound because as the decks wear, these each become thinner. This same premature aging will happen to handrails and bare trim if you use a bristle brush. So the all-around most satisfactory way of maintaining bare wood is a once or twice a year scrubbing with warm salt water, some dish soap and a pot scrubber. Scrub in a

---

*The holystone, a flat block of soft sandstone, was the old-fashioned answer to scrubbing and sanding at one time.

circular or across the grain motion. Try to minimize scrubbing with the grain as the pot scrubber can also press into the softer grain and scratch it out a little. With this method you should be able to go five years with only slight grooves developing in your edge grain deck or trim (1/32-inch deep.) When these grooves get deeper the deck and bare wood parts should be sanded almost flat. Use a belt sander or do it by hand with 100 grit wet and dry sand paper. Sand only until the gray in the little grooves is just visible. This way you remove as little wood as possible. If this lower grain is still black from air pollution instead of light gray, a light bleaching with oxalic acid should return the wood to an even light tan color. I avoid regular use of oxalic acid or harsh cleaners on our bare wood. I feel the cleaners pull out the natural oils which protect and harden most good decking woods.

The regular use of salt water is critical to the maintenance of scrubbed decks. So a canvas washdown bucket is a must if you opt for lots of bare wood. The salt left on the wood attracts moisture and holds it there. Wet or damp wood resists checking and cracking because it doesn't shrink and swell as much; the salt soaks into the soft summer grain. This salt dries and toughens the wood so that the regular wear is kept to an absolute minimum. And finally, salt is a preservative—it minimizes wood rot. Keeping your decks swollen up helps the paying compound to stay adhered to the sides of the seams, thus you have less wood shrinkage, and less paying compound-seam separation.

The best time to wash down with salt water is just before dark so the decks and bare wood can absorb moisture all night long. We try to wash the boat with salt water at least once a week. In hot dry climates we try for every night.

To clean common deck stains, oil spots, food spots, drips of varnish or paint, we use acetone and a pot scrubber as soon as possible. We rub with the grain only if necessary. We don't try to get every last bit of oil stain out because we find that a few weeks of sun and salt water does the work for us. The black stains caused by iron tools or tin cans can be removed by soaking the wood with a 5 percent solution of oxalic acid crystals and water. (If oxalic acid is not available where you live, look for one of the solutions recommended for removing rust stains from sinks; Qwink is one brand that is oxalic acid in disguise.) Repeat the soaking until the stain bleaches out.

Bare wood on your boat's exterior can be worked on any time it suits

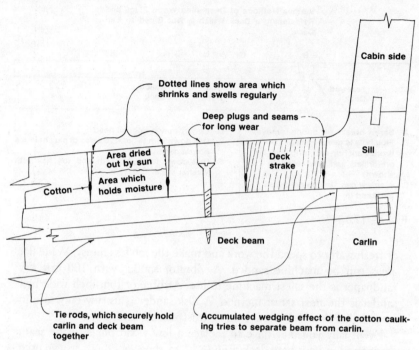

Cabin side

Dotted lines show area which
shrinks and swells regularly

Deep plugs and seams
for long wear

Area dried
out by sun

Deck
strake

Sill

Area which
holds moisture

Cotton

Deck beam

Carlin

Tie rods, which securely hold
carlin and deck beam
together

Accumulated wedging effect of the cotton caulking tries to separate beam from carlin.

FIGURE 17.12

your schedule, rain, shine even late at night. This means that during fine
weather you can spend more time out sailing, less time sanding, painting
or maintaining your boat.

Below decks, fresh water can be used exclusively for scrubbing counters or floor boards. Extreme moisture loss and the resultant checking
is not a problem here. Lin keeps her bare ash sink counter and bare
interior teak surfaces clean by using a solution of one-fifth bleach, a
squirt of liquid soap and hot water with the plastic pot scrubber every
three weeks. For extreme spots, such as the one caused when an exuber-
ant guest dropped his pizza then stepped on it, she adds a bit of scouring
cleanser and a few curses.

Even the most kindly treated scrubbed decks will eventually have to
be carefully sanded or scraped down. The safest way to do this is to hand
sand them or use a hook scraper. Both methods can be used with salt

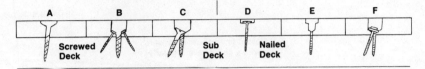

Various Methods of Deepening Wood Plugs and
Refastening a Deck Which is Not Glued to Sub
Deck

A Screw breaks off during removal.
B Plug hole is deepened and two
   bronze anchor-fast ringnails are
   pre-drilled and toe nailed as
   shown
C A screw can also be predrilled
   and toed in.

D Center punch ringnail head
E Drill down with ¼″ drill so sides of plug hole are
   not damaged.
F Drill down to plug depth and toe nail with
   washer under nail head.

FIGURE 17.13

or fresh water to speed the work and make the job less messy. Wide flat
areas can be machine sanded. A vibrator sander with 100 grit dry
sandpaper is the safest machine to use. A three or four-inch wide belt
sander is the next safest method. A disk sander is usually only safe in
very skilled hands. I know I don't trust myself to use one.

Eventually you may have to replace a few wood plugs or the seam
compound in your bare deck. Figure 17.13 shows methods I have used
to refasten old decks when I did boat repairs as we cruised.

Although I have only discussed poles, decks and cabin trim in detail
in this article, figure 17.14 will give you some ideas about where you
might use bare wood to improve the appearance of your boat. It also
shows some of the woods besides those I've mentioned that could be left
bare.

Wherever you choose to use bare wood remember to avoid leaving
expensive, wide boards or large solid spars unfinished. No bristle brushing, scrub or lightly sand the high grain only. Keep exterior bare wood
parts moisturized with salt water to minimize checking and harden the
softer grain. Scrubbed wood is one of the favorite choices of boat
builders and ultimately the user—the sailor who has to maintain the
boat. It saves them both time and materials. So they can both kick off
for a great weekend of sailing or racing with their no-press faded jeans
and scrubbed woodwork.

Commonly Left Bare	Values / Variable Costs								Scrubbed Uses	Comments.
	Low shrink & swell	Cost	Availability	Resistance to wear	Resistance to rot	Ease of working	Non skid	Weight per cu. ft. in lbs.		
Ask a local boat-builder about local woods suitable for leaving bare.										
Teak	10	2	8	9	10	8	10	45	Decks trim gratings hand rails cabin sole etc.*	Natural oil keeps teak stable. Too heavy for spars or oars.
Elm (American) (Canadian Rock Elm)	8	?	?	8	6-8	9	9	37	Railcaps gratings pin rails sink counters cockpit coamings hatch coamings	Available in U.K. or east coast of America.
Ash	7	9	9	7	4	10	3	42	Oars railcaps sink spinn pole interior trim	stains easily cheap & available
Fir	5	9	9	6	3	5	9	37	Decks only	Only use tight close grain 16 rings per inch.
Cedar Port Orford	6	2	?	5	10	10	1	28	Decks only	Expensive & rare.
Iroko	5	8	?	8	9	9	8	43	Decks gratings small parts	Hairline checking when scrubbed.
Beech Queensland	8	?	?	8	?	10	8	?	Decks	Australian deck material.
Pitch Pine	10	?	?	10	10	9	8	40-48	Decks railcaps	Should be full of pitch & heavy 40-50 lbs per cu.
Spruce	5	4	6	3	2	8	?	26	Small spars & oars only.	Oil for 12 months before leaving bare

*Other uses of teak pads on mast for winches, cleats. Dorade boxes. Companionway sill and dropboards riser for sail & spinn track seraffyns teak tramsom was bare dinghy rails & knees.

FIGURE 17.14

18

Nuts, Bolts, and Screws

The fasteners catalogue from the boat builders' supply house we used during *Taleisin*'s construction ran thirty-eight pages and listed almost one hundred possible choices in forty or fifty different sizes. Six types of metal alloys, bolts or screws, four different head styles, two different slots plus sheet metal screws, nails. escutcheon pins and pop-rivets. Then at the end of the catalogue there was a note, "Other types and styles available by special order." This seemingly endless list of choices can be quickly pared down for the yachtsman who is working on a spring refit. The place to start is with type of metal.

Hot-dipped galvanized fasteners are rarely used today except for refastening older wooden boats or building large new wooden boats. Although galvanized fastenings cost about 40 percent less at the retail level, corrosion problems give them a limited life, especially in smaller sizes. Bleeders and wood deterioration are also a problem with galvanized screws and bolts, even those set in red lead. In recent years some boat builders have been substituting stainless steel screws when they refasten older wooden boats that were originally galvanized fastened. This seems logical as the metals are similar, but only time will tell if this is a good practice.

Brass is also a poor choice except for decorative interior trim or for tacking protective copper or stainless steel sheet in place. Brass is a brittle metal that can deteriorate quickly in the marine environment. The most frustrating problems boat repair carpenters encounter are caused by brass screws that snap off when they try to remove planks, fittings or joinery.

Silicon bronze fastenings are a fine choice for any use on any repair job above or below the waterline except through aluminum such as spars. The galvanic action between aluminum and bronze will turn the aluminum to powder with or without saltwater contact. Silicon bronze is almost copper-colored when new, Statue of Liberty green when it has been exposed to salt air. Brass is gold when new, gray when it ages.

Copper fasteners such as rivets or boat nails are used most often on wooden boats. They are non-corrosive and perfect for holding wood together, but not as strong as silicon bronze fasteners. For holding chainplates, bow rollers or other high stress fittings, bronze is far better.

Stainless steel fasteners are strong for their weight, relatively inexpensive and easy to find at most marine hardware stores. Unfortunately they are not the perfect fitting for all uses. Although they are the best choice for fastening fittings to aluminum masts, they will eventually cause some pitting and bubbling on the metal near them. Stainless steel should not be used externally below the waterline of your boat as it deteriorates in salt water.*

Stainless steel fasteners above the waterline can become an eyesore since the most common type of alloy used for marine fasteners is not stain proof, it only stains less. So rust will occur and can occasionally be so bad that red teardrops will run along the deck and down your hull. This is especially a problem if you bolt wood onto your hull such as a rub rail. The rust stains will bleed between the hull and wood and create a problem that is impossible to solve short of removing the whole rail and refastening it with bronze.

Stainless steel and bronze get along quite well on deck and aloft.

*Theoretically, high-quality stainless steel such as alloy no. 316 should work below the waterline. Unfortunately, it is difficult to be sure all of the bolts, screws and fittings are of an equal quality alloy, especially if there are welds. Naturally the least noble of your stainless steel fittings will suffer first from electrolysis.

Stainless rigging wire attached to bronze turnbuckles was the norm for decades. But below the water these metals should not be mixed. Bronze gudgeons and pintles require bronze bolts or copper rivets.

Monel used to be a good choice for those who wanted the strength of stainless combined with the corrosion resistance of bronze. Unfortunately monel fastenings are becoming difficult to find and therefore quite expensive.

The choice of bolt or screw depends on what type of stress your joint

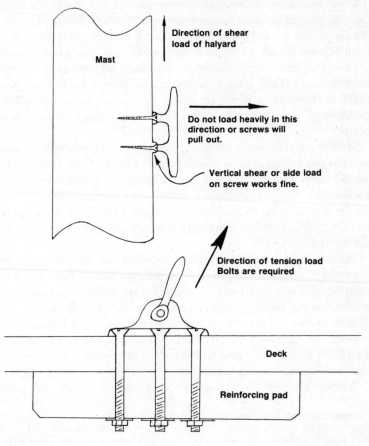

FIGURE 18.1

will be asked to bear. (See figure 18.1) In all cases, your best and strongest fastener is a through bolt such as a carriage bolt, hex head bolt or machine screw with nut and washer. (Hex head bolts are used primarily on metal work, carriage bolts on wood or wood to glass.) Unfortunately, it is not always possible to have access to the opposite side of your fastening so you will have to settle for a wood screw at times. The rule of thumb used by wooden boat builders is that a screw needs to have a gripping depth of at least six times its shank diameter to develop full strength in hardwood and eight times its shank diameter to develop full strength in soft woods. If you must screw into the end grain of any kind of wood, especially plywood, it would be wise to increase this depth (figure 18.2). For safety and conservatism, always choose a through bolt where the gear you are fastening could cause injury or boat damage if it pulled loose. Choose screws for interior joinery or fittings that bear little strain.

Head styles are usually an aesthetic choice based on tradition. Flat head screws are usually covered by wood plugs. Oval heads are used to attach finish trim where the heads will be left showing, such as oil lamps, towel racks and clothing hooks. Round head screws are the choice for attaching thin metal fittings in place if the metal is too thin to counter sink for an oval head screw.

Phillips head screws are a great advantage to the production builder. Air driven screw drivers have special bits that grip these screws and drive them quickly. In large quantities Phillips head screws are not too difficult to get. But for the average yachtsman they are not the convenient choice, first of all, because they require a special set of screw drivers; secondly, it is harder to clean their slots if they become filled with putty or the edges become burred. And finally, most marine stores and foreign chandlery's carry only a limited selection of Phillips head screws. During our fifteen years of cruising we found that slotted head fasteners were the norm in both foreign shipyards and marine stores.

For metal working jobs on board such as spars, stoves and tanks, there are special fasteners including pan head screws, self-tapping screws, (sheet metal screws) machine screws and pop rivets. Since a special tool is required for the use of pop rivets, they are once again a fastener that is of more use for boat building shops than for repairs afloat. Self-tapping screws in stainless steel are useful for sheet metal work. We recently used

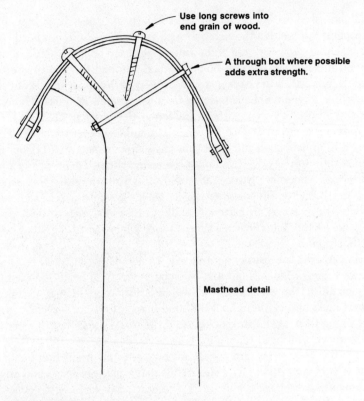

Use long screws into
end grain of wood.

A through bolt where possible
adds extra strength.

Masthead detail

FIGURE 18.2

them to relocate the vent on the side of our propane oven. But for
spar work where the fastening will be going into softer, thicker metal
it is usually better to drill then tap and use a machine screw. For
high load fittings such as spreaders, sheaves or winches on aluminum
spars it is best to choose a through bolt with a compression sleeve
(figure 18.3).

As the catalogue stated, space constraints limit this discussion to the
most common types of fasteners used by yachtsmen during a refit.
Unusual applications such as bolts for propellor struts might require
custom-made fastenings. In this case it is best to talk to the foreman of
the machine shop in your local shipyard.

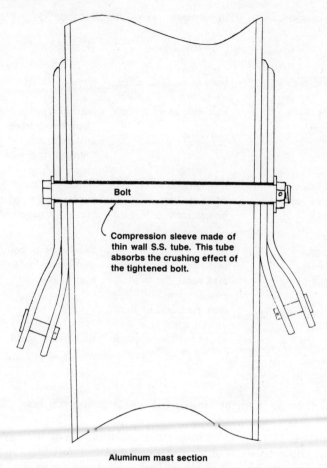

Bolt

Compression sleeve made of
thin wall S.S. tube. This tube
absorbs the crushing effect of
the tightened bolt.

Aluminum mast section

FIGURE 18.3

When you are shopping for fastenings, take along a small magnet.
Lower quality stainless steel in alloys such as no. 302 and no. 304,
those used in almost 50 percent of marine fittings including rigging
wire and fasteners, will have a strong, definite magnetic attraction.
Higher-grade stainless such as alloy no. 316 will have little or none.
Bronze and brass fasteners should have absolutely no magnetic attrac-

FASTENERS FOR SOME COMMON MAINTENANCE JOBS AFLOAT

Job	Fiberglass boat	Wood boat
Exterior		
Hull to deck joint	bolts or machine screws with nut and washer	screws or bolts
Cleats	bolt with backing block	into deck beam—use long woodscrew into deck only— through bolt with backing block
Chainplates	through bolt	through bolt
Fair lead or track	bolt	bolt or long woodscrew
Seacock	bronze carriage bolt	bronze carriage bolt
Interior		
Grab rails	bolt	woodscrew or bolt
Oil lamps	oval head wood screw	oval head woodscrew
Hinges	into wood, flat head wood screw into glass, bolt or sheet metal screw	wood screw
Clock and barometer	round head wood screw	round head wood screw

tion, if they do it might mean some one is selling you brass plated steel.*

A final word that may save many curses and moans a year or two down the line. Dip every screw or nut you use into a bit of waterproof marine grease before you screw it in place (don't use soap, it is corrosive). Not only will the grease help the fastener drive more easily, but it will make it easier to unscrew without breaking when the time comes to replace or change a fitting.

*Although this magnet test by no means gives positive identification because machining can often cause stainless to be magnetic and electro-polishing can sometimes remove magnetism, we have found the less magnetic stainless is, the less tendency it has to bleed rust.

For offshore voyagers, we recommend Jamestown Distributors, Jamestown, Rhode Island 02835 USA, phone (401)423-2520 or (800)423-0030. It is their catalogue we describe on the first page of this chapter. They give quantity discounts, ship anywhere in the world and accept credit cards. Their catalogue is a permanent part of our library.

Taking Care of Yourself and Your Crew as You Cruise

Shipboard harmony comes not only from having a well-thought-out, well-prepared cruising home and confident skipper, but from having a confident, communicating crew as well. Knowing each crew person can safely go aloft and inspect the mast, adds confidence. Keeping lines of communication open as the second chapter discusses, adds harmony. The third chapter in this section will, we hope, encourage those readers who might like to try the most portable profession of all, writing.

19

Safety Aloft

I'll never forget the first time I went aloft. I didn't really want to. In fact I felt a bit like I was being conned. "Check everything out and put a touch up coat on that spot right below the masthead," Larry told me as he checked the gantline. He could have done this himself, but as I climbed into the chair and untangled the safety line Larry said, "This is important. Some day you may need to go aloft when I'm not around."

I struggled to keep from banging against the mast as he hauled me up. My work bucket snagged under the lower shrouds. I yelled "stop" when my feet felt the comfort and safety of the first set of spreaders. I was only one third of the way up the mast and already the boat was shrinking beneath me. When I cleared the upper spreaders I could keep a hand on each cap shroud but looking down became frightening. The only thing between me and shattered bones was that halyard and a safety strap. I'd never had any particular fear of heights, just a responsible respect for the edges of steep cliffs. But now I didn't look down as I did my bit of work. I was nervous about taking both hands off a shroud at the same time. Only when Larry started easing the gantline did I glance around me. The view was magnificent. I could see over the sand spit to the huge bay of La Paz. Seagulls flew below me. But I was glad to feel my feet hit the main boom and relieved when I scrambled out of that chair and stood on deck.

As we voyaged, going aloft became a part of my life. In fact I came to look at it as a sort of nerve relaxant. Each time I slid up that spar and checked the gear, I came back to deck assured I had nothing to worry about. Like checking the steering linkage and brakes on a car, a three times a year trip to the masthead could mean spotting problems before they happened.

Even if you are not planning to cross oceans, even if you do not have to varnish or paint your spars, a biannual trip aloft is top priority for safe sailing. The equipment you'll need for this job can be made at home or bought quite inexpensively. The safety procedures are simple but extremely important.

If your boat has a mast that can be taken down once a year for maintenance and if you do not plan on making any long offshore passages, you only need a bosuns chair, a safety line, and a good bucket for your inspections aloft. But if your mast stays in place for three or four years at a time, it will pay to add a proper gantline (workline) to your equipment locker.

We made our own chair for *Seraffyn* out of a piece of bare teak 18 by 12 by 13/16 inches. Larry drilled a 5/8-inch hole through each corner of the seat 1½ inches from the edges. Then he covered the edges with a piece of old ½-inch dacron line. This line was tacked in place and not only protected the varnished mast but kept the wood from biting into our legs while we worked. He ran a good piece of ½ inch three-strand dacron line through the holes and criss-crossed it under the seat with a short splice so that we ended up with a doubled up support line that was siezed to a shackle just above chest level. The only improvement I'd like on this design would be a seat pad of canvas and foam for those times when we varnish the mast. After an hour aloft that wood seat gets hard.

Several sailmakers and canvas shops offer chairs made of dacron fabric, and we chose one like this for *Taleisin.* The features to look for are a wooden seat board with good padding, large pockets, an adjustable back strap and loops for things like pliers and side cutters, plus good reinforcing. Remember you are trusting your life and limbs to this chair, so look at the stitching and lifting ring carefully. Chairs that do not have a bottom board may feel more comfortable when you first use them, but when its time to shift yourself so you can reach above your head, the wrap around bucket type seat will not give you the support you need.

Next on the list is a good bucket. If you use a wooden chair like we did on *Seraffyn* this is important, the bucket will hold your tools and

FIGURE 19.1 Larry in *Seraffyn*'s homemade wooden bosuns chair.

varnish can as you work. If you have a canvas chair with large deep pockets, the bucket is only used as elevator to send tools aloft as the mast top person needs them. We like a canvas one with a rope bail that is spliced through strong grommets. Because the canvas is flexible, it will be less likely to catch on the rigging as you go aloft. But if you can't buy a proper bosun's bucket with a wooden bottom, either make one or find a plastic bucket with a bail that goes all the way around the rim, not just through two holes in two little tabs. Remember, your bucket will occasionally snag or be jerked by shrouds and halyards. Bails that poke through tabs can be pulled loose and tools that are dropped from forty feet in the air become lethal weapons.

A proper gantline is essential for both long-distance racing and off-shore cruising. If you have a varnished or painted spar it is even more important. A gantline is simply a four-part block and tackle arrangement that lets you haul yourself aloft with ease. We used two neoprene shelled double blocks (one with a becket) a 250-foot long ⅜-inch line (the same one we used as a stern anchor line) on *Seraffyn* plus a galvanized hook for this purpose. This made a gantline sufficient for work on any mast up to 45-feet tall. If we put a tail on the warping line we could stretch the gantline to work on spars up to 52-feet tall. On *Taleisin* we still use our stern anchor line plus two double blocks, the gear is slightly larger. But then so are we.

When it is time to use the gantline we secure the double becket block

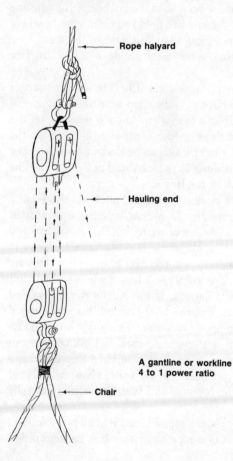

Rope halyard

Hauling end

A gantline or workline
4 to 1 power ratio

Chair

FIGURE 19.2

directly to our halyard. The other double block is secured to the chair (figure 19.3). Then we feed the line through the blocks as we haul the gantline aloft until it is snug against the masthead and we secure its end to our anchor windlass. (This keeps the secured line away from the spar while we varnish. The four ½-inch bolts holding the windlass in place will definitely make any one in the chair feel well supported.) It's amazing to see how versatile this rig is. Because it increases your pulling power by four, you can pull yourself up the mast. (Even I can do it alone.) If you add a galvanized hook (or a small cleat) to the shackle on your chair, you can be in complete control of your assent or descent. Simply take three turns around the hook with the tail line of the gantline and the weight and friction of the line will hold you right in place where you want to work. Ease the line, you'll slide slowly down the mast, haul on it, up you'll go. This gantline leaves your deckbound assistant free to get you the parts you need.

If you plan to work aloft on a complex job, it pays to rig a messenger line with a bucket so you can have your assistant send you that special screw driver or seizing wire. In our case when Larry is working on the varnish and has to be aloft for three or four hours at a time, we use the messenger bucket to send up a light lunch so he doesn't have to come down until he has finished varnishing. A spare halyard or the hauling line on the gantline will usually work for this job.

Mast steps are one piece of equipment we definitely do not recommend. They are bulky and unsightly. They snag halyards and chafe at sails. Their increased windage causes boats to wander at anchor and wind whistling through the steps can cause nerve-wracking whines in heavy winds. Worse yet, because they are so easy to use, mast steps are often the cause of accidents. We lost a good friend who climbed aloft at sea on steps just to retrieve a halyard. It was a calm day, he figured he'd only be aloft for seconds. But the boat lurched, his foot slipped through the step and he hung upside down until his ankle broke. Then he fell and hit the deck. This is a gruesome case. But going aloft can be dangerous and must be taken seriously. If you have to prepare and check your gear each time you head up the mast, chances are your subconscious mind will get the message and keep you acting carefully each step of the way.

When its time to go aloft, choose a rope halyard if at all possible. You can visually inspect every inch of a rope to be sure it is in good order.

FIGURE 19.3
Seraffyn's gantline
block and hook
showing the
connection to the
bosuns chair.

Wire or its end connection is more difficult to be sure of. Never go aloft on a halyard with a rope to wire splice. It is impossible to see what is going on inside that splice. So why take a chance?

Unless there is no other choice, don't connect your gantline or chair to a snapshackle. Choose the eyesplice behind the snapshackle and use a screw type shackle instead. Remember, you want a definite nonopenable connection holding you to the halyard. A snapshackle pin should be taped or wired so it won't snag and open accidentally.

Never go aloft on a wire reel winch. The clutches on these winches work only on friction. They have no definite lock and you can't cleat the tail of the halyard. So if anyone happens to bump the clutch handle, or if the clutch fails you could be in for a quick trip to the deck. A self-tailing winch cleat is also unsafe for the same reasons. Take the

FIGURE 19.4
Lin hoisting
Taleisin's
gantline aloft.

safest route, use a regular winch that is securely bolted to the mast. Then secure the tail of your gantline around two cleats just for a bit of extra security.

If someone else is hauling you up the mast, have them keep three turns around a regular winch, then lead the halyard or gantline end under a cleat. If the strain gets too heavy, they can quickly cleat the hauling line off. Do not let them hoist you aloft on a reel winch. If they loose their grip on the handle and the clutch is not fully engaged, your assistant could end up with a broken wrist and you could end up worse.

Okay, now we are ready to be hoisted aloft, the chair is all rigged, the gantline secured or the crew ready on the winch. Here is the most important safety test. Get in the chair, haul yourself up so your toes just touch the deck and bounce as violently as you can, sort of like a baby in a jolly jumper. If nothing creaks or groans, if the halyard holds, you are on your way safely up the mast.

We use a simple safety harness every time we go aloft. We tie a seven-foot-long piece of one-inch-wide nylon webbing around our waist, then tie it around the mast with about two feet of slack. That way if some unexplained accident happens such as a halyard breaking or the chair slipping out from under us, the line will hold us against the mast and act as a brake, controlling our assent and arresting the fall at the spreaders. This is far better than an uncontrolled fall from forty-five feet in the air. The only time our safety line is untied is when we reach another set of spreaders. Then we put an arm over the spreaders while we retie the line. Once we get to a place where the shrouds are quite close to the mast, we tie the line around the shrouds too. That way we can't slide as far in case of an accident. Up or down we keep this safety line secured. Slow? yes. Safe? yes.

I know we must sound like nervous hens with all of this talk about each detail of going aloft safely. But we know of one fine yacht skipper who walks with a permanent limp due to a fall from aloft. Even more poignant is Larry's picture of the yacht rigger in his home town. The rigger retired at a very young age and is now getting around in an electrically powered wheelchair because a halyard broke while he was aloft. If your goal is to be an old sailor, make going aloft as safe as crossing a street. Look everyway you can before you leave the deck.

One thing I learned the hard way is to wear long pants when you go aloft. Innocent looking sail track can give you a nasty bruising pinch on the soft inner flesh of your thighs. Also try to have someone always standing by on deck. Otherwise you just might not finish a masthead job properly. I know I wouldn't want to let myself down the mast, then haul myself aloft again just to get the wire to put one seizing on a shackle. But with someone standing by I'd wait until they found the seizing wire and sent it aloft.

If you have to go aloft at sea and there is a swell running, it pays to secure a tagline to the bottom of your bosuns chair. That way the person on deck can control your swinging and help keep you from banging against the mast on each roll. If this doesn't help, tie your safety line so you can untie one line when you reach the spreaders and secure it above, then untie the second line. Then you will never be detached from the mast. This extra security counts because the pendulum like motion of a spar in a seaway could rip you loose otherwise.

Each time you go aloft, even if it is between your regular inspection trips, look for any changes on the spar or its gear. If you see wear, scratches or dents in the mast finish, try to figure out what is causing them. If the fittings show signs of movement, secure them better and check your leads. I remember going aloft in Spain just to free a flag halyard. I noticed the varnish around our spreader fitting seemed to have pulled away about ⅟₃₂ of an inch. Larry went back up to take a look. There definitely was a change from his last trip aloft. It took an hour to figure out the problem. We had run into the overhanging branches of an ancient pine tree when we sailed alongside a pier in Falmouth Bay, England. It had seemed a laughing matter when we ducked from falling pine cones and needles a month before. But now we spent three hours refastening the spreader fitting.

While you are being hauled aloft, check each wire for broken, rusted or cracked strands. These are a sign of wire fatigue and could snag or stain your sails. Inspect each swage for signs of cracking, move each shackle and check its wire seizings, move each sheave and make sure it runs free. Then check for any cotter pins or seizings that can scratch your sails. We watched our brand new mainsail rip open for three feet just like it had been slit with a knife. Close inspection showed one stainless steel seizing on a shackle near the spreaders had a projecting wire that scored the sail.

Finally, while you are aloft, think of any parts you may eventually want to replace or change. Make a list of the parts and tools you'll need. Then two or three months later when it is time to make the modifications, you can carry everything aloft at one time. Planning like this can turn a horrendous looking task into two hours work.

Going aloft is one of the skills of seamanship that should be practiced before it becomes a dire necessity. Like man overboards, or kedging-off procedures, practice drills for going aloft insure you against real emergencies. If every person on board has gone aloft while the boat is lying securely tied in a marina or anchored in a quiet cove, they'll know and trust the equipment they need to use. If each person knows what good spar and gear condition is from a personal inspection trip up the mast, they'll be able to spot potential problems before they can cause emergencies. Going aloft even at sea can be safe and relatively easy. Don't wait until you've lost a halyard 200 miles from land, find out now how your bosun chair and gantline work. You might just enjoy the view from the top.

20
Cut the Shouting
Out of Sailing

I guess we could sense trouble even before it started. The 35-foot sloop was making a downwind approach into the crowded mooring area, its engine running, a spray dodger in place so the helmsman had a hard time seeing the lady who stood on his foredeck armed with a boat hook. The ten-knot breeze blew their shouted words down to us. "Head more that way," she yelled. "Where's the mooring?" he yelled. "Head more that way," she yelled again, obviously unaware that the noise of the engine, the dodger and the wind kept the helmsman from hearing her words. We could see the helmsman's plan, a quick round up into the wind with the tide to slow the boat down right next to the mooring pennant. But his lady on the foredeck didn't seem to know. Between her drowned yelling and confusion they missed the mooring pickup and had to try again twice. By that time a shouting match developed that embarrassed both of us into going below with our drinks.

An hour later I was in at the club showers when the same lady walked in. "I quit," she said. "This is the last time I'll get on that damn boat with him. He never tells me what's going on then he shouts at me until I get frazzled. Then when we go home he spends hours blaming me for making him look foolish on the boat." She was embarrassed by their foul-ups too. "Why can Old Bailey sail a 64-foot, engineless yacht up to his mooring everytime, no shouting, no hassels, almost like a precision dance team?" she asked.

I knew what she meant, I'd watched Mr. Bailey sail his 12-meter *News Boy* through the tightly packed moorings in Newport Beach. I knew some crews who could sail into the tightest situations and look cool and relaxed. The key to their success is careful communications, good planing, crew cooperation and lots of practice.

The first link in any communications chain is making sure everyone on board is speaking the same language. This may sound corny but if you call your small genoa a lapper one day, genoa the next, you are bound to confuse the person who is handling the foredeck. It goes back to the old sailing ship days when every line, every sail and halyard had its own distinct name, and its own distinct position on board all ships. This is not just tradition, it allows for concise communications and for sailors to step on board any ship and set to work immediately. In the old days, every sailor, no matter where he was trained, knew what a top gallant sheet was and where it was on the pinrail. So calm or storm, there was no excuse for misunderstanding. On board your much smaller cruiser these names are just as important, maybe more so since you've got less crew to do the work. A mistake won't be remedied by another crew man who understood exactly what you meant.

The old-fashioned sounding words port and starboard, fore and aft are still by far the best words to use in all on-board communications. Left and right will only cause confusion. If you are at the helm and call an order to your wife on the foredeck, "Put the mooring line on the left cleat," who's left are you talking about, yours as you look forward or hers as she looks aft at you? Help everyone on board learn these designations so they become as natural as foot and hand. Put red tell-tails on the port side of the boat, green on starboard, put signs on each side of the cockpit. But get communications started on the proper footing and you'll be on the route to hassel free sailing maneuvers.

The next step is to call a huddle before each maneuver. Whoever is in charge should explain what he/she has in mind, which person should do each part of the job and when each move should be made. Even after sixteen years of sailing together Larry and I still confer each time we get ready to get underway or come into a mooring, dock or anchorage. This war council not only makes later communications more effective, it helps you make sure everyone is ready to go.

Two friends of ours were leaving for a month of cruising. They'd just carried the last minute stores on board then John set to work removing sail covers, clearing the deck, untying the safety line on their mooring. Meanwhile Ellie was busy below rushing to put away stores in the bilge, in settee lockers and behind the bunk cushions. They were in a hurry to catch some friends who wanted to rendezvous in Catalina, so maybe that's why John decided to set sail and cast off the mooring without calling a huddle. He didn't even make sure Ellie heard his call of "Everything ready? I'm getting underway." Just when John steered clear of the mooring bouy he realized he'd forgotten the jib sheets. He rushed down the companionway, tried to stop but it was too late. His foot went past the open floor boards, into the bilge and there he stood, up to his calves in seven dozen crushed eggs. Needless to say, that day's voyaging got off on the wrong foot.

In tight situations such as sailing or powering out of a crowded marina, it pays to spell out each part of the planned maneuver, then have each crew person check the gear they'll be handling. Are the jib sheets lead correctly, is the boat hook free of its holder, are the mooring lines ready to run freely? Don't let anything rush this pre-maneuver check. The one time we didn't follow this rule, I ended up with a broken leg and that was after eleven years of voyaging together. We were hurrying to catch the tide under the Second Narrows bridge so we would be in time for opening day maneuvers at our own yacht club (West Vancouver Y.C.). There were a lot of friends on the dock at the Royal Vancouver Yacht Club, they'd come to see us off. Some were helping us put the sails on, three cast off our mooring lines. So instead of having our normal conference and quick gear check, I hoisted the lapper, then went back to steer after we'd cleared the dock. Everything seemed fine until we tacked 200 yards from the club. Larry put all of his strength into pulling the genoa sheet. Someone hadn't tied a proper bowline. The sheet came loose from the sail, Larry fell back across the cockpit, landed against my leg and I had a nice clean fracture of the fibula. We were both at fault for not taking the time to confer, then check our gear.

If the maneuver you are planning is something new to you and your crew, or if there is something like a swiftly running tide or unusual wind shifts that could cause a foul up, take a dry run. Sail or power past the place you want to moor. Check the position of bollards or cleats, make sure there is sufficient room for your boat. Discuss anything that could interfere with you or your crew doing a neat job of landing. Then sail back to clear water for that final check on mooring gear. Larry would have avoided an ugly scrape on *Seraffyn's* topsides if he'd taken a dry run before sailing up to the seawall at Brindisi, Italy, when he was out alone one day. He would have spotted the pipe protruding from the seawall and saved himself from a nasty bruise, too.

You'll notice that all of these suggestions seem to be aimed at a skipper who must be both commander and scapegoat. This may not seem democratic, but on a sailing boat, democracy doesn't work. We've seen the chaos that happens when four or five experienced skippers end up on the same boat. Everyone wants to issue orders, no one really wants to take them. This leads to mistakes and temper tantrums. So choose a skipper for each day or each passage if there isn't already someone on board who has assumed that position. Larry and I take turns being in charge. We change off almost every time we enter a new port. That divides the responsibility up and gives me a chance to learn more about making sailing decisions.

But just because you don't happen to be skipper for the day doesn't mean you have no responsibilities for the safety or smart handling of your boat. During the pre-maneuver huddles mention any facts that may be helpful. Point out the wind wavelets being caused by a gust coming into the anchorage, mention the unsecured halyard tail or partially unpacked stores below deck. Even the most experienced skipper has a hard time noting everything on deck, below and ahead.

Once you start any maneuver, every person on board must learn to repeat every order and make sure the skipper knows each job is complete. Sure it seems formal to call back, "anchors coming up" or "staysail's going up" after the orders are called to you. But this is the only way each person on board knows what's going on. It's very easy for the person on a windy foredeck to miss hearing a call of, "Is the mooring clear?" If the engine is running, this is even more important. Remember the engine is louder in the cockpit than it is on the foredeck. Don't be afraid to yell to make sure you are heard, even better yet, arrange for hand signals when you must maneuver with the engine. But with either hand signals or shouted orders, repeat each order. It's far better to repeat orders than to get into a shouting match when a maneuver deteriorates into a mishap because someone aft didn't hear you.

This repeating of orders is one of the biggest weaknesses Larry and

I have when we sail together. I hate to yell. He sometimes doesn't hear me and so assumes everything is done. Then I end up rushing or tangled in a mooring line I didn't have time to flake down completely. The British Navy felt this repeating of each command and order was so important that men who failed to comply where put in the brig for three days. A cruising boat is not a naval ship but crew cooperation makes life in close quarters and tight situations far safer and more comfortable.

Half the fun of sailing is talking over the near misses or neat maneuvers afterwards. This is an important part of learning to sail as a team. Once the laughs are over, a careful analysis of each crew's part in the "almost" situation will help the next time you are out sailing together. At first I put all of the blame for one of our most embarrassing sailing stunts on Larry's shoulders. We were flying down the Solent on a sunny Sunday afternoon in May, spinnaker set, 4 knots of tide under us, 15 knots of breeze shoving us at a combined speed of close to 10 knots. Just ahead lay the river Cowes with a sand bank stretched out into our path. We could already see binoculars flashing from the verandah of the Royal Yacht Squadron headquarters. "Let's make this look real smart," Larry suggested. "You take the helm, I'll lead the spinnaker halyard back to you. Then when we're right abeam of the club house we'll drop the chute behind the mainsail, jibe and round up into the river. Okay?" "Sounds great," I answered, as I lead the spinnaker guy so it was clear and ready to run. I took the halyard without even glancing down. Larry went forward. The club house was right on our beam maybe 400 yards away when he called, "Ease the halyard," I did. "Ease the halyard," Larry called even louder. I did. "Ease the G-- D--- halyard!!!" he yelled. I looked aloft to see what was wrong as we rushed ever closer to that sand bank. "Larry, the mainsail is coming down." Well, we did a Chinese jibe, put our tails between our legs and didn't moor near the Royal Yacht Squadron that day. But later when we were having our post mortem, I realized I was just as much at fault as Larry. Each halyard on *Seraffyn* was slightly different. The spinnaker halyard was thinner than the main halyard. If I'd been doing my part, I'd have looked at the line Larry handed me and noticed the difference. Careful smart boat handling only happens when everyone on board takes responsibility for more than just their own job.

One lesson I have learned the hard way through twenty-two years of sailing with various crews on deliveries and race boats is that few women are able to unemotionally accept the occasional yelling that is part and parcel of any physical sport. Unless these same women have been involved in team sports during their school days, they may never have been yelled at by a person who is reacting to the emotional pressures of the situation, the tension of the moment, not at the person or people he is working with. When I took an introductory course in karate, I was surprised to find that we were actually instructed to shout as one of the ways to increase the power of each action we made. The shout was supposed to release tensions and direct power. The men in my beginner's class had no trouble at all in letting out full-powered *keii*'s. The women had to have separate practice sessions, shouting at each other to overcome our ingrained reluctance to making agressive sounds. Eventually I came to rather enjoy the chance to make big noises. The next step in learning to live with this shouting problem was to depersonalize it. I'd listened to men on race boats, on football teams, in beach front volleyball games, using abusive and rude words toward each other, then ten minutes later laughing together over a mug of beer. I'd even heard this tension-caused yelling from all-women sailboat racing teams. Yet as a wife of my sailing partner I occasionally came close to tears or rebellion when Larry used his fore-topsail voice during a race and yelled, "put your G-- D--- back into it, haul on that f---ing downhaul!" Fortunately Larry would usually notice my stiffening back, my angry face then defuse the potential crisis by calling, "Don't take it personal, just keep the boat moving!" Eventually I came to accept this and actually laugh it off. "Calm down you macho turkey," I yelled back one day. Larry grinned back at me. The whole crew began to laugh and I was on the way to living more comfortably with this least pleasant aspect of sailing.

No matter how much you practice together. No matter how meticulous you are about planning maneuvers and relaying orders, just enough foul ups will happen as you sail together to make two last things very important. Tension-free shipboard life can only happen when you keep a sense of proportions and refine your sense of humor. When the tide back eddies and the captain of the day nips a quarter of an inch off the end of the freshly varnished bowsprit, when your crew jumps for the dock, slips on a fish head and misses the cleat so you end up with a 12-inch scratch on the topsides, remember this is a sport and a boat can always be repaired with a bit of paint, a bit of putty. The only catastrophies worth more than an evenings rehash are human injuries or lost tempers that lead to marriage partners refusing to sail together. If you work to make sailing into a sport. If you learn to plan and communicate then remember your sense of humor before it is too late, you may find the same rules can extend into other areas of your lives.

21

Writing and Cruising—Does It Pay?

I can't think of a more portable profession, one more suited to the needs and pace of offshore cruising, than writing. All you need is pen and paper, occasional access to a typewriter and a simple 35mm SLR camera. Your cruising life will probably give you the free, undisturbed time a writer needs for thinking, planning, outlining, and if you are at all successful, the extra freedom chips you earn will give you more free time to cruise so you have more things to write about and more free time to do it. So if you have a new how-to idea, if you have a new wrinkle to contribute to the age-old problems of boat handling, or if you are a good writer who has had a unique sailing adventure, there is an excellent chance of earning extra funds as a cruising writer.

But, before you dream of financing your cruising life with your trusty pen, we'd like to share some of the realities we've learned from fourteen years of selling over 200 articles and seven books about offshore voyaging.

A few years ago we visited the offices of two major American yachting magazines. At both offices editors showed us stacks of unsolicited manuscripts waiting to be read. The success rate for these manuscripts turned out to be identical at each magazine. One editor told us, "We get about 50 manuscripts a week, reject 46, buy two outright and encourage the authors of the other two. We either ask them to rewrite and expand their idea, or sometimes we like their writing but feel we've already covered that subject so we suggest they write something different."

At first the rejection rate might sound formidable to the potential cruising author. But if you compare it to the success/failure rate of the number of people who dream of cruising to those who actually get out there and do it, you'll find once you have actually made the break from a life ashore, you have overcome a far greater hurdle than the one you face as a writer. There are only a relatively limited number of people out cruising who are self-motivated enough to sit down and take the time to write. It is far easier to get involved with the day-to-day pleasures and chores of a cruising life than to set aside time for an endeavor that might or might not pay off. The same editor told me that less than half of her unsolicited manuscripts came from people who were actually out there doing it. She said, "I dream of going cruising one day and I am sure I give closer attention to articles submitted by people who are off in some exotic port than I do to an article that arrived from Norfolk, Virginia."

Another editor stressed, "We always need new writers. Even more, we need new approaches to old ideas." Many editors said they'd rather have good ideas set down clearly by people who know their subject than articles that are well-written in a broad, literary sense. Patience Wales, editor of *Sail Magazine*, suggested that potential writers read at least six recent issues before submitting any articles to a magazine so they will know the magazine's goals and attitudes. "If they send a self-addressed, stamped envelope, we will send a specification sheet with our editorial and photographic guidelines spelled out. I wrote for these guidelines from 3 different magazines and found they were helpful."

Patience asked that I include a special plug for her. "We need these stories about cruising in home waters just as much as we need offshore stories. But they are even harder to write so they will capture and hold the readers interest."

Fourteen years ago Monk Farnham, the then editor of *Boating Magazine* told us, "If a foredeck hand writes about foredeck work and comes across as an experienced foredeck hand, we'll buy his article. We don't expect or want him to write like Hemingway. No one would trust his advice." Monk also said the secret of success for yachting writers is to write about practical subjects.

We have heard this many times since Monk retired, and went crusing off to Europe. Cruising stories are the hardest articles to sell.

The best way to break into boating journalism as a freelance writer is to write about basic, practical subjects. Len Barton, who lived on his small cutter in Southern California received two checks for his first two articles, first try, no rejections, no delays. His subjects: tips on working to windward in a cruising boat and how to build your own navigation equipment drawer, complete with diagrams and high-quality color photos of the finished project.

Maureen Fassbough found an immediate market for her first article. She wrote about caring for a two-year-old child in the confines of a 28-foot boat as she and her husband lived on a mooring in Newport Beach, California and worked toward a cruising kitty. Her story was accompanied by six or eight handsome photos of a happy shipboard child.

Photos are the second key to success as a sailing writer. Unless you have an exceptional story to tell, such as one we read a few years back about the crew of a 30-footer rescuing survivors of a schooner which was sinking during the height of a hurricane, editors will probably reject your story if there are no photographs or accompanying illustrations. Photos attract attention, they help sell magazines and they help sell your article.

To print well, photos must be sharp and clear. Black and white photos should be glossy and preferably 5 by 7 inches or larger. Color transparencies are even better since they can be used as color or black and white. Color prints are the editors last choice, for they do not reproduce well.

We know photos helped sell some of our so-so articles because an editor faced with an 18-inch thick pile of manuscripts will react just like a reader at a newstand. He'll thumb through the manuscripts. If he sees a photo that attracts his attention he will probably give that article more careful or maybe more sympathetic appraisal. That is why we write very short cover letters giving only three or four lines of background information, then place our best photograph on top of the manuscript.

Presented in this manner, your article becomes its own best salesman. It arrives at an editor's desk ready to use, making him more eager to buy

FIGURE 21.1   We originally shot this photo as a point picture to illustrate an article on buying stores. It was used as a cover photo on *Cruising World* and earned us $400. That sure paid for some extra stores.

it. Provide a variety of good photos and make sure the manuscript is easy to read. If a chart or route map is needed, include one.

If you are not interested in writing how-to articles, you can still use the same basic approach as you try selling your cruise story. Send good photographs, not only of the place, the boats, and the people on them but of details of the boats that are mentioned in your article. Send good charts and if you describe some special maneuvers you used to get your boat out of or into a tight situation, include a clear diagram. We recently read an interesting story about two boats that went aground inside a reef in the Solomon Islands. The writer's description of how the boats were successfully relaunched confused me because she didn't clearly state the wind direction, the direction of deep water, where anchors were lead. A diagram would have solved this complex description problem.

Though you may be interested only in the flow of your cruising narrative, remember, most readers are trying to learn from your experience, so include as much technical data as possible, concisely and with sizes and strength factors. One very exciting story about the only boat to escape the fury of Hurricane Issac in Neiafu Harbor, Tonga, didn't describe what sized ground tackle the writer or other people on 27 boats used, what size chain or rodes, what scope. He wrote only "anchor chains and rodes snapped," but didn't say why. We later learned both chain and line snapped because they wrapped tightly around coral heads. Six or eight sentences on the technicalities would have turned this cruising catastrophy into the thing editors need most, an exciting how-to-cruise-more-safely story.

The very best cruising narratives include emotions, yours and those of the people around you. If you admit to fear, felt childish, overjoyed, worried, got angry, share this with readers. The more you do, the more chance your cruising story will be successful. If you learned something new about seamanship or relationships on board a cruising home, share this too. Though the best cruising stories show the downside of this life style—the cold, the wet boredom of a long night watch, the fear of a stormy passage—they also reflect on the fact that to be free enough to cruise or explore on a small boat means you are very fortunate. Maybe it is this sense of good fortune that makes me persist in writing cruise stories in spite of the fact that our how-to articles and books sell far easier and earn more for us. I feel compelled to share the wealth our cruising life has given us—friends, memories, new ideas, new goals—so other sailors are encouraged to take the first step because they know the dream is possible.

It is almost impossible to sell a logbook-style cruising story. You might occassionally be able to include a few paragraphs from your log as proof of how you recorded a certain exceptional event, but more than that and an editor will almost immediately pull out one of his Xeroxed rejection slips. The only exception to this logbook style I have seen was done by a woman who drew beautiful water color sketches in her log book along with descriptions of her emotions in almost calligraphic handwriting. I wish I'd kept that article, just for its fine art work.

Humor, especially gentle humor, can also help you over the hurdle on a cruising story. Editors need a break from the hassel of shorebound office life. Make them laugh with you and you've probably made a sale.

Short news stories are another way to gain the attention of editors. Most yachting magazines dedicate several pages to news items that are

FIGURE £1.£   Don't forget mood photos.

concisely written and would be of interest to a broad cross section of their readers. One or two black and white photos might be helpful here. If you provide half a dozen news stories as you cruise, the editor will remember your name and read your first full length articles with a more sympathetic eye. If you are fortunate enough to be in the right place at the right time and have either very exciting photos of a sailing event, or can write the only eyewitness report, don't be afraid to negotiate with magazine editors for a price you feel more fairly reflects your efforts or luck (see yachting magazine payment rates which we discuss later). A coastguardsman on board a rescue cutter took black and white photos of a schooner rolling over during a gale. Those photos earned him top rates because he asked for top rates.

If paying for your cruising by writing becomes one of your goals, remember that you need new experiences to interest editors and readers, new cruising goals, new interpersonal relationships. Although you don't have to cruise as far afield as Deborah Shapiro who writes wonderful stories about overcoming her fears as she explores Antartica under sail, you will have to leave the well worn routes like the west about circumnavigation with major stops at Panama, the Marquesas and Tahiti to have the best chance of success with cruise stories especially when you are first breaking into the writing game. Too many people have already written about these places. You'll also have to get away from other cruising sailors at least fifty percent of the time because a good cruising narrative needs the spice of encounters with local people to make it interesting, we can all read about the other cruising sailors from our own country in the "who's going where" columns.

Even if how-to articles are your forte, the more cruising and sailing you do, the more often you explore unusual places, the more likely you are to have new ideas to write about. I know we have learned some of our best tips, ones that not only made our own boat more fun to sail, but also became the basis for good articles, by leaving the normal cruising grounds and finding semi-sophisticated sailing centers where we could get out racing on *Taleisin* and meet racing type sailors. The broader your sailing experiences are, the more confident your writing will appear and the more editors will be interested in what you have to say.

Many potential and actual cruising sailors we have met have told us of ideas we know editors would find interesting, but these people are worried about the technicalities of submitting articles. This is really the least worrisome part of writing.

Double-spaced typewritten pages with good margins give editors room to work. They need to correct spelling and grammar, need space to give instructions to typesetters and paste-up artists. Leave at least one-inch margins on each side of the copy. Handwritten manuscripts rarely stand a chance unless the text or accompanying photos are really exceptional. The only yachting writer we know of who gets away with submitting handwritten articles is Sven Lundin, but then few people can match his style.

Don't be scared off if your typing skills are limited. No one expects freelance submissions to be letter perfect. Correct typographical errors clearly with black pen and you can send pages that have six or seven errors on them and never slow an editor at all. Put your full name and address on every page of your article and on each photograph. Be sure to choose an address that will be good four or five months down the line. I've seen letters from magazine editors languishing at the Port Captains offices in places like Tahiti and Samoa because the intended cruising recipient had sailed onward.

Mark your manuscript "first serial rights." This means you are offering the magazine the right to publish your article first and use it only once. If you dream of making writing your main source of cruising income this could be very important. You will then be free to try to sell the same article to magazines in other countries. Be leery of any editor who askes for world rights. This could cost you a lot of cruising funds. One of our favorite articles, a photo study done by Larry on rudders, sold to seven different publications. Had we given away all rights, the first time we sold it, we'd have earned only one third of what it eventually made us. The same holds true for photographs.

If you've been scientific about freelance writing, you've probably purchased the *Writers Guide* or *Writers Market*, both well known guides for freelancers. Forget their advice on query letters. Yachting editors don't like queries except from writers they already know.

"People who write great letters, often can't keep an article-length idea together," we were told. Invest the time to put your whole article on paper, then send it in and wait. (Patience Wales at *Sail* said she disagrees with me on this. Mike Davidson, editor of *Cruising Skipper* in Australia, who also edited this chapter, says he agrees. We took an informal poll among editors we know and found four preferred complete submissions, two preferred queries.)

That's the hardest part of this whole game. Most editors need six or eight weeks to make a final decision on a new article. There is no special person on a magazine staff who just sits and reads unsolicited manuscripts. Instead, articles are doled out to the editor most likely to be interested in your subject or passed around for several comments. A features editor or technical editor may have to read several dozen unsolicited manuscripts each month on top of his already busy work schedule. Magazines from countries like Australia, New Zealand and some of the smaller English periodicals may have only two editors trying not only to take care of putting together this month's edition, but also to plan and write articles for future issues. They probably have to carry unsolicited works home to read at night. So by the time you wait for him/her to make a decision, then add mailing or cruising delays, it may be four or five months before you find out if the article was a success. If it is rejected by one magazine it is time to start the whole process all over again.

When we were cruising in Europe on *Seraffyn* we'd often receive a check seven or eight months after sending a finished article. It pays to be an optimist. On the other hand, send a back-up postcard if you haven't heard anything for three months. There might have been a foul up at the post office, or, as happened to us once, your return address might have been incorrect. A back-up postcard also might jog an editor into finally making a decision.

One way to learn about the writing game without the pain of rejection slips is to first publish articles in local sailing papers and the small give-aways found at marina stores. Payment rates for these publications are much lower, sometimes only a penny a word, but far fewer writers are trying to sell articles to these non-slick publications so competition isn't as fierce. This experience can serve as a stepping stone to higher paying writing jobs.

And now, the all-important question: Can you earn enough to make investing in a good camera, photo-processing, plus postage, worthwhile? Only four or five yachting authors survive completely on their freelance writing income. Payment at the best U.S. yachting magazines for good feature materials varies widely from $300 to $1,000 or more. Rates in England are about half of this with top features earning only $300. New Zealand and Australian rates are two thirds of English rates. New writers are likely to find their submissions accepted at the lower end of the scale. Even recognized authors are fortunate to hit the top-dollar jackpot more than once or twice a year. Our second year as freelance writers we earned $2,400 on twelve articles submitted to three countries and we felt like absolute winners since we'd gained almost two thirds of our cruising funds just by sitting down on rainy days and sharing some of the things we'd learned.

While we were building *Taleisin* I worked four hours a day, five days a week at writing. Larry added another eight or ten hours each week. Together we earned about $8,000 a year. That isn't much figured on an hourly basis but it allowed us to work at home and I was always available to hold the end of a plank or rush to help Larry get something out of his eye while he worked on our new cruising home.

For people out cruising this $2,400 to a potential $8,000, if you are willing to be a prolific writer, can be a tremendous advantage if you keep your budget low. We've seen far more people on smaller, lower-budget boats, cruise and write successfully than people at the more expensive end of the scale. The reason is simple. If one article sold for $500, gives you a month and a half of freedom, the sacrifice of working at your chart table every morning for a week seems less tiresome than if the same work only gains you a half month of cruising funds for a higher budget boat.

The fringe benefit of writing—one we think may be far more valuable than cash—is the dimension writing has added to our cruising life. We never run out of things to discuss even after twenty-two years of sailing, cruising and delivering boats together. Our articles provide a constantly changing source of topics. Cruising could have become less stimulating after four or five years if we hadn't started writing. We had some very special days and met some very interesting people because we set off to research or photograph an article instead of goofing off.

One day in Malta when the wind was blowing force seven gusting eight, we'd have sat in the local pub for the third day in a row, swapping the same old sea-stories with other harborbound cruisers. But Larry got the idea of doing a photo essay on rudders. So, camera in hand, we wandered through the dry storage yard on Manuelo Island where more than two hundred boats were waiting out of the water. We shot two rolls of film and ran into a delightful old-timer who invited us to spend the afternoon at his typical Maltese home drinking hot chocolate and playing with his children. Those photos led to an article that earned us $900. Several years later when it was time for us to make the passage from Japan to Canada, a voyage we both knew would take at least 45 days, I used writing as a way to avoid the boredom of a cold weather sail. I spent most of my night watches putting down my thoughts. An hour or two each afternoon was filled as I read what I'd written to Larry and he added his comments and ideas. By the time we reached Victoria I had filled 300 pages with what soon became several articles and later a book called *The Care and Feeding of the Offshore Crew.* Without that writing, that book goal, I am sure I would have hated that extra long passage.

The process of writing articles that eventually become the basis of a book, is an old one. L. Francis Herreshoff's *Commonsense of Yacht Design,* Uffa Fox's and Bill Atkin's books on boats, Eric Hiscock's first cruising books, Bill Robinson's book on his favorite islands each started as a group of articles. I think this is the easiest way into that magic world of book writing. Not only does it seem less intimidating to finish a book that has already been half written as you collect articles together, but publishers feel better about investing money in an author who has already proven there is an interest in his ideas by selling articles. The publisher also feels the book is pre-advertised to readers who are familiar with the cruising writer's name.

But be forewarned, books are harder to sell than articles and they take far longer to earn you cruising funds. Spencer Smith, the editor of Dolphin Book Club, probably sees every new nautical book as soon as it is published. His club doesn't subsidize or publish books, but if he agrees to buy a finished book to add to his selections, it's more probable that a publisher will invest the money necessary to bring a book from rough manuscript to bookstore copy. Spencer said between 150 to 200 guides, cookbooks, cruising stories, navigation manuals and practical books are published each year. Only ten of these are cruising narratives.

Publishers are leery of cruise books because a good one probably will sell less than 3,000 copies off bookstore shelves over a two year period, perhaps another 10,000 through the book club. How-to books, on the other hand, have been known to sell close to 20,000 copies through bookstores and another 50,000 through the Dolphin Book Club, Spencer said. Donald Street's *Ocean Sailing Yacht; Dutton's Navigation* by Elbert Maloney; Ferenc Mate's *Finely Fitted Yacht* are each in this category. Wally Ross's book, *Sail Power,* sold an astonishing 90,000 copies during seven years, but Spencer says books like these come along infrequently. (So far not one of our books has come close to these sales figures.)

It is common knowledge that authors get ten percent of a book's retail price. So what is shoddy about royalties on 3,000 books at retail outlets and another 10,000 through the book club, especially given the $24.95 cover prices common today? Here unfortunately comes the fine print.

The ten percent royalty only applies to *retail* bookstore sales. Canadian or English sales pay only four percent. Regular sales through the Dolphin Book Club pay ten percent, half of that, five percent, for books included in special promotional sales. Of that the publisher keeps half. Books sold by mail order in the publishers catalogue or through advertisements in magazines, pay only five percent.

Our first book, *Cruising in Seraffyn,* was published in 1976 with a cover price of $11.95. So far we've received $16,410—or an average of 4.7 percent a copy (as of the spring 1986). That is a tidy sum to add to a cruising kitty. But we wrote the manuscript in 1974 so the earnings must be spread over 12 years and we didn't earn the first royalty until 1977. That first book was a combination cruising/how-to book and did very well. Our later cruise story books sold only one half the number of copies our *The Self-Sufficient Sailor,* a purely how-to book, did.

Some sailing writers have tried to beat the royalty problem by publishing their own books. They know it only costs about $4 to print each copy of a hard bound book in lots of 5,000, so figure if they do most of the editing and lay-out work themselves, they can pocket far more than the royalties offered by publishers. They are sometimes right, but the figures are rarely as good as they look. Bookstores demand up to a fifty percent discount on the books they buy, advertising costs money, going to boat shows to self-promote your own books costs money, so does warehousing, packing, mailing and distributing them. Even more important, distributing and publishing your own book means staying in one place for at least two or three years.

Steve and Linda Dashew, who cruise at the other end of the financial scale from us, went back to California after three years of voyaging on their Columbia 50 sloop so their children could finish their educations. They had already had one book published by W.W. Norton & Co. Steve resented the low royalties and liked the challenge of doing it himself. He and Linda spent about five months getting the book ready for publication and invested several thousand dollars to produce and print the 14,000 copies he needed to satisfy the book club and distributor he found. A year after *Blue Water Handbook* was printed it had sold 4500 copies through the bookstores and about 8500 through the book club. Steve wrote that his per book earnings were double what he would have earned on royalties. Was it worthwhile? Steve says, "It's better than straight percentages. But also a lot more work and it required the risk of our capital." We had glimpses of Steve working like a devil as he put it all together and know he enjoyed the learning procedure and the work. But Steve is a super-dynamic person who likes trying anything new, and he is backed up by a determined partner, Linda.

Some self-publishers have chosen soft cover, low-priced editions for their books and been relatively successful. Two of my favorites are *The Cruising Chef,* by Mike Greenwald and *Sailing the Farm,* by Ken Neumeyer. Whether either of them made money to cruise again from these books is something I'd like to know.

We have few complaints about book royalties, especially because we were thrilled that any publisher cared enough to put our name on the spine of a book. But we've learned it's necessary to write four or five books and continue writing articles if a substantial amount of our cruising fund is to flow from our pen. Few free-lance boating writers make much more than $8 to $10 per hour—less than a teacher or carpenter. But, there is no other job I know of that fits a cruising life as perfectly.

Work permits are not required for free-lance writers. Who else can practice a profession in a laundromat, under a banyan tree or during a night watch? More important in some ways than the money is the pride of seeing your work in print. You open the pages of your favorite magazine and there it is: your photos, your name, your words. One Sunday afternoon, while you are sitting on your boat, someone will come by and say, "Hey I tried your idea. It works. Thanks." And you'll glow. You'll also end up with a new friend. That glow will never seem to fade. We still feel it each time we meet another sailor who has enjoyed something we wrote.

If you really want to try free lancing, listen to the questions local people and yachties ask about your boat. If more than half a dozen people ask the same thing, get your ideas together and write on that subject. Then take your camera and shoot off a roll of film. Remember, the reader will not be sitting on your boat while he reads your article. Show him the secrets and angles that will make the idea come alive.

Write up the article with opening paragraphs that will attract your reader's attention. Subject your manuscript to its first test, let a few friends and sailing mates read it. Listen to their comments. Something that seemed perfectly clear to you might not come across in the writing. Re-edit your work and type a clean manuscript before sending it off.

FIGURE 21.3   Yes, I still use a manual, nonelectric typewriter. (Photo by Bob Greiser.)

It's a gamble but one that pays off far more often than people expect. Yachting magazines need interesting copy, and writing sailors go into more lucrative fields or stop sailing and therefore stop learning and their writing grows stale while sailing magazines grow thicker with ads. The editors need at least 40 percent articles to 60 percent advertising or readers feel cheated. I counted 19 to 24 free-lance contributions in the first three 1986 issues of *Cruising World* and 10 in *Sail Magazine* if you include technical, feature and news articles. Ten American yachting magazines and maybe another 100 smaller regional publications need new material. Five Australian and four New Zealand magazines are looking for offshore cruising articles, so are half a dozen English publications.

If you don't get into free-lance writing with unreasonable expectations, the investment of a few hours—hours that might otherwise be spent gloomily whiling away bad weather in port—can pay wonderful dividends, both to your cruising kitty and to your self-esteem.

22

Getting the Photos that Sell Cruising Articles

Nothing sells articles to boating magazines faster than good, sharp, informative and pleasing photographs. Inexpensive cartridge-style cameras might work in a pinch. But anyone seriously interested in making a steady income from free-lance writing will eventually have to invest in a good 35mm camera.

Our first camera was a Nikonus II underwater camera with a 35mm lens. It was fine for shooting details for a how-to article or for taking deck shots in wet stormy conditions. It got us some nice general cruising shots as long as we remembered to carry it with us. But as our writing became more of a paying proposition, we purchased two second hand Nikkormat SLR bodies and three Nikon lenses, ranging from a 28mm lens to a 200mm. (Just last year we added a 35mm to 105mm zoom to our kit.) Then we learned we had to shoot at least one roll of film to be sure of getting two or three usable photographs.

Most top professional photographers find one good photo per roll is a normal success rate. A *National Geographic* editor told us their photographers average one high quality photo for each six rolls of film. Our slightly better average is due to the far less demanding tastes of yachting magazines and the fact that so many of our photos are of technical details taken when we can control the light and content of the picture.

At first we practiced with black and white film which we could get processed into inexpensive proof sheets from which we could select the photos we wanted to print. Then we started using Kodachrome 64 ASA slide film, which seems to be the film preferred by most major magazines.

Apart from learning the basics of photography and spending the time necessary to become comfortable with a camera, the next biggest problem is finding ways to have your camera with you at the right time. Not only are cameras bulky to carry, but a trip ashore in a windy anchorage can threaten a very large investment due to saltwater spray and a possible dunking should the dinghy capsize.

A waterproof camera solves part of the problem. We had a Nikonus II for *Seraffyn* that lived in her cockpit for hundreds of hours of sailing; rain or shine, spray or calm. It proved to be amazingly rugged. Because it was always in the way, we remembered to use it. We now have a Nikkonus V, a fancier camera with internal light metering. It is not as rugged so it is kept stored away and I think we tend to miss some good photos because we forget to get the camera out. But, we do willingly carry it when we dive overboard to go skin diving, when we go ashore for a walk on the beach. But since it doesn't have interchangeable lenses, we use our Nikkormat cameras far more than the waterproof one.

Keeping those non-waterproof cameras with us on forays ashore was a problem. To keep them handy, dry and avoid the worry of theft took some clever planning on Larry's part. His solution was very inexpensive. He took one of my large rectangular Tupperware storeage boxes and lined the bottom with the shipping styrofoam our cameras came in. This already had shapes cut into it to position the cameras and keep them in place. It also added buoyancy. On each side of the box he drilled a 3/16 inch hole and secured a piece of one-inch nylon sail webbing with small bronze bolts and washers imbedded in silicon sealant. This made an adjustable handle. Two hours after he started we had a waterproof camera box that has lasted twelve years. Two bodies, three lenses, lens wipers and four rolls of spare film fit inside. We leave it in the pilot berth ready for instant use. No fear of rust, so it can sit out in the cockpit even on damp days. Even better, the cameras are safe to row ashore.

Part of our homemade camera kit's charm is its corny, unprofessional look. No one seems to suspect the battered plastic box conceals expensive, easy-to-fence cameras. We accidently left the box in a restaurant in Sri Lanka and came running back worried only to be told, "You left your lunch box, here it is." For longer forays ashore we have a small nylon zipper carry bag that slips over the box.

Between our underwater camera and our box full of SLR gear, we have found we have the right combination. When we set off just to take photos, we carry the heavier, bulkier camera kit. When we head off for a picnic ashore, for a bicycle ride around an island, we carry the underwater camera. It also serves well for walks around the marina.

We've learned not to try to make every photo we take a perfect sailing shot. We use lots of film to snap pictures of interesting fittings we see as we take a late afternoon walk or row past other cruising boats. Those snapshot photos make great point pictures, as editors call them. You've seen them—photos that show how someone attached his boom gallows or stantions, pictures of broken equipment. You don't need a fancy camera for them but you do need a camera with you when the subject materializes.

Seamanship as You Cruise

The basis of seamanship is knowing how to recognize danger, then learning to take the often boringly obvious steps necessary to avoid it. Knowing that a clove hitch used accidentally in the wrong situation could jam just when you need to free a line to avoid a collision, knowing that the lack of one cotter (split) pin could case the loss of your whole rig, recognizing a cloud formation that is the first forerunner of a quickly deteriorating weather pattern that could catch you on a lee shore—each of these small unrelated items is part of the overall picture you must be aware of to voyage safely. The following section is about this never-ending list of details that makes up the skills of seamanship. It also shows that all of us have to keep an open mind and learn to recall the seaman's rules we need to win this most exciting and fairest of games. I call it the fairest, because it is the only one I know of where we can use experience planning and research to hedge our bets and swing the odds so they stand 96 to 4 in favor of our being complete winners.

The following letter appeared in *Latitude 38*, a California publication, in spring of 1983:

The first rule of seamanship:
The man who lives and works in the city develops skills to allow him to survive in the city. If he is sufficiently good with his skills he may accumulate enough money to buy a boat. After he has the boat his inclination will be to operate the boat the same way he operated in the city, his cars, his house or apartment and his business life. Few people seem to know that they need a

new set of skills to survive at sea. Perhaps a better way to say it would be they need a new awareness.

When a man learns to fly the first thing he learns is that he and the plane are perfectly safe—even upside down and backwards—as long as the plane stays away from the land. A boat is the same. The greatest danger is close to land. Rule number one for the sailor should be: beware the land.

This is where the transition begins, for the landsman has this belief that there is security in being close to land. When a man becomes a sailor he will look askance at the land for he knows it to be his foe and its proximity will cause him to be always on guard. The sailor's eyes see differently from the landsman's. Don't take your landsman's eyes to sea.

Paul Stead
Sausalito, California

23

Coral Reef Cruising: The Sailors' Venus's-Flytrap

"Please break open five or six coconuts and set them near the front porch to feed the chickens. The machete is on the wall next to the books." As I read this sign tacked to the front porch of the deserted house on a deserted island on the edge of a normally deserted atoll, my mind tried to blank out the incessant sound of surf, the rustle of wind-tossed trees, reminders of an angry sea only 300 yards away. Here I was on Anchorage Island, Suvorov, the refuge where New Zealand hermit and author, Tom Neal, found solitude and contentment for sixteen years. The nearest inhabited land lay 400 miles away. That sign, the well stocked trading library, the swept paths and neatly kept homestead were like a balm after a stormy passage from Bora Bora. I too wanted to fall in love with this place, wanted to leave it just bit better than I'd found it, just like almost 200 other cruising sailors had done during the eight years since Tom Neal died. I spent part of that first afternoon reading their names in the carefully wrapped guest books that formed a history of this unique place. Then a French cruising couple walked up the path from the lagoon and we sat in quiet companionship, sipping cool sweet rain water as they filled jugs from one of the half dozen 200-gallon catchment tanks around the homestead. "This is like the ultimate cruising sailor's park," one of them said. "No one can get here except by sailing across an ocean. It's the best place in the Pacific!"

That afternoon I agreed completely. As Larry and I rowed past the seven other yachts lying between us and *Taleisin* we commented on the wish we and each person we met at Suvorov had had, that we'd find ourselves completely alone in this romantic spot. Yet here was a truly international group of sailors, French, American, German, Australian, Belgium, on eight yachts and each had a special story to share. "Besides," Larry reminded me, "there are several other places to anchor inside the atoll, so when we're ready to be completely alone, we just have to sail four miles east or west."

It wasn't until a few days later when the incessant 22- to 28-knot easterly trade winds increased just a bit and began to swing slightly to the south, that Suvorov's charm began to get just a bit frightening. Like so many South Pacific anchorages this one could turn out to be a watery version of the flower called Venus Flytrap. A 30-degree wind shift, a sudden squall from the south could and often did, turn this bit of heaven into a sailor's image of hell. It was Larry who finally crystallized our thinking about the voyaging we'd been doing since we'd left Mexico. "Some people call this route from the Marquesas, through the Tuamotos and Societes then eastward, the 'Milk Run.' But I don't agree. The passagemaking may be easy, it's almost all downwind. The weather is warm, the water is warm, even *we* can catch fish here. But as soon as you get near the atolls and islands the demands on your seamanship and navigation is tougher than any other place we've been. The reefs, the currents, the lack of navigational aids, the poor anchorages—cruising down here means constant concern. "Then if you find you have to go home for some reason, all of that neat running downwind means you have to beat back against those same strong tradewinds. It sort of reminds me of what our old cruising friend Gordon Yates used to say, 'If you aren't afraid you just don't know the facts.' " Then the splash of a school of fish leaping nearby, a shout from new French friends of "lets go diving," brought a smile to his face, "but the skin diving . . ."

Coral reefs have always made experienced sailors nervous. Even the advent of modern electronic navigational equipment hasn't kept com-

FIGURE 23.1   Shipwreck on the reef at Suvorov.

mercial ships off the sheer cliff a coral reef presents to the unwary. There
is no shoaling, no gradual change in the wave patterns as you approach
most of these atolls since they leap straight up from depths of 2,000 feet
or more. Worse yet, most reefs are only visible at low tide unless a sandy
motu or island has formed and trees have grown. Then on a clear day
the watchful sailor could spot the tops of the trees from six or eight miles
off. Otherwise it is hard to see a coral reef from a mile away. At night
you have no chance at all until you are right in the surf line. Add to this
a fact we have personally seen and tested, the fact that normal ocean
currents increase their velocity and often change their direction close to
coral reefs and you'll understand why the British South Pacific Sailing
directions devotes several pages to a section on navigation among coral
reefs.

   We were reluctant to sail among the Tuamotos, an archipelago of
dozens of coral atolls whose name translates to "Dangerous Islands."
Several people we know who are professional delivery skippers had come
to grief there, even on boats with powerful engines. We'd planned a
route to take us from the high volcanic islands of the Marquesas, to the
3,000-foot volcano of Tahiti clearing these atolls by 50 to 60 miles. But

then we met Frank Corser, a cruising sailor who'd been seduced 15 years ago by the South Pacific and now owned a tiny hotel in Taiohae Bay on Nuku Hiva. Frank had been through the Tuamoto Islands a dozen times under sail. He felt we'd regret passing without visiting at least one of the atolls and he had a seamanlike set of rules for approaching the Tuamotos: plan a course that will make your approach up wind and beam on to the current. Make your approach from the north and east, so if you don't get good conditions and have flukey winds, squalls or poor sights, you can reach north and clear the whole island group. Only approach within ten miles of the atoll on sunny days after you have confirmed your position. Don't be too determined to get in.

We took his advice and chose Rangiroa, one of the most northerly atolls as our goal. For three days before we expected to make our landfall, we began practicing star sights to brush up our skills. The night before our landfall we shortened sail to get the best possible conditions for our evening sights. We precomputed the heights and azimuth bearings of the seven brightest stars recommended in our 249 Air navigation star tables and Larry presented me with a fix that showed five of our LOP's crossing within a quarter mile. "Even if you allow for the thick pencil I used, I'm confident we're forty miles north, north east of Rangiroa. It's ten hours until daylight and we're making five and half knots. Should we sail on until 0200 and heave to?" Larry asked, "or should we heave to now and get up at 0300 and sail in then?" We tossed the pros and cons back and forth and decided to heave to right there. The next morning when I spotted the tree tops of the northernmost motus two hours before I expected them I was glad we'd chosen to heave to forty miles out. We'd been set ten miles toward the reef during that night for a rate of 1 and ¾ knots southeast when the charts showed a due easterly current of less than half a knot for our area. Glen, a New Zealander on a cutter rigged H28 whom we met later at Rangiroa, had chosen the opposite tack. He'd hove to only ten miles out during that same night and gone below for four hours of sleep. When his alarm clock woke him he was only a quarter mile from the breakers. To quote Glen, "only ten minutes more sleep and I'd have hit the reef."

Our first atoll landfall increased our confidence and by the time we approached Suvorov, we'd become comfortable with our routine of keeping an offing until we confirmed our position and could approach in daylight. During this time we'd met dozens of sailors who told us, "If you had Sat Nav, these reefs wouldn't be any bother at all. We also met several new to cruising people who were changing their plans to visit certain reef areas because their Sat Navs weren't working.* As much as these magic little boxes intrigued us, five incidents that occurred as we sailed in these waters reminded us of the warning manufacturers put on each instruction sheet, "This unit is only an aid to navigation." Two cruising boats were damaged when they approached within four miles of the Tuamotan reefs after dark using Sat Nav fixes. They hove to and while they waited for daylight the currents did the dirty deed. Another family bumped their boat onto the reef at Ahe when they came into the pass on a Sat Nav fix in spite of squalls and rain. Fortunately their boat hit on the weather side of the pass and suffered little damage. A fourth yacht was gouged badly when the owners used a Sat Nav fix and came into the pass in one of the Cook Islands during a squall only to hit a piece of coral that projected into the channel. In two of these cases there was up to a four-hour lapse between satellite passes. In between these passes the DR is updated with information the skipper gives it. These yacht positions were updated with current speeds, current direction on log speeds that were inaccurate.

The skipper of a large charter boat told me he'd been quite upset with his newly repaired Sat Nav when he started it up in Cooks Bay, Moorea. His position put him on top of the mountain a mile and a half away. A careful search of his chart showed Moorea as being incorrectly plotted. Many of the islands and atolls of the South Pacific are slightly to the east or west of their plotted position since the majority of charts still in use were drawn before it was easy to determine accurate longitude. A study of the chart notes usually tells you of any error. But if you should miss the small type, your Sat Nav could lure you into trouble.

The most worrisome aspect of Sat Nav in our opinion is that some sailors have come to regard it as a substitute for the skills and practice required to learn celestial navigation. A respected American magazine contained a letter from the owner of a 45-foot ketch who had just returned from one year of cruising in the Pacific in 1984. He wrote, "Sat Nav has made sextants obsolete." He was being quoted by several newer sailors we met along the way. To us this sounded just like saying, "I've

---

*Our interest in Sat Nav was dulled when Fred and Helen, the owners of a Lion Class 35-foot sloop *Amigo*, surveyed more than 50 Sat Nav owners in Polynesia during 1985 and found 50 percent of their Sat Navs were not functioning for various reasons.

got an outboard motor for my dinghy, now my oars are obsolete!" This wondrous piece of equipment can be a great way to confirm your navigation and give you confidence in your celestial observations, but it is not a substitute. We'd go as far as saying the skipper who fails to learn and practice navigating with a sextant and depends only on Sat Nav is endangering the life of his crew since he places them all only a diode away from disaster.

We watched an extreme example of reliance on electronic navigational aids a few nights after we anchored at Suvorov. A large New Zealand ketch came in to anchor a few hundred yards from us late in the afternoon. We saw the crew launch an inflatable and load a pile of gear into it, then zoom off at high speed towards the atoll pass. We soon forgot about them as some French cruising friends came over to share the fresh cake we'd baked. It was well after dark when one of us noticed a light on the horizon to the west. The light seemed to be approaching dangerously close to the atoll. Then we saw a swing of green, red then white that showed it was the masthead lights of a sailboat. The light continued east and disappeared behind anchorage island. Our six guests joined us in breathing a sigh of relief. The sailboat had seemed perilously close to the north-jutting portion of the atoll. Later as we scrambled into four separate dinghies to adjourn to Martine and Benoidt's ketch for a fresh fish dinner, we were stunned to see the lights of the sloop coming through the atoll pass in spite of the cloudy, moonless dark, in spite of the breaking coral heads dividing the main channel. They rafted alongside the New Zealand ketch that had arrived earlier that day. Benoidt, our host, chuckled and said, "How would you have done *that* without a motor?" We laughed and replied, "We wouldn't even have considered it." Later we realized our engineless state did force us to be more acutely aware of possible dangers. It also might have made our coral reef cruising safer since we were already accustomed to being patient and heaving to to wait for ideal conditions before we closed the land or entered passes. It had been standard procedure for us for twenty years, as had choosing anchorages with an eye to getting out as soon as we felt the boat was threatened, and usually having a plan A, plan B and sometimes plan C in case the wind shifted or conditions changed.

We came to know the whole story as we helped the professional delivery skipper of the ketch try to locate the beacons he'd set to guide his friends in. "They'd been beating from Samoa into 25-knot tradewinds for six days and really wanted to get a good night's sleep," he told us. "We'd been in radio contact all along. They'd asked on the radio if I'd come out and guide them in and I really couldn't say no on the air. So when I arrived I checked the channel over and decided if I set two lights as leading marks, then guided them into position using my radar, they could come through the channel and I could then use my anchor light as the last leading mark to guide them past the inner reef. I had a hand held VHF in the dinghy, my crew with the radar was in radio contact with all of us. The radar showed the reef and their boat clearly. It was sort of a fun exercise, laying the lights, planning the bearings." Unfortunately the current in the atoll entrance dragged one of the man-overboard lights and its 150 feet of line and 12 pound anchor under and about $250 worth of gear was lost. The delivery skipper came over for coffee two days later and seemed a bit less sure of his late night piloting. "They really had to trust me to come in like they did," he said. "They also had to trust my radar. When you think about it, they were putting their boat and their lives in the hands of my electronic system. They cleared ten foot breakers by only a 100 yards on a dark windy night." We too could enjoy the adrenalin charge of planning and executing that nighttime entrance. But we agreed with the skipper it had been an unnecessary risk since no one on board the other boat was sick or injured. "If they'd hove to and waited twelve hours they could have come in the next morning with no risk at all," was his final comment.

One of my main concerns about sailing into the atolls and into the lagoons of the reef ringed islands of Polynesia had been locating the passes. At places like Rangiroa where the pass was bordered by two sandy islands with distinctive churches as guiding marks there were no problems, but what about places like Tahaa where the pass was only a break in the coral fringe and over a mile from the nearest land? That concern fell quickly by the wayside as we visited a dozen different atolls and lagoons. At first the excellent navigation markers of French Polynesia helped build our confidence until by the time we reached unmarked Suvorov we knew we'd be able to sight a lagoon entrance just by the change in wave patterns, the curling of breakers around the end of each projection of the reef, the smoother backs of the swells that found their way through the reef entrances, the color changes. Just to refresh our memories we consulted our up-to-date pilot books to confirm the colors and shapes of channel markings as we visited different parts of Polynesia.

The bouyage systems changed from French areas with lateral markings, American Samoa with red right returning, British influenced Tonga with red markings on beacons or the port side when approaching shipping ports.

Deciding which way the current would be flowing through atoll passes was the hardest problem to solve. Throughout French Polynesia and the mid-Pacific, there is less than a 14-inch rise and fall of the tide. Wave and swell patterns often influenced the amount and direction of the current more than the diurnal tide changes. The size of the lagoon, how much of the fringing reef was bare, how much covered by motus or land, also determined the amount of water trying to get out through the narrow passes. The Pacific pilot books list a complicated formula of moonrise combined with tide table data to determine when we would find slack water to sail through the pass into Rangiroa. We arrived off the pass at Tiputa at the correct time (according to the pilot) and we could see spectacular tidal overfalls accentuated, believe it or not, by dolphins leaping from top to top. The current was definitely running out, at a rate we later learned could attain nine knots. We sailed six miles west towards the second pass at Avatura, remembering the advice of the skipper of a trading schooner we met in the Marquesas, "Moon over head, moon under feet, go!" We consulted our almanac moonrise and moonset columns, hove to off the pass, saw the overfalls calm and, exactly as he'd predicted, the current stopped flushing out when our almanac showed the moon to be directly under our feet or midway between rise and set. We sailed into the lagoon on flat calm water.

We watched the overfalls, the flashing current and leaping dolphins in the passes of Rangiroa for several days and learned more about reading the current direction. If the overfalls occurred in the narrowest part of the pass, the water was running in. If the overfalls and rough water were just outside the pass, where the reef fell steeply off into the ocean depths, the current was running out. We rarely saw rough overfalls inside the lagoon no matter how strong the current.

Although we only experienced a slight bit of current once we were a quarter mile away from the pass inside an atoll, we did find some fierce currents inside the fringing reef of high islands. When we lay at anchor about a mile from the entrance to the reef at Huahine and again five miles from the reef entrance in a secluded safe spot behind Bora-Bora, we had as much as four knots of current rushing past. In both cases ferocious winter storms two thousand miles south of us were sending large southeasterly swells crashing across the low lying southern fringes of the lagoons. At low water when the fringing reef on the south side of the lagoon was exposed, less water flowed over it into the lagoon and the current slowed a bit. But at high water the crashing waves piled huge amounts of water into the lagoon and it had only one way out, through the narrow reef passage. For four days in each case there was never a slack or incoming current. So at times like this you can have trouble getting into lagoons.

Navigating inside coral atolls and lagoons seems deceptively easy. The natural breakwater of the reef calms even the largest swells so only a small wind chop develops within a mile of the inside of the reef even on the roughest days. The lack of swell means there is little danger other than to paint and pride even if you do bump a coral head. The wondrous underwater visibility along the inside of the reefs made exploring under sail one of my favorite sports. As all the guides suggested, we tried to sail when the sun was well above the horizon and behind us. We tried polarized sun glasses and found they weren't absolutely necessary to differentiate between the dark blues that meant deep water, the turquoise that spoke of shoaling, the browns that meant coral heads. I was sometimes shocked when I took soundings on a coral head I felt was only a few feet below our keel only to find it was 20-feet below.

Although it might have been fun to have a set of ratlines and climb to the spreaders to con from there, we found standing on the gooseneck next to the mast let us see far enough ahead to sail among the uncharted coral heads of Suvorov at the modest speeds of two and one half to three knots we found comfortable. It was in the relatively well marked lagoon of Raiatea where we had our only mishap. Because of the fine new French chart we carried, because of the bouys and markers we could see ahead of us, we relaxed and forgot about keeping a watch from the gooseneck or foredeck. We kept sailing in spite of the sun going behind a cloud. We clipped a coral head at two knots. *Taleisin's* eight and a half tons kept her moving, a hard swing to port got us back into deep water and two hours work with a hammer and putty eight months later covered the signs of our lapse. The anchorage we found later that day, secluded, fine skin diving, deep firm sand for our anchor to dig into only

12-feet below us and almost 360 degrees of protection made that mo-
mentary heart-in-throat, stomach upside-down feeling our prang on the
coral left behind seem worthwhile.

When anchoring among the atolls and islands of the South Pacific is
discussed, my memories are of constant concern and rare feelings of
complete security. From the time we left Mexico, until we reached New
Zealand we only encountered harbors with 360-degree protection and
good holding ground with limited fetch in four places. Everywhere else
other than in the three small marinas of French Polynesia, we had to
settle for 180-degree anchorages like we found at Suvorov. Although the
trade winds are amazingly consistent during the nonhurricane season
each year, we did experience several sudden shifts from the normal ENE
or E trades to SE and once, to south. The switch to south is the one
most atoll dwellers find disconcerting because this wind can be quite
fresh and will sometimes blow for two or three weeks at a time. The
storm shutters ready and waiting on all the south facing walls at the
charming Kia Ora resort on Rangiroa reminded us of this. About 90
percent of the best anchorages among the atolls of the Tuamotos and
Suvorov, are on the northern fringe. A southerly wind turns them into
a dangerous lee shore. The far edge, which is often ten or fifteen miles
away, cuts down the ocean swell, but a tremendous wind chop can
develop in minutes. If this happens in daylight with good visibility it is
only an inconvenience. Lift anchor and head out to sea or sail to the
opposite side of the lagoon and find an anchorage there. But when the
wind shifts occur at night (and in the tropics nights are always at least
nine hours long because of the proximity of the equator) you are caught
in a trap. There are few coral reef areas in Polynesia where you can safely
move at night except at the main harbor of Papeete or with local
knowledge near a few of the main villages in places like Rangiroa and
Bora-Bora. Even in daylight, these sudden windshifts can become more
than an inconvenience if you have not found a perfect anchorage because your rode can catch under a coral heads' overhanging edges as the
boat swings. Unless you can dive to clear your gear, you will have to buoy
your anchor cable then sail back later when the weather reverts to
normal and retrieve your gear.

Choosing a good place to set your anchor is always a problem in coral
areas. You have to search hard to find a patch of sand completely clear
of coral heads in less than 60 feet of water. So you can either search out

the shallow spot, lay out your ground tackle and hope the wind holds steady, lay out a stern anchor to keep your rode in the clear area or anchor in deep water, water of 90 to 115 feet where coral heads are much less common. Any of these choices have major drawbacks.

We found clear sand patches to set our anchor in several places as we cruised through Polynesia. In each case the time we spent searching for these areas was well worthwhile. Instead of the horrid, wrenching, grumbling sound of chain grinding its galvanizing off against coral heads, we had only the swish of chain on sand. To find this peace of mind we often had to anchor a mile or more from villages. But we felt the extra rowing, the trouble of putting our outboard motor on the dinghy, was worth the effort. Besides, we usually ended up closer to the best skin diving areas this way. We did find a few places where the clean clear areas of sand were a potential trap. In these rare spots, the sand was only a thin layer on top of dead coral. So we usually watched our anchor dig in or dove to inspect the depth of the sand.

Our second choice was usually the deep water one. Near the high islands of Polynesia, rivers wash mud into the rifts in the coastline and good coral-free holding ground exists in most waters deeper than 80 feet. I worried about retrieving our gear when we let out 275 feet of chain plus 50 feet of nylon snubber to get a minimum three-to-one scope in 90 feet of water, yet never, in two dozen anchorages in Polynesia, Tonga or behind Anchorage Island at Suvorov did we encounter coral heads in deep water or hear any grinding noises transmitted up our chain.

When we sailed to the seclusion of Bird Island on Suvorov's far eastern edge, we came up against the third solution, using a stern anchor to line up our gear along a coral-free alley of clear sand. But here one of Suvorov's unique problems forced us to try a new anchoring solution. We let *Taleisin* drift back gradually away from her anchor in the largest sandy alley we could find. Massive coral heads rose to the surface within 50 yards on either side of us. Another lay 50 yards astern. Larry put on a mask and dove overboard to set our light weight stern anchor by hand so it was well clear of coral heads. He was out of the water before I could turn around. I looked where he pointed and counted over half a dozen sharks—sharks up to six feet long—cruising below our keel. "I'm not so sure I want to set the stern anchor where I might have to dive to retrieve it," he said. "But we can't let the boat swing or the main chain could catch a coral head and I've got the same problem." We came up with a solution that used our obstacles. Larry rowed our stern anchor out 150 feet and hooked it into a crevass on the coral head that reached within a foot of the surface astern of us. Then he arranged the chain so it lay across the rough area on top of the coral head to take any chafe.

Neither chain nor line are perfect solutions for anchoring where there are coral heads. Line will chafe through in minutes if a wind shift lays it against coral. So if you use line for your rode, you must buoy it so it stays clear of the bottom. To get the seven-to-one scope required with a line rode for safe holding, you will need to carry several buoys. Chain will let you use slightly less scope, as little as five-to-one in well protected waters of twenty feet or more. But if you swing and your chain wraps around a coral head so that the chain has absolutely no slack to absorb shocks, a three- or four-foot surge can cause a ten-ton vessel to pitch so violently that it will snap the finest ⅜-inch chain. Letting out more chain will temporarily solve the problem, until this chain also finds the ever-present coral head to snag. One solution found by a sailor trapped in this situation at night, was to buoy the extra chain he let out so it couldn't reach the coral head studded bottom. His solution was shown on a note pinned to the bulletin board at Suvorov along with handwritten personal accounts of seven hapless voyagers who had all been blown onto the insides of the reef at Suvorov atoll one August night in 1983. Five of the boats were eventually salvaged, repaired, and their cruises continued. Two were too badly damaged. Six of the boats at the atoll that fateful night had been laying on line rodes, two were on chain, when the normal trade winds suddenly turned to the south and freshened just after dark. The chop and waves reached heights of six feet within a few minutes. Every boat broke its anchor rode and was washed ashore except for the one whose owner buoyed his extra chain as he let it out. Below these accounts a later visitor to Suvorov had written, "Why didn't they get out to sea?"

It was the hint of a wind shift, a WWV report that a band of southerly squalls was moving slowly closer to our area, a slight drop in the barometer from its normal diurnal rise and fall, that sent us scurrying out of the intriguing atoll at Suvorov. We'd only been there a week. Yet we longed for a 360-degree anchorage, a firm mud bottom and no coral heads just for a while to relax after five months of semi-safe anchoring. Pago Pago, 700 miles west offered that. Six hours after we set sail, the reinforced trade winds (strong trades) slowly veered until by nightfall we were reefed down for a fast beam reach with the wind due out of the south. Larry and I were seriously concerned about our cruising friends back at the Venus Fly Trap called Suvarov.

As we rested and reprovisioned in Pago Pago for two weeks, several of the eight cruising boats we'd seen behind Anchorage Island sailed in. Most had stayed only through that initial restless night when the trade winds shifted to the south for the first time in three months and two- to three-foot chop turned their previously dreamlike tropical haven into a restless, nerve-racking threat. The two most novice boat owners stayed three days more because the fear of the 30- to 35-knot winds outside the atoll were more frightening than the existing devil inside the lagoon. They arrived in Pago Pago exhausted and frightened and tired of it all.

Now as *Taleisin* lies with her ground tackle in clean soft mud, four miles up a river in New Zealand, we look back at Suvorov as one of the highlights of our South Pacific crossing. We miss the marvelously clear waters, the days without any need for clothes other than the diaphanous wrap of a pareau I used to "dress up" for dinner. But now I understand completely why so many South Pacific cruisers actually look forward to the hurricane season. The constant vigilance needed to explore among the coral reefs of Polynesia can eventually be unnerving. The chance to find a safe anchorage, to forget about your anchor dragging, chafing, grumbling against coral, to give up the concern of coral reef navigation, the chance to reflect on what you've seen, all make the five- or six-month pause in the safety of Pago Pago, Suva, Neiatu or as we have, south of the cyclonic storm belt in New Zealand or Australia, a welcome relief.

P.S. Unfortunately for the majority of cruising voyagers, a few people have forgotten that Suvorov is not only part of the Cook Island Nation, but also a wildlife sanctuary. Several people have tried to homestead, others have anchored for more than the eight to ten days suggested by the authorities and some have collected hundreds of wild bird's eggs to eat. An official of the Cook Islands related how investigators who went out to the island found one yachtsman with a freezer jammed with 200 lobster he had caught at Suvorov. Because of this, late in 1985, officials camped on Anchorage Island until the beginning of the hurricane season to keep visiting yachtsman from staying more than three days. They are no longer there and the commissioner for the Cook Islands in New Zealand told us, "If yachtsman write and request permission to visit two months in advance or stop first at Roratonga or Atutaki and clear, permission will normally be granted for visits to Suvorov."

24

"No Oceans to Cross"

"Wise men learn from other peoples mistakes, average men learn from their own mistakes, fools never learn," Anonymous's saying kept running through my head as I braced myself in the clammy bunk reeling from a headache brought on by seasickness and trying to justify one of the lousiest dinners I'd ever served a crew at sea. I thought of the stew or chili I should have prepared before we left port. I tried to avoid thinking of the three quarts that made up our total reserves of fresh water just as I tried to forget about the lines that were rigged to hold the skeg and rudder onto the poor battered boat we were delivering north from Turtle Bay to a woman who's problems were far worse than mine. When Larry came in to ask if I'd be able to stand my watch I began telling him I belonged in the fool category. "Don't be too hard on yourself, this is a different kind of delivery job than we're used too. We're getting her home and we've learned a few more lessons."

He was right about this job being different. I'd been Larry's mate and cook on ten delivery jobs and in each case the boat we were to move lay within a mile or two of *Seraffyn*'s well-stocked tool locker or in the midst of a major yachting center. So we'd been able to prepare and outfit the boat with abundant supplies after we'd made a survey and inventory.

Not so this time. *Matani Vahini* a Mariner 39 sloop, had been the victim of a pair of thieves. There'd been a murder on board and she'd run onto the rocks at the entrance to Puerto San Bartolomé, one of the most inaccessible spots on Baja California's west coast, 330 miles south of San Diego. (See following section for the story of how *Matani Vahini* came to be in this position.) Turtle Bay, a cannery village of 3,000 people lay at the head of the port and from what we knew from previous delivery trips, the only supplies easily available were tortillas, beer and diesel fuel. A naval detachment had a small compound next to the village and the officers had agreed to watch the boat after she'd been pulled off the rocks. We knew of the well meaning but lackadaisical manner of the Mexican Navy towards yachts, of the southerly exposure of the anchorage where *Matani Vahini* lay on her single anchor and of the official beginning of the Mexican hurricane season only six days away. So when it became obvious we were the only available delivery crew willing to take on a crippled boat we decided to bring the boat north even though we were only three weeks into *Taleisin*'s first, away-from-her-home-port sea trials.

"It's only three or four days of sailing, no oceans to cross," Larry reminded me. "Allow three days to get there and prepare the boat, its a week. What's that to us?" Larry had really been disturbed when he'd heard about Marlene Pugh arriving in San Diego alone with two dead bodies late at night, battered and bruised, out of cash. Her boat was uninsured and sitting in a position that we knew was precarious. "If you were ever in a position like that I'd hope someone would help you." I agreed with him then and still do, but his estimates were off as far as sea time, ridiculously wrong about getting there and as time went on, four words from his statement came back to ring in my mind, "no oceans to cross."

One problem all delivery jobs have in common is that the skipper needs documents to satisfy port officials at both ends of the delivery route. The boat owner has to legally relinquish control of his boat to the delivery skipper, yet retain his ownership. The delivery skipper has to be sure he can show he has not stolen the vessel. Usually the owner writes a letter stating who the skipper is, the approximate route and duration of the delivery then includes a photocopy of the ship's registration or documentation. With *Matani Vahini* we had to be sure our documents were flawless because we knew that the boat was under the jurisdiction of the court in Santa Rosalia, 250 miles from Turtle Bay where the murderers were awaiting trial and the authorities we'd be dealing with in Turtle Bay would be junior naval personel, men who would be extra cautious because their superiors could not be contacted by telephone since no lines ran to this isolated village. This quest for proper paperwork eventually taught us two important lessons.

When we spoke with Marlene's lawyer he said he'd be most willing to help with the documents except for one technicality, Marlene did not legally own *Matani Vahini,* her late husband's estate did. When the boat was purchased the state registration slip was made out in Bob Pugh's name only. Because of children from a previous marriage, Bob's will contained a relatively common clause stating that his estate became Marlene's property only if she survived for 120 days after his death. With a confusion of estate laws ringing in my ears I called the American consul in Tijuana. They had been trying to assist Marlene right from the beginning. A dozen conversations finally produced a solution we hoped would work. We'd present a copy of the will, Marlene and Bob's wedding certificate, a statement from her attorney and bank manager that said they were still married at the time of the "incident" plus the boat's registry and a power of attorney giving us control of *Matani Vahini.* The consul would then write a letter in Spanish describing the above documents and adding their suggestion that we be allowed to prepare, provision and leave with the boat if the court gave us clearance. The attorney for the U.S. consul stated, "All of this would have been unnecessary if Mrs. Pugh had only carried a letter making her legal captain of the vessel in the event of the death or absence of her husband." Lesson number one, my document folio on *Taleisin* will soon contain another letter (see figure 24.1).

Lesson number two came a week later when we'd finally gotten through to the courts in Santa Rosalia and learned the boat was no longer needed as evidence. We called the American Vice Consul in Tiajuana and said we'd be at her office Monday morning by 11 AM and needed our documents ready. "Can't be done," was the immediate answer. *Matani Vahini* had already been sitting in the unprotected bay for three weeks and the first hurricane of the season raged only 900 miles to the south of her. We didn't have too much time to waste. After exhausting my patience with a half dozen calls I finally pulled out a trick I'd been taught by Mr. Smith, the American Consul in Malta. "When

278 Seamanship as You CruiseSeamanship as You Cruise

POWER OF ATTORNEY

To whom it may concern:
I, Lawrence F. Pardey, owner of the vessel *Taleisin* of Victoria, Canadian registration number 802991, registered tonnage 7.46, do request that in the event of my absence, death or incapacitation due to illness, my wife, Mary Lin Pardey be afforded all rights as captain of said vessel. She shall have the right to operate and sail said vessel, make arrangements for its trans-shipment, storage or hire another competent captain if necessary. Her name shall in this event serve as a replacement for mine on any legal documents pertaining to this vessel and its operation.

Signed this_____day of_____1986.

_____
Lawrence F. Pardey

Witnessed by
FIGURE 24.1

all else fails, start yelling the name of your senator. No government employee wants to have a mark against him in a senator's book."

"I don't know any senators," I protested.

Mr Smith persisted, "Look up a senator's name and the address of his Washington, D.C. office and use it whenever American Bureaucracy overseas forgets it's there to help American Citizens." I mentioned having met Chuck Percy, the senator from Illinois one afternoon in Tunisia. Mr. Smith dug out his address and a letter to Percy's office solved my Maltese problem like magic. On my seventh call to the American Consul in Tijuana I remembered that magic and marched in waving Chuck Percy's name like a Crusadors banner. Our papers were typed in Spanish, notarized, gold-sealed and Xeroxed within an hour of when we needed them.

During the ten days I'd been fighting with paperwork, Larry had been trying to establish the exact condition of *Matani Vahini*. We knew her rudder and skeg had been badly damaged while she pounded on the rocks. Larry tried to use the local ham (amateur) net to find yachtsmen in or near Turtle Bay, but after four days of good wishes and well meaning advise, we were no closer to our answer. Then Hank Durant, a sportfishing skipper we knew in San Diego, suggested we use the singlesideband network maintained by the fuel docks who service

sportfishing boats. This is a commercial radio network used to keep track
of charterers, arrange stores, transfers and fishing schedules. Larry called
Bob Bisbee's fuel dock in Newport beach and within 24 hours was told
that Mike Hope, a delivery skipper on his way north would divert into
Turtle Bay that afternoon and survey *Matani Vahini.*

The next day his survey report was read to Larry over the telephone.
He'd actually put on diving gear and inspected the hull, started the
engine, listed the gear he'd found on board. We were impressed with
the professionalism of the SSB network and the generosity of Mike, but
depressed by his report. There was no guard watching the unlocked boat.
He'd been on board for an hour and no one even said hello to him. The
skeg holding *Matani Vahini*'s rudder was cracked right through so that
Mike could actually move the bottom of the rudder over an inch side
to side with very little pressure. The boat had been burglarized. There
were no oars or outboard left for the dinghy, no radio, no overboard gear
or life jackets. His report helped us make one of our best decisions of
the whole trip.

We have always made it a policy to choose our own crew for deliveries,
people who realize this is a job not a pleasure trip. But when Marlene
Pugh mentioned that Bob's 24-year-old son who had worked for a season
on a fishboat in Alaska, wished to go with us for one voyage on the boat
that had been his father's last home, Larry and I decided to break our
rule. Not only did Bruce Pugh prove to be hardworking crew in spite
of this being his first time on an oceangoing sailboat, his presence also
meant that we wouldn't have to explain what happened to all of *Matani
Vahini*'s missing gear.

So on a sunny Monday morning, the three of us set off by taxi from
Tijuana, legal papers in hand, *Taleisin*'s sextant, Sony shortwave receiver, handbearing compass, navigation books and sleeping bags sur-
rounding us, a kit of possible repair equipment, charts and a portable
auto pilot with our foul weather gear filling the trunk. Sixty dollars, two
hours and 50 love laments later traveling by taxi we reached Ensenada
where we learned just how isolated Turtle Bay can be. The twice weekly
flights run by the cannery co-op had been cancelled for that month. We
had three choices; wait ten days, charter a plane for $600, or take an
eight hour busride to Guerro Negro and hope to find a taxi there
willing to take us across 100 miles of salt flats and desert rubble to
Turtle Bay.

We chose what seemed like the fastest, least expensive way and two days later again sat in a Mexican taxi surrounded by our gear as the taxi driver loaded extra gas, two spare tires and an extra driver. We set off into the black desert night just after nine o'clock and began a saga of flat tires until midnight when we were finally stuck in the middle of the Visciano desert with two flat spares and two more flat tires. We spent a restless night trying to get some sleep in the dust-filled taxi and hoped the driver was right when he said someone had to be along soon. By 10 AM the next morning when we were picked up by the fish and game warden for the last 30 miles of the ride into Turtle Bay, we were convinced the worst part of this delivery job was behind us.

In spite of her battered appearance, *Matani Vahini*, sitting three hundred yards offshore, beckoning with her promise of hot showers, looked like heaven. A local fisherman offered us a ride out to the boat and as we approached we saw that our instincts had been correct. In spite of their sincere promises to Marlene, the Mexican naval contingent had lost interest in guarding the boat within a day or two. It was obvious that boats had been coming alongside without fenders, that gear had been taken since no one was watching. We were on board for over an hour in broad daylight before a submachine gun armed guard arrived to ask us what we were doing. The lesson we filed in our minds for future use was, in spite of the earnestness of officials, the promises of locals, never leave a boat without hiring a specific person to be in charge and responsible for its condition with payment based on performance. A young person from the village would have been willing to sleep on board as a guard and would have saved many times his daily pay by eliminating theft.

While I went through every locker on the boat taking inventory, Larry donned mask and fins for a survey. His report was more encouraging than mine. The only hole in *Matani Vahini*'s hull was a six-inch crack above the waterline, easy to patch with the kit of underwater putty we found on board. The bottom of the external lead keel looked like a dog had been chewing on it, but Larry said that damage wasn't a problem. He was impressed with the amount of pounding that outside lead had stood up to. "The soft metal absorbed a lot of the shock load. It probably saved the boat from leaking," he said. "It will be a relatively easy problem to fix when the boat is hauled, just a hammer and bondo should do it." Our only real problem was the rudder and skeg.

As Mike Hope had told us, the fiberglass on the skeg was broken just below the propellor shaft bearing. Fortunately, the fracture was spiral shaped, running around the skeg in such a way that on the port side there was still a three-inch strip of glass holding the lower portion of the skeg onto the hull. A further check inside the boat showed that the rudder was supported not only by the gudgeon at the heel of the skeg and at the stuffing box but also at a bearing attached to the bulkhead under the after bunk, an arrangement designed to allow for the use of an emergency tiller. "That bearing almost makes the lower one redundant since the rudder shaft is 2 inches thick and solid," Larry explained to Bruce and me. "We could probably sail her back without the skeg if it fell off. Only problem is, if it broke in a seaway it could jam the rudder or hit the prop, so we have to figure some way to hold it in place for 300 miles." His solution looked obvious when it was completed the next morning. Larry borrowed some gear and spent three hours with the mask and snorkel, jury rigging the skeg to the boat just like a mast, only upside down. First he filed a radius onto the bronze heel fitting of the skeg, then used some half-inch polypropylene line to tie a clove hitch around the skeg through the prop aperture (figures 24.2 and 24.3).

He ran a line up to either side of the deck through some fire hose we'd scrounged on shore, through the turning blocks to the sheet winches. Then we tightened the lines until they worked just like underwater shrouds. Larry rigged a set of intermediate shrouds by securing another set of lines below the swelling of the skeg where it widened towards the prop shaft bearing. Bruce and I tightened all four lines until they seemed to be equally bar tight and Larry could get absolutely no movement, no matter how hard he shoved the bottom of the skeg or rudder. We tested the wheel, and the rudder still turned freely. Then Larry gladly climbed out of the 58-degree water into the hot shower we had waiting for him.

On deck and in the stores department we had problems of a different sort. Not only had every can of food, every roll of toilet paper been taken but most of the tools, general spares, mooring lines and linens were gone. Our supplies consisted of five hose clamps, some hammers and drills, three pillow cases, two rags, pots, dishes and twelve jars of spice. We knew that Marlene had offered all of the food stores to cruising people who had helped her during the days following the "incident," but the rest had definitely been stolen. A consensus of both yachtsmen and local

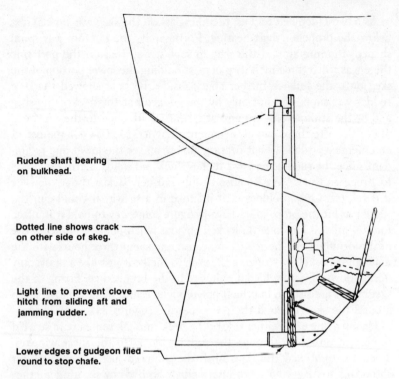

Rudder shaft bearing
on bulkhead.

Dotted line shows crack
on other side of skeg.

Light line to prevent clove
hitch from sliding aft and
jamming rudder.

Lower edges of gudgeon filed
round to stop chafe.

FIGURE 24.2

authorities was that both northbound cruising sailors and Mexican fishermen could have gone on board the unlocked, poorly guarded and obviously distressed vessel at night without being seen.

Fortunately Jim Kirby the owner of *Mile High,* a 50-foot steel ketch, had enough spares in his tool box to fix us an assortment of screw drivers, socket wrenches and vice grips that we arranged to return once we reached San Diego. Rich and Shaun Tempesta, the crew on *Orcas,* fixed us dinner that evening and split their meager supply of canned meat, fruit and peanut butter with us since they knew we'd have a hard time getting any kind of stores in the tiny shops in the village.

Larry's reminder that we had no oceans to cross rang through my mind as I spent the second morning in Turtle Bay trying to get basic food stores, some towels and anything we could find to help the boat.

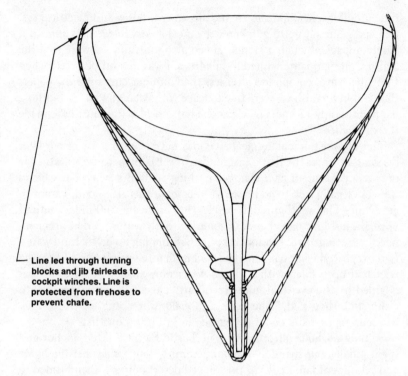

Line led through turning blocks and jib fairleads to cockpit winches. Line is protected from firehose to prevent chafe.

FIGURE 24.3

My luck was marginal, the butcher had no meat, the baker's oven had caved in a week before so he had no bread. A careful tour of all the shops in town turned up tortillas, frozen chicken legs, canned ham, a package of American bacon, eggs, tomatoes, potatoes, and onions so we'd eat, not well but sufficiently. I was able to locate two flashlights and two towels in a tiny shop full of hair preparations in a ladies' front room. Soft drinks and beer were available so I bought two bottles each per day for the three of us to last five days figuring that would give us plenty of leeway for a slow trip.

When I brought the stores on board Bruce was busy washing a quarter inch of desert dust off the boat and supervising the Mexican driver we'd hired to scrub five months growth off the boat's bottom.

Larry was in the engine compartment changing fuel filters, wiring up the autopilot, checking the engine alignment, hoses and electrical system and generally getting to know the mechanics of *Matani Vahini.* I'd barely unpacked when a launch pulled alongside and we were told the Naval Commandante wished to talk to us. I was in a bit of a daze when I left the Naval compound after less than an hour clutching the papers that said in Spanish we were free to leave with *Matani Vahini.* Nothing happens in only 15 hours in Mexico! That consular seal must have made the difference.

This almost miraculous clearance may have lead to some of our later discomfort, or maybe that is just hindsight speaking because an extra day or two in port might have changed nothing at all. But when Larry heard we were legally free to go he said, "Lets leave this afternoon. I want to get home. The weather seems steady, that hurricane 800 miles south of us might just give us a chance of some southerly winds." I don't remember disagreeing at all. I think I asked about topping up on fuel and water. Larry repeated what Marlene had told us before we left San Diego, the boat had been filled with fuel and water only an hour before she was boarded by the eventual murderers. Larry checked the fuel tanks with a dip stick then said, "She holds 240 gallons of water and 90 of fuel. Marlene figured she could power about 340 miles on that."

So only 28 hours after arriving in Turtle Bay, we lifted anchor and spent a half hour swinging *Matani Vahini*'s compass against the lights and prominent landmarks of this rugged desert outpost, then headed to sea on the last of the day's light, just as the Pughs had planned to do three weeks before.

Thirty-six hours later we began to re-learn old lessons. We'd isolated each of the boat's three water tanks as soon as we came on board, choosing the starboard tank as our reserve. When the port tank ran out of water 12 hours out of Turtle Bay I did some rough calculations and concluded we could have used 80 gallons of water cleaning *Matani* and showering, especially if you figured the people who had helped Marlene prepare to leave had also cleaned up the blood spread during the horrible incident on board. So it was more than a bit of a surprise when the port tank ran dry the next day. The 60-gallon reserve tank began to sputter after only one gallon of water flowed into the plastic milk jug I all of a sudden decided to use as an emergency rationing precaution. We gathered every container we had and by heeling the boat first the port, then to starboard and pumping each tank in turn, we managed to get a total of 2½ gallons of water. That, with our soft drinks and beer totaled 3½ gallons of liquid to carry us 240 miles more, and Larry's sights second day out made that bad news. The heavy northwest winds and choppy seas we were experiencing meant we were motorsailing with our main sheeted flat and making tacks of about 70 degrees on the compass. Our rhumbline course lay dead into the wind, our speed through the water was less than four knots. If we pushed the engine speed past 1400 RPM, the engine overheated.* At this rate we had at least three and a half days more sailing. That translated to one third of a gallon of total liquid per day, per person. Five cups of liquid to drink, cook with, brush teeth with. Then the wind began increasing.

The weather reports we picked up on our Sony carried an ominous note. The hurricane that was so far south of us two days before had taken a turn to the north where it began applying pressure to the high that lay along this coastline in spring. Our northwesterly winds began increasing until *Matani Vahini* could no longer carry her full mainsail. The furled 150 percent jib was far too big to let us motorsail close to the wind. We had no smaller headsail to set. The wind increased to over 30 knots and we motorsailed onward with the mainsail reefed, the engine turning at its self-imposed top RPM of 1400, our speed through the water only three knots. And I became seasick. Larry thinks my seasickness is a sign of worry and as he sat on my bunk and talked with me that second evening I had to agree with him. He was concerned too. "If we had lots of water, this would be no problem at all. We'd just heave to and wait it out, we've got lots of searoom, if we lay to on the offshore tack we could easily get more room." His words made me even more angry with myself. Why had I forgotten my promise never to leave on any voyage without topping up our tanks just before we set sail? Larry's reminder that I had tried to find some way to sound the tanks didn't ease my guilt.

The storm lasted only 24 hours and as it passed our wind backed until we could beam reach with both main and jib set. It seemed great to unroll that furling jib but when the wind began to lighten then die we once again had reasons to be unhappy with the actualities of using roller

*We'd been told of this problem before we went for *Matani Vahini.* The charter company that had used her felt the heat exchanger was too small for the engine.

furling sails. *Matani Vahini*'s roller furling jib was the kind with a slotted headstay foil. We found that the foil extension had come apart at a joint about six feet from the top bearing. It would still roll and unroll but it meant we couldn't take the headsail down unless we went aloft in a bosuns chair because the sail groove was misaligned. When I began to gripe, Larry reminded me, "Even if we got the sail down, we don't have another one to set in its place." (Larry and I figure we are now batting 1,000. We haven't yet delivered a boat with a roller furling jib that worked correctly in all situations.)

After four days we were 80 miles south of San Diego almost becalmed on a slowly flattening sea, trying to urge a heavy undercanvassed boat to windward with an engine that had run dry so we relearned another pair of lessons. Number one, you can't depend totally on your engine; and two, those four jerry jugs in the cockpit locker were what made up the final 20 gallons of *Matani Vahini*'s 90-gallon fuel supply. Someone had stolen the diesel they held. Had we gone into the pier for water, we would have filled those too.

We sailed slowly northward for most of the fifth day, eating the last fresh vegetables and hording our private last quart of water. Then we saw a Mexican tug standing by as a tanker unloaded fuel for the huge power plant 20 miles south of the border. We hove to and received immediate assistance, ten gallons of diesel and five gallons of water. That led to the last lesson of a voyage we'll not soon forget. As Bruce and I resumed sailing into the five-knot breeze, Larry slaved and cursed in the engine room, trying to remember the proper sequence to use to bleed the air from the fuel injection system of a Perkins diesel. When that machine finally sputtered to life after his tenth attempt, Larry vowed once again, "I'll never leave on a delivery without the engine shop manual. We could have bought one for only $12 in San Diego."

And so as we powered towards the finish of a job that had stretched to cover almost three weeks, we tried to make excuses to ourselves and probably to Bruce too. On the surface the delivery had been very successful. We'd brought poor, crippled *Matani Vahini* home safely with no damage from the voyage. She looked better than when we first saw her. Larry's underwater rigging job had held up well. But underlying this success was the awareness of the mistakes we'd made, mistakes that with a bit of bad luck could have lead to serious problems. As we powered between San Diego's entrance buoys thinking of the steak dinner and cold drinks only two hours away, I looked at the calm sea behind us and remembered that every time you go outside the breakwater there is a chance you'll hit a storm and even more important—every voyage is an ocean passage.

25

Murder in Turtle Bay

"The saddest thing about this whole affair was that it had nothing to do with cruising, nothing to do with Mexico or Mexicans, we just happened to be in the wrong place at the wrong time," Marlene Pugh told us when we returned her boat to her. "I'm worried that other people will blame the Mexicans or our cruising life style when the same thing could have happened anywhere, even right here in California."

Fifty-one-year-old Marlene and her fifty-four-year-old husband had cruised the Pacific together for five years. They returned to work in Northern California and to keep in touch with the life they loved, began purchasing another boat through a Caribbean lease/buy back chartering firm. When the boat was fully paid off they flew to the Virgin Islands for what was to be virtually a delivery job back to California where they planned to sell the 39-foot center cockpit boat that had been designed for the charter trade but not for the long-term sailing the Pughs had in mind. Enjoyable events and encounters in Central American and mainland Mexico ate into the time they had set aside for the voyage. So it was almost May when they sailed into Turtle Bay, halfway up Baja California with the last of the season's cruising sailors who were hurrying north to avoid the hurricane season.

They arrived late Friday evening with plans for a quick morning shopping tour in the small cannery village while they took on diesel for the last 330 mile slog north into the almost constant northwesterly swell and wind that lay between them and San Diego. Then they planned to leave late in the day to take advantage of the lighter night winds to make their way north past Cedros Island.

All went according to plan until about four P.M. on Saturday when Bob decided to take his dinghy ashore for extra motor oil. His outboard sputtered and stopped and two Mexican men came alongside in an inflatable to offer assistance. Bob had no way of knowing that these two men were desperate, the inflatable stolen. According to later reports, the Mexicans had been invited aboard another of the American yachts, *Anak,* a 41-foot ketch. They'd begun drinking with the owner and gotten into an argument which turned into a fight. The American, Bob Kavani, was stabbed and died. The two Mexicans, one of whom was on the run from American authorities, knew there was no easy escape route by land from Turtle Bay. They tried to start the engine on *Anak* but couldn't find the switch. When they offered to assist Bob they had already decided to steal another yacht.

Bob asked only for a tow back to *Matani Vahini.* The Mexicans obliged but when they arrived there, forced their way on board, pulled a knife and began a 45 minute reign of terror during which they tortured Bob in front of Marlene, hoping to get more than the $200 cash the Pughs had on board. They also said, "You are Americans, you must have a gun on board," and though the Pughs tried to convince them otherwise and offered to give the whole boat to them if they'd let them go free, the Mexicans used physical abuse and threats of sexual violence to get Marlene to surrender the pistol which was fastened behind a panel in the cabin. Finally they demanded to be taken to sea. Marlene tried to stall in the hopes that someone on the other American yachts in this open Bay might come back from shore. The Mexicans tied her badly wounded husband below and began helping her load the dinghy on board. Then Marlene saw a boat put off from shore. She shoved her dinghy against her captors. They fell and she dove overboard and swam towards help. The captors forced Bob on deck where he started the engine. The Mexicans cut *Matani Vahini*'s anchor rode and headed for the open sea while Marlene's saviors rowed to the nearest boat and sent out radio warnings on channel 16 VHF telling of the escape attempt.

Meshach, a large American trimaran, picked the message up as it turned to enter the bay and took chase. The Mexicans began firing the stolen gun and became distracted. *Matani Vahini* powered onto a rocky ledge and ground to a halt, crashing in the three-foot surge. By the time the first boat, a Mexican fishing ponga, reached her position, the murderers had fled on foot. Bob Pugh lay in the cockpit bleeding and only semiconscious. He was taken to the small local clinic with 14 knife wounds. When he died 12 hours later it was found that the real cause of death was a bullet lodged against his brain, a bullet from his own weapon.

The crewman who had come from Cabo San Lucas on the *Anak,* went back after an afternoon at the local cafe and found Bob Kavani dead. The crewman arrived at the police office as Marlene's story was being told. Since he had seen the Mexicans who had gone out to *Anak* with his skipper, he was able to corroborate Marlene's description. In a town of only 3,000 people, it was easy to ascertain the murderers. The police went to their homes and found both men and the goods they had stolen. Within two weeks they were on trial for the murders and soon were sentenced to 35 years in jail according to the last report we had.

Matani Vahini was pulled back into the harbor and since it was not taking on water it was left sitting on its spare anchor and rode with the local Navy guard promising to watch until Marlene sent someone to take it home. After two days of packing and paperwork, Marlene chartered a small plane to fly to San Diego with the body of her husband and of Bob Kavani, then went north to Redding for hospital care, funeral services and to try to gather the pieces of her life together again.

26

The Jinx

We were jinxed. That was the only explanation I could find. How else could we be having problems in such perfect cruising conditions. Tonga's weather was warm and sunny, its winds steady, its waters filled with sea life and best of all, its people so glad to have visitors they made us feel more like long lost cousins than the tourists we actually were. Yet like a threatening cloud hanging over all the pleasures of exploring under sail was the worry caused by seemingly unexplainable navigation foul ups.

We've always enjoyed navigating with simple tools, cautiously and accurately. We've sometimes had to heave to and wait for an extra sextant sight to confirm a headland or check for currents. But usually our fixes work out fine, few surprises, few moments of anxiety, just a feeling of doing a job "by the books" and having it turn out right. After twenty years of sailing together we've developed a pleasant routine. Larry does the celestial navigating and recently I've been taking a few sights on each passage to keep up to date. I do all of the piloting if it isn't during my off watch at night. I can remember very few times before we started sailing from Niuatoputapu, the northern most point in Tonga, south through the 300-mile-long chain of islands, shoals and reefs that make up this special little kingdom, when we'd had many startling navigational surprises. Yet as we sailed through the Vava'u and Ha'apai groups, the Nomuka islands and finally toward Tongatapu, navigational errors began flying into our lives like pesky mosquitoes, then frightening wasps.

The first error only gave us a start. We came within twenty feet of hitting a coral head as we worked into the lee of Ha'ano Island to anchor. We blamed that problem on inaccurate charts or coral growth. But the errors continued and began increasing until three weeks later when the biggest error started a frightening chain of events piling on events, the way most major sailing mishaps grow. After a 60-mile close reach through rough seas shoved by 35-knots of wind, we were shocked to find we'd missed the Tongatapu approaches light by over five miles. We were to leeward of the reefs we needed to clear, it was getting late, we had to beat into eight-foot seas on a wind that had us reefed to storm canvas. The roaring, breaking reefs caused the marching seas to deflect so that on one tack we were hard on the wind with the seas almost on our beam, but on the other, the seas were almost on our bow. So *Taleisin* plunged and struggled, waves crashing across her foredeck as we drove her to try to get to the leading lights of the big ships channel before dark. We just made it but still had twelve miles to sail through reefs and isolated dangers to reach the relative calm of Nuku'alofa's anchorage. Then as we eased sheets to reach past the first buoy, Larry noticed the foredeck seemed too clean. It took us both a few minutes to believe that some time during that crashing beat, our working jib had been torn loose from its lashings and washed overboard. It was no use going back to look for that jib in the dark, it probably would have sunk like a stone.

Loosing that expensive 420-square-foot, two-year-old sail really battered our egos, even more than being down to leeward on the 60-mile reach to Nuku'alofa had. And our Tongan jinx had yet another surprise for us that long hard day.

Soon after we began tacking up the nine-mile-long harbor, we became lost. We could still see the last lighted buoy of the main ships channel astern of us, but we couldn't find anything reliable to use as a cross on that bearing. After half a dozen long tacks I said, "Larry, I want to anchor. I don't feel comfortable about my compass bearings. I feel like we're close to the reefs." We hove to while I tried to distinguish the leading lights and reef lights that should have been four miles ahead of us from the confusion of shore lights behind them. But nothing seemed to make sense. Then Larry tried to take bearings to pinpoint our position. But neither of us could find any way of knowing how close we were

to the reefs that lay between us and the anchorage on that dark stormy
night. We both agreed that the best thing to do was to anchor while
we still had water under our keel and our large flashlight beam showed
no apparent dangers within its 300 yard scope.

Reefs four miles to windward of us were breaking down the ocean
swell so we set our anchor in three feet of wind chop and 17 fathoms
of water to wait for dawn. We spent an uncomfortable night rolling and
lunging, but at least we were safe. I do remember being ticked off at
Larry because he instantly fell asleep behind his lee cloth in the starboard pilot berth while I lay awake behind my lee cloth almost half the
night trying to figure out what we were doing wrong.

We sailed safely into the anchorage the next morning and stayed
anchored near the Tongan capital for seven days, licking our wounded
egos, reviewing our navigation, looking for errors in Larry's celestial
navigation calculations, in my plotting, then finally saying, "Well, I
guess we just have got to be more careful, got to stay to windward." But
we both still felt puzzled by our Tongan jinx and plagued by the feeling
that somehow our sailing lives were slightly out of control.

When we'd finished taking on stores, had some quiet nights of very
sound sleep and waited for a gale system to pass by, we set sail with a
storm jib borrowed from David and Doreen Samuelson on *Swan 2,*
another boat cruising toward New Zealand. Within two hours of lifting
our anchor to beat the 12 miles out of Nuku'alofa my piloting again
proved in error. The errors compounded until we had to spin 180
degrees and reach clear of a coral head strewn area where we should have
found deep clear water. Larry's trust in my piloting was shattered, so was
mine. We found the correct channel markers and worked clear. I was
silently castigating myself, wondering if I was competent, trying to find
excuses for my errors. For two hours after we'd come within a few feet
of hitting those coral heads I tried to decide what to say to Larry, how
to apologize, how to regain his confidence. Then a simple difference of
opinion sparked an argument that solved my problem.

There is a dangerous reef two miles west of Tongatapu Island and on
a direct route between it and the Minerva reef, our turning point on the
way to New Zealand's Bay of Islands. The Duff reef breaks in a spectacular swelter of waves that can be seen for miles, even during the calmest
weather. We were broadreaching with the spinnaker set in very light
breezes on a course that gave us a mile and a half clearance on the Duff

reef. I was below making lunch when Larry called, "Let's jibe, we're too
close to the reef. It's less than a mile off and I feel like we're getting
set onto it." I came out to help and commented, "It looks more like two
miles away to me." After arguing for a few minutes I said, "Okay, I'll
take some bearings and show you." My bearings, taken with the same
handbearing compass we've used for seven years of cruising and yacht
delivery work, showed the reef to be over two miles south of us. Larry
was still adamant, saying the reef was too close. He became obstinent
and thank God he did. "You watch the main compass and tell me the
reading when I line the land up on the back stay. Then *I'll* go down and
plot our position!" His bearings were each seven degrees different from
mine. We were only 1¼ miles from that boiling cauldron of breaking
waves, a minimally safe distance, but the proverbial light began to come
on. I got the handbearing compass and as Larry called the readings from

FIGURE 26.1   Lin with *Taleisin*'s hockey puck-type handbearing compass. (Photo by Bruce Laybourne.)

our main compass, I sighted along the straight edge of our cabin sides, along the cabin back, down the centerline of *Taleisin*. Every reading was off by at least five to seven degrees. We'd swung our main compass twice during two years of sea trials and cruising, but in all the time we've owned that handbearing compass we had done nothing more than make occasional cursory checks against the main compass readings. Never had we formally checked it against fixed landmarks.

I got out the charts we'd used since we left the Vava'u group. Every problem we'd encountered had been caused by that handbearing compass deviation. We'd taken bearings on a distinctive hummock as we tacked into the lee of Ha'ana Island; replotted, the correct bearing put us right on top of a just submerged coral head that was clearly marked on the chart. We'd faithfully taken bearings on various small islands when we left Nomuka for the 60-mile reach south to Tongatapu in gale force winds and also taken a noon sight which we crossed with a bearing on an island to the northeast of us to determine our exact course for the last 30 miles when we would be out of sight of land. Each fix had shown us being set eastward. When I recomputed these fixes using my new information I saw we'd not been set at all, we should have been holding a course five degrees closer to the wind. Had this been an error in the opposite direction we could have sailed right into an area of unmarked shoals and breakers. (The sights Larry took both at noon and later in the day had been absolutely correct. If we'd used Lines of Position obtained with the sextant instead of bearings that day we'd have had no problems at all.) We'd used that handbearing compass to try to locate the leading lights inside the huge bay of Nuku'alofa, because of the error, we'd been looking for them in the wrong places that jinx-ridden night. And so it went as my confidence in my piloting and Larry's navigation slowly came back.

When I showed him the reasons for each of our Tongan troubles, Larry asked, "Didn't we use that handbearing compass to come into Santa Maria bay at night last year?" We began listing the night bearings we'd taken as we cruised along Mexico's Baja California coast and I shuddered to think that we may have sailed within yards of rocks or reefs, completely unaware of the danger. Yet we could remember no navigational surprises in Mexico. Then as we talked of the last year of sailing we realized we hadn't had the handbearing compass out of its box for ten months. Maybe it was age, maybe the tropical heat, maybe the metal objects stored near it. But the handbearing compass had lost its accuracy during that time.

So now there is a new item on our New Zealand shopping list and a new addition on the calender we keep to remember maintenance check dates. What ever handbearing compass we buy, it will be swung twice a year.

I resented loosing a very good jib just to learn what now looks like a fairly obvious lesson. But as Larry reminds me each time I gripe, the compass didn't cause the jib to go overboard, sun-weakened lashings did. "Besides, I think you should be grateful we got off so lightly," he says. "It could have cost us more. It could have cost us our boat."

A few days after we reached New Zealand, we visited Trans-Pacific Marine Limited, the main instrument and chart suppliers to big ships in Auckland. When I asked why a hockey puck-type handbearing compass would suddenly develop an error, the specialists there listened to my comments on the age of the compass, the fact that I had twice dropped it onto the wooden cabin sole and that it had come through a year of heat in the tropics then commented, "Those are pretty tough units, maybe you should bring yours in and let us see it." Connie McCann, a cruising sailor who is now working as the chart corrector and assistant to the compass specialist then made a comment that stopped me short. "It is a compass that's compensated for the southern hemisphere, of course." I thought she was joking, special compensation for the southern hemisphere? I'd never in my life heard of that. But to allay my doubts she showed me several brand name compasses in the store room, each labeled, "Compensated for southern hemisphere." Then she got out a book called, *Notes on Compass Work* by Hemp and Young, published by Stanford Maritime, Ltd, in London which explained, "*Angle of Dip*—at positions other than on the magnetic equator, a freely suspended magnetized needle will lie in the plane of the magnetic meridian but will be inclined at an angle to the horizontal. This angle is known as the angle of dip and is said to be positive in the northern hemisphere where the north end of the needle is inclined downwards and negative in the southern hemisphere where the north end of the needle is inclined upwards."

In simple words, once you reach the southern hemisphere your northern compass is almost trying to turn itself inside out. "If you go look at your main compass," Connie said, "you'll see the card is tilted ten or fifteen degrees with the north side higher." (We did check the minute we got back to *Taleisin* and she was absolutely right.) In a freely suspended bowl-type compass such as our Danforth Constellation main compass, this dip is not a problem because the card can still swing freely. But inside a flat handbearing compass the card bottoms out at the edges and starts to drag. To make the compass card move freely, you can try tilting the compass, but then it becomes difficult to read and the bearings become inaccurate.

Connie explained, "A compass compensated for the northern hemisphere that is to be used south of the equator over a long period should be adjusted or the bearing may wear unevenly. If you intend to sail south of 40 degrees, this tilt will make the compass very difficult to read. Southern hemisphere sailors who go north of the equator have the same problem in reverse. That's why we recommend compensatable compasses for cruising."

If your compass is not a sealed unit, i.e., it has obvious screws holding the top in place or securing the two halves of the bowl together, the adjuster can remove the card and remagnitize it. For handbearing compasses, the choice for people who plan to sail in both hemispheres is between a unit with a larger float bowl (the type that looks like a flashlight with a compass perched on top) or two smaller units, one compensated for each hemisphere.

"But," as Captain Oates and the compass adjuster told me when I called to confirm this information, "Don't forget to swing your handbearing compass as often as you do your main one. Keep it well clear of the main compass as you do so. Electronics, fields created by alternators, other magnets, shocks, age and improper storage can all eventually cause a compass of any sort to change its deviation."

At Anchor

Although the skills you need to choose an anchorage, to evaluate the safety of the one you do choose and to have the equipment on board to cope with the variety of situations you'll encounter when you try to anchor, are all elements of seamanship, we have chosen to separate the following chapters and discuss various aspects of anchoring in detail for three reasons. First, over 150 offshore cruising boats suffered major damage in the 1982–83 Pacific cruising season while they lay at anchor in places like Cabo San Lucas, Tahiti and Neiafu, Tonga. Each of the people we later met who'd been involved in these storms, was surprised at the intensity of the winds, the seas, the problems they encountered in places where they expected storm free cruising. Each of these people told us they would have done something differently had they been able to exercise hindsight. We've learned no sailing area is immune to storms. Far more boats are damaged at anchor than at sea. Secondly, we are frequently asked to recommend an anchor type for new cruisers, the implication being that one type of anchor is better or worse for cruising, when in fact the anchor you use is only one part of the whole system of gear and techniques you need to get a good night's sleep when you reach port. Finally, once you are off cruising you'll spend 90 percent of your time at anchor. Your success at anchoring securely, the ease with which you can handle your ground tackle, if you decide to move to a better anchorage, could determine the comfort, satisfaction and safety of your whole cruising life.

27

What Happened at Cabo San Lucas?

The familiar sandy beaches and bold headland of Cabo Falso were a welcome relief after six hours in the cramped confines of a small plane. Larry and I started pointing out landmarks we recognized from our cruising and yacht delivering along the barren, desert coastline of Baja California. When the stunning gold-colored rocks that mark the very tip of the peninsula passed beneath us, I noticed Larry had a misty look in his eyes as he recalled the partylike atmosphere of the small Mexican village that nestled in a fold of hills behind the crescent shaped roadstead of Cabo San Lucas.

Today, the clear blue water lay still, protected from the prevailing northwest winds, warmed by a semi-tropical sun. From 1,000 feet we could see two dozen 50- and 60-foot sportfishing boats lying to their permanent winter moorings only 300 yards from the sandy beach. Another two dozen sailboats lay scattered among the fleet and I mentally pictured the day when our *Taleisin* would be somewhere among them, her decks bathed in sunshine. Then as we flew closer, I saw a sight that turned my stomach. The normally clear, cream-colored beach now looked like a trash dump for broken, discarded boats. Scraps of wood, bright fiberglass slabs, torn shreds of fabric, twisted masts and even

FIGURE 27.1

worse, at least 12 shattered but recognizable hulls lay at crazy angles along more than a mile of sand only 100 feet away from the thatched roofs of cafes where we once sat and watched the late afternoon shadows play across calmly anchored boats. I started to cry as I looked down at the shattered remains of so many dreams. My first reaction was, "What can I say to those poor people?"

But two hours later Betty Bower from the 28-foot Cutter *Vagabundo* which lay on its side in the sand made a statement that we heard at least a dozen times over the next two days, "The one thing all of us want is to be sure everyone knows what really happened at Cabo San Lucas."

It is easy to understand why Cabo San Lucas has become a favorite Christmas rendezvous for Pacific Coast cruising sailors. Most of the voyagers who set off from ports as far north as Alaska have meandered slowly south toward the Mexican border all during the summer months. They've congregated and made friends in San Diego while they waited for the end of the Mexican hurricane season in late October. Then like birds suddenly released from a cage, they flocked south away from the first of the cold winter nights and tested their boats and skills against the barren coast of Baja. Only half a dozen headlands offer some shelter from the constant Pacific swell, only two small ports on this desolate 720-mile-long coastline offer the most basic of supplies. So when these voyagers turn the corner and sail into the amazingly warm, beautiful bay at Cabo and see Latin-style outdoor cafe's lining the beach, next to handsome hotels, then hear the beat of the disco music late into the night, they fall into the mañana spirit, relaxing and putting away the cares of voyaging for another day or three. In 1969 when we first felt this partylike atmosphere, only three other cruising yachts lay anchored 300 yards offshore, bows pointed seaward, sterns held toward the beach by stern anchors while fourteen large sportfishing boats swung to permanent moorings set in 90 to 100 feet of water. In spite of its charm, its easy-to-catch seafood, its low prices, sweet freshwater and fine cafe's, the Cape is a difficult anchorage. The beach shelves quickly to a deep underwater trench near the nightlife areas. So voyagers have two choices, anchor a mile down the beach in eight fathoms of water about a quarter of a mile offshore, or try to find room right in front of the cafes and hotels. By December 6th, 1982, the popularity of Mexican cruising and sportfishing had drawn close to 60 boats into the Cape. Instead of a single row of boats moored and anchored with their bow hooks in 90 feet of water, sportfishing boats crowded with sailboats in four ragged lines (figure 27.2), the innermost less than 120 feet from the sandy beaches. Some boats including the bright red steel hull of Bernard Moitessier's *Joshua* lay as close as 75 feet from the beach, their stern anchors right in among the six-inch-high line of gurgling, miniature breakers.

Parties and friendships grew as the normally warm, calm weather eased any memories of Pacific storms. The ham radio net buzzed with plans for fishing trips and shopping tours. The coin laundromat in town was like a central meeting place where voyagers talked of January departure for the big plunge into "real" cruising, voyagers with goals like Tahiti or Panama. It's not surprising that an 0530 report by the high seas radio operator in San Francisco that quiet Monday morning wasn't heard by anyone we met at the Cape. Only someone planning to head offshore would have been interested in an unseasonable cold front stalled 300 miles to the west. On Tuesday December 7th two more cruising yachts joined the fleet at the Cape. They both complained about heavy swells and unstable winds for their voyages south along the peninsula.

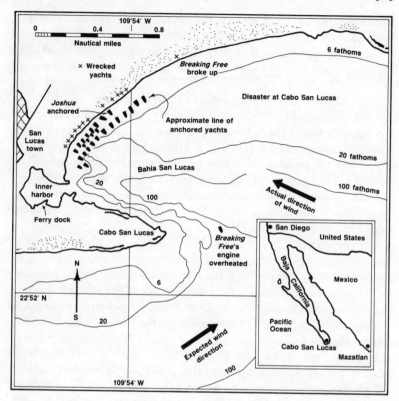

FIGURE 27.2

One boat had had its engine break down. Several people noticed its crew maneuvering the boat smartly into the bay under sail. That lone boat anchored in an open area about a half mile from the main fleet.

No one was awake for the 0530 weather report from the high seas operator on Wednesday morning. Only one person I spoke with mentioned that between December 6th and the morning of December 8th the barometer fell four tens of an inch from its normally stable position. In fact several of the newer sailors I met after the incident said they didn't have a barometer on board. I wonder if anyone would have expected the storm that was to come, even if they had noted the falling barometer and heard the operators report of a major disturbance centered 300 miles north of Cabo San Lucas and 100 miles offshore, moving southeast at 6 knots. The radius of gale force winds was only 100 miles; the morning report indicated they were blowing from the southwest. The warm water currents around the cape usually turn any winter storms away from the land.

By 0900 when several people were chatting over the ham radio the day was already warmer than usual and sultry. But the skies were clear, the water in the bay still, the cafes onshore busy with sailors, tourists from the campgrounds a half mile inland and hotel guests.

At 1100, the professional skipper on a large sportfishing boat finished doing a minor repair to his main engine and recorded it in the ships log. He also recorded the barometer reading and commented to his crewmen, "That's two tenths of an inch lower than this morning. Must be some kind of blow coming."

Fifty-five minutes later clouds rolled across the bay and almost without warning a 40-knot squall struck from the southwest then swung to southeast. Heavy rain obscured the horizon and a three-foot chop built up. Three sailboats began to drag their anchors. The squall lasted less than fifteen minutes and the sky cleared to let a steamy hot sun shine through. Mark Lewis, one of the crew from the 68-foot schooner, *Elias Mann*, chuckled when he recalled that squall, "We loved it. It never rains down here. It was nice to finally have some different weather." Most of the other sailors dismissed that squall, saying in effect, "It was a fluke, the hurricane season is a month behind us. Shouldn't be any bad weather at the Cape this month." The three boats that had dragged were re-anchored. One owner tried to find room in the already crowded inner harbor but was warned that the 250-foot-long car ferry was due from the mainland that evening. Photographs in one of the hotels showed the damage the ferry could do while it maneuvered into place —dismasted cruising boats, crushed launches—so the warning was heeded.

Sometime during the normal Mexican siesta hour three Cabo veterans, professional skippers on sportfishing boats that had spent ten or twelve winters here, got together for a beer at the fanciest cafe on the beach. "There's going to be a real catastrophe here some day. There are just too many boats trying to anchor in too little space," one of them (who asked to remain anonymous) commented. "Look at that line of sailboats, there's less than 50 feet between. Besides, the holding ground in close just isn't good. The last hurricane piled a lot of loose soft sand in next to the shore."

Susan Mitchell on the 60-foot Alden Schooner *White Cloud* is a keen ham radio buff. At 1600 she began talking to the skipper on a sportfishing boat that was halfway between Cabo and Magdelena Bay. He reported that his weather-fax print out showed a general area of bad weather lying 100 miles offshore from San Diego to Cabo San Lucas with gale winds predicted to blow from the southwest. At the normal 1630 ham net time, Susan repeated this warning to anyone listening. Someone on the net commented that the Cape offered good protection from southwest winds.

Betty Bower from *Vagabundo* watched a 30-foot boat set sail and leave on the moderate West Southwest wind a few minutes after that broadcast. She remembered that this was the boat that had sailed in the day before with its engine broken down. Betty noticed the low barometer but said, "That's no lower than it was when we had a gale from the west three weeks ago. Besides this is supposed to be a safe month here at the Cape." So when clouds began to gather and the wind began to increase and swing to the southeast thirty minutes after she watched that lone boat set sail, Betty and her husband Richard said the same thing everyone of the people we interviewed said, "Probably another squall, just like the one we had at noon."

For another hour the wind gusted from a direction between south and southeast and by 1830 when Bill Peterson decided he'd better get back on board his 36-foot cutter *Kama* just in case things got worse, he had a rough time getting his dinghy launched through the surf which was now breaking four-feet-high all along the beach. "It was almost dark by the time I reached *Kama* and I was soaked to the skin. *Kama* was moving around a lot but my crew, Linda, wasn't too worried."

Nobody we met remembers actually seeing Bernard Moitessier's red ketch drag its anchor then hit the beach. *Joshua* had been the boat closest to the beach, moored like Bernard was so used to, Tahitian-style with a line to the beach held this time by an anchor right in the surf instead of a palm tree. Sometime between 1830 and 1930 someone reported that she now lay on her side in surf that was quickly growing until by 2000 it was breaking ten or twelve feet high, driven by 35 knots of wind. Susan Mitchell reported *Joshua's* situation to anyone who happened to have their ham radio's on and added, "The waves passing

FIGURE 27.3

us are 8 feet high, gusts must be 50 knots." Occasional rain squalls swept through the frightened fleet and with each one someone would say, "This must be the worst of it. It will soon be over!"

The crew on the 55-foot yawl *Severance* decided to get out at 2000. Charley Beasley, Sr. was at the helm. He tied a buoy to the stern anchor line while his two sons Charley, Jr. and Vince went forward to bring in the bow anchor. "We figured it wasn't worth trying to get that stern hook in, we'd just come back the next day and get it," Charley, Sr. said. He threw the buoy and the last of the line over the stern and got a preview of one of the worst problems that lay ahead for the yachts closest to shore. That nylon line refused to sink. *Severance* bucked against her bow anchor as the 8-foot swells lifted her bow and 40 knots of wind dragged her chain out straight. Charley shut the engine down to keep the propeller from catching the drifting stern line. "Bring the anchor chain in," he called through the din of wind and seas. At first the boat began to pull away but as the chain grew short she started to drag until her stern lay over the floating line. "It was five minutes of Hell!" 25-year-old Charley, Jr. told us. "The waves growling past us, the anchor trying to drag, our engine off so we wouldn't snag that line. If we wrapped our prop we were in real trouble because we didn't have much room around us to maneuver under sail." The line finally did sink and *Severance* powered clear of the moored boats and headed offshore until there was room to heave too. "Next time there's an emergency we'll haul that stern line in tight and cut it so it springs away from the prop," Charley, Jr. told us later.

By 2200 ten foot waves were running through the anchorage, their steep tops curling and breaking along the decks of any boats within 100 yards of the beach. At least ten more crews tried to get their boats out into open water. The husband and wife crew on *Vixon*, a Challenger 41 had arrived just one day before. They were low on fuel and water but decided to wait a few days at the Cape before maneuvering into the hard-to-reach fuel dock. They were reluctant to leave in spite of waves that seemed to tilt their boat to a 35-degree angle. Their anchor was holding well, they were among the boats furthest from the breakers. Then without warning a gust of wind or a breaking wave turned their boat at an angle that pulled their one inch nylon anchor rode right off its chock. With unbelievable speed the line ripped their bow pulpit off the deck then snagged against the sharp edge of one of the pulpit bases and parted like an old rubber band. The owners cut their stern line and motor sailed out of the bay. Less than thirty minutes later they ran out of fuel and sailed on to La Paz. They returned after four days hoping to find the two anchors and dinghy they'd left behind and told us, "We learned several lessons, the first was, have an anchor rode fairlead that can be closed completely. If our line had stayed in the chock we probably would have been fine. The second lesson was even more important. Get water and fuel as soon as you arrive in port so you can leave for sea the minute you first think you want to."

The crew on the schooner *Elias Mann* had a different problem. They had specific orders from the owner who had flown back to Seattle, Washington to be with his wife while she had their first child, "Do not move this boat until I come back." The temporary skipper, Joe Daubenberger of Port Townsend is an experienced racing sailor and had things pretty much under control until the heavily built replica of a Newfoundland fishing schooner began to come up short against its half-inch chain. As the schooner plunged and reared the chain actually leapt off the cathead and threatened to break free and play havoc with the forward part of the boat. So Joe worked with his crew of four to rig a three quarter inch nylon line as a snubber. They tried a rolling hitch to the chain just forward of the chock then let out 30 feet of line and 40 feet of chain, then secured the line to the bitts so it took the first strain. The line lasted less than ten minutes before it snapped like a piece of string. Joe had the crew set to work again. This time they secured four nylon lines to the chain and led each one aft to a separate cockpit winch and adjusted the lines so they seemed to be taking an equal strain. The added length gave the stretch the nylon needed and everything again seemed under control. The crew did have the decks cleared for sea and at 2215 their preparations paid off. The waves that had been breaking at least 150 yards astern of them suddenly changed their pattern. A new set of waves broke right against the bow, jerking the schooner almost beam onto the seas. Almost simultaneously another boat lost its anchor and rammed against *Elias Mann* ripping loose her rub rail and stoving in a plank.

Joe didn't wait one minute more. His crew buoyed the stern line and worked like demons to cut the anchor chain. In the confusion of shrieking wind, breaking waves and horror of watching other people's boats thrown 14 or 18 feet into the air only to be smashed into the sand 300 yards astern, not one of the crew actually noticed what snapped their whisker stay. The 453 GMC engine worked perfectly and the crew of *Elias Mann* received high praise from the owner when he arrived a few days later to assess the damage to his boat. In true seamanlike fashion they had returned to recover all of the ground tackle they'd left behind that stormy night.

The crew on board *Breaking Free* were far less fortunate. Joe Pikus, and his wife, Donna, owners of this Force 50 ketch, knew they did not have the experience to handle the boat alone so they asked two friends who'd cruised before to join them for the first leg of their cruise. They'd also taken on an experienced crewman as extra insurance. Unfortunately, the crewman was on another boat when the storm blew in. He tried to get back on a borrowed rubber dinghy but couldn't make any headway. The husband of the couple who were guests was not on board. His wife and the frightened owners tried their best. They kept the engine running to take some strain off the ground tackle. They tried to leave soon after the blow started but couldn't get the anchor up because other boats had come in to anchor after they arrived and a 30-footer now lay right over their ground tackle. Since the anchor seemed to be holding well, the small crew on *Breaking Free* decided to wait just a bit longer. Then the engine overheated. "I looked overboard with my flashlight and the water was like pure sand," their crew, Pheobe Law, told us. Joe cleaned the strainer and got the engine going again. This happened twice before a sudden wave turned *Breaking Free* broadside. "The next one slammed against us so hard the electric anchor windlass ripped right out of the deck and jammed in the pulpit. That's when we cut our gear and headed out." They dodged dragging boats and fortunately didn't catch anyone elses lines in their propeller but they decided to keep their sail covers on so the sails wouldn't get loose and flog against them in the 45 to 50 knot gusts. They were almost three quarters of a mile away from the beach when the engine overheated again. This time it was too late. *Breaking Free* was blown onto the beach well away from the center of the tragedy and shattered into unidentifiable pieces just 40 feet from a jumble of rocks. Her terrified crew of three reached the shore soaked, but uninjured and began the one mile trek through soft sand toward the line of car lights that now illuminated the boats being pounded by the surf closer to the village. *Breaking Free* was uninsured and the only possessions the owners saved were their wallets and one set of clothing, the clothing they had on when they lost their dream.

Linda Gervasoni who was crewing with Bill Peterson on his 36-foot cutter *Kama* said she'd been a little embarrassed when people would come in and try to anchor within 150 feet of them. "Bill would row over and tell the skippers, 'we were here first.' So we were sort of alone in the middle of the fleet."*

Bill had a 50-pound COR set on 100 feet of chain and 100 feet of nylon line. After the squall at noon he set a 45-pound Northill on chain and line and at 1830 another, smaller, COR. Then when the gusts

*In accordance with U.S. Admiralty court decisions, Bill Peterson was definitely acting within his rights. On page 310 and 311 of Knights Modern Seamanship 12th Edition, published 1956, the Juniata decision no. 124–5861 is shown in its entirely. The basic reasoning of the courts was; "A Vessel shall be found at fault if it . . . h-anchors so close to another anchored vessel as to foul her when swinging, i-fails to shift anchorage when dragging dangerously close to another anchored vessel. Futhermore, the vessel that anchors first shall warn the one who anchored last that the berth chosen will foul the formers berth."

It has long been accepted yachting etiquette that the first boat in has the right to ask that others give it not only room to swing, but also room to maneuver out safely. So although Bill Peterson may have offended some people who arrived at the Cape after he did, his actions probably saved his boat.

started backing he pulled in his stern anchor so the boat could swing freely in the open space he'd argued to keep around him. "I was still worried and I was ready to slip all the anchors and sail or power out. I'd doubled the lines and rigged buoys just in case," Bill told me. One boat did slam into *Kama* when its anchor line sheared. It hit only once and bent *Kama's* spreader. The next second the hapless boat was thrown into the surf. "The boat to windward of me was a Hans Christian 38. It really was snubbing at its anchors because the wind and sea were hitting it almost beam on. I yelled at them to cut their stern line and finally they did. Then their boat rode it all out held by the two big COR's they had down."

Room to swing wasn't enough to save Jerry and Gail Sieren's Tayana 37, *Sea Wren.* After the noon squall they'd decided to re-anchor in a more open area down the beach. They had two bow anchors down, a 30-pound Danforth and a 45-pound COR. Each one was set on 50 feet of heavy chain with enough line to give what Jerry estimated was a 30 degree angle to the water when the boat came to the end of its swinging arc. "When things got bad we cut our stern line and began running our engine and steering to keep the strain even on both anchors. Then about 2030 waves actually began breaking in front of the boat. One slammed us sideways and the arms on our steering quadrant broke." Jerry said. "So we couldn't leave even if we wanted to." About 2300 they watched *Jolena* a 32-foot cutter power out with no apparent problem. Then *Amola II* a Cal 40 near them tried to power out and snagged their prop on one of the many lines floating in the turbulent water. Her crew hauled up a storm jib and heavily reefed mainsail that had been rigged and waiting then sailed to the safety of the open sea. Meanwhile the crew on *Sea Wren* waited and prayed, but at 2330 the line on their COR anchor chaffed through and they began to drag. Minutes later their boat was on the beach being shattered by breakers that most people agreed reached 18 feet by midnight.

Amazingly, the only injury occurred on board a boat that left the anchorage at the height of the blow right at midnight. The husband and wife team on *June Eighth,* an Endeavor 37 had just lifted their bow anchor when a wave washed the length of the deck. It caught the husband who was forward near the bowsprit and threw him halfway down the deck to smash against a Dorade ventilator. The helmswoman

powered clear and reached La Paz the next day where doctors set her
husband's broken leg.

On board *Ayorama,* an Endurance 36, things looked bad right from
the beginning. Soon after the blow started, their propeller became
fouled on their stern line. Grant Nicholas said he would have sailed out
but there just wasn't any room since boats were anchored within 50 feet
on each side. Then the genoa that was stored in a zippered bag on the
headstay broke loose. It went halfway up the headstay, filled, pulled
Ayorama's beam to the wind and sea and she dragged her bow anchor
until she was into the crushing surf.

Susan and Paul Mitchell spent three hours being quite sure they were
the next to lose their boat. They had set their main anchor, a 66-pound
Bruce on 125 feet of ⅜ chain in 35 feet of water about 100 yards from
shore. There was another line of boats anchored inshore of the schooner.
By midnight most of that line of boats was breaking up in the surf. Susan
and Paul watched in horror as *White Cloud's* stern began getting closer
and closer to the breakers. then they realized they weren't dragging.
Their anchor was holding, but as each wave lifted their bow at angles,
beach side observers said often approached 45 degrees, a few more links
of chain would leap out over the solidly clutched cat head. "We dropped
our 75-pound Danforth over on all line and when we'd drifted far
enough back for that to take the strain, *White Cloud* began to hold her
own. But we were only 100 feet from shore when the wind began to ease,

FIGURE 27.4

FIGURE 27.5

FIGURE 27.6

the barometer started to rise at 0100 Thursday morning. Then a huge downpour seemed to lay the seas flat and we could breathe again. We knew we'd just been lucky. We should have left the anchorage by 2000 like *Severance* did. We broke our bowsprit, overheated our engine but we still have our boat."

By daylight the waves were down to two or three feet. The clouds began to break up and the anchorage looked like it had been pruned. Twenty-two of the sportfishing boats which had been secured to permanent moorings in 90 feet of water still sat in the same position. Two sportfishing boats from this group were now safely anchored in the inner harbor where they'd gone after they had rescued a sailboat during the night. Six sailboats still remained at anchor and several could be seen on the horizon struggling back after a stormy night at sea where some reported winds reached 70 for the hour after midnight and others reported only 50 knots, but seas as high as 20 feet. On the beach the remains of 27 large boats lay scattered among a dozen open sportfishing launches and another dozen smaller boats. The Mexican villagers, poor as they are, immediately came to offer clothing, homes, hot meals and bedding to the dazed sailors who crowded into the beach front cafes. The government officials sent a dozen federal soldiers to patrol the beaches and keep away looters. They made three arrests that first day,

FIGURE 27.7

all American tourists from campers parked just over the rise from the beach.

The owners of two boats that had broken up so completely there was nothing to identify or save, left on the first flight to the United States. The ones that stayed to try to salvage something of their dreams came

FIGURE 27.8

FIGURE 27.9

up against understandable but frustrating bureaucratic hassels. They were forbidden to sell or give away any gear they salvaged without first paying duty on it as imported goods. They also could not leave Cabo San Lucas until the beach was cleared of all wreckage. The government did provide trucks and local people willingly offered assistance to drag away shattered pieces of barely recognizable hulls and cabins. But still it was a bleak task for people like Joe and Donna Pikus who couldn't even find one piece of wreckage to call their own.

As we walked along the beach five days after the storm the final toll was apparent. Five hulls were salvageable, the caved in steel hull of *Joshua,* the expensively built Bristol Channel Cutter *Vagabundo* (figure 27.8) and equally expensively built Olson 40 *Notorious* (27.9). *Grace,* (27.10) an Omega 44 that had snagged its stern anchor on its prop and slowly eased through the surf, bow always pointed toward the shore, was virtually undamaged, lying with its deck tilted away from the breaking seas at high tide. *Dancing Bear* a Cabot 36 was the final intact, salvageable hull and we watched it being refloated before we left.

Twelve other hulls were recognizable but damaged beyond repair or sinking beneath the sand in the river's mouth at the far end of the beach where heavy equipment could find no safe place to work. Several of the less expensive, oriental hulls had split open like apples just aft of the chainplate area where the extra build up of glass necessary for the bolts ended abruptly. Six other large boats were shattered beyond recognition, six were missing completely. Of the 27 large boats that were shoved

FIGURE 27.10

through the surf late that night only ten were insured. This led to the worst part of the whole experience. We sat and listened as people dressed in "Welcome to Cabo" T-shirts donated by a Mexican vendor tried to decide, what next? One gentle woman in her fifties, owner of an uninsured boat that had been sucked out to sea and disappeared minutes after it hit the surf, struck the saddest note of all when she said, "Go home? We can't. We sold our home to go cruising."

28

Voyagers Lament

"I was stupid, just stupid," Bernard Moitessier kept repeating as we sat together on the sand behind the battered hull of his steel ketch *Joshua*. Around us half a dozen volunteers reluctantly began admitting they could no longer keep ahead of the sand and water being carried into the hull by yet another high tide. The brand new gasoline powered pump loaned by a local sportfishing skipper, refused to start. There were no other pumps to be had that day. As I looked at the meagre pile of salvageable goods that now represented Bernard's total worldly possessions, I could understand his depression, his reluctance to try to restore the remains of the boat that had carried him twice around the world and made his name synonomous with the mystique of singlehanded voyaging. All that remained of *Joshua* was her hull and deck. Her mast lay in two buckled pieces, her steel bowsprit lay bent at a 45-degree angle, her rudder head was snapped off, her engine was buried under tons of sand. the tattered shreds of her sails were now rough bundles on the beach, books swelled four times their normal size on top of soggy rice, battered fruits and saltwater soaked hemp bags of walnuts.

Larry and I had first heard of Bernard 13 years before when he confused the sailing world by refusing to sail the final 5,000 miles to claim the $15,000 prize that went with an almost certain, first to finish in the original nonstop, around the world singlehanded race. He'd pressed on for six months nonstop, sailing *Joshua* from England, around

FIGURE 28.1

the Cape of Good Hope, south of Australia, around the horn, then had been becalmed for over a week just north of the Falkland Islands. He'd heard radio reports of the strange death of one of his fellow competitors, Donald Crowhurst, he'd heard of the loss of two other competitor's boats, he was aware of his probable lead, but a strange transformation happened as his boat lay absolutely still. He realized it was peace of mind he'd sought by going to sea. He turned his boat away from England and for four months more battled the unfavorable winds of the Southern Ocean winter season to reach the tranquillity of Tahiti after ten months alone. He tried to explain his reasons in a book that became a bestseller throughout Europe. But I never understood until we met in California a year and a half ago and he said, "Sailing is a private experience. I knew if I returned to Plymouth the press would hound me and steal it all away piece by piece."

For ten years *Joshua* and Bernard stayed in French Polynesia with his second wife and son, farming on a tiny island in the Tuamotos and living on the dwindling proceeds of books including his first which described the beginning of his sailing career in Indo-China, the wreck of his first boat on a reef in the Indian Ocean, the loss of his second on a Caribbean

Island and the first voyage of his seemingly indestructable dream ship, 38-foot *Joshua*, built of 5mm steel plates, rigged and outfitted with absolute simplicity.

In early 1981 Bernard finally left French Polynesia, frustrated by the politics and fascinated by the picture visiting American sailors had drawn of California. He set off on a direct singlehanded voyage to San Francisco where he hoped to show his sailing film, give lectures and enjoy the companionship of cruising sailors who would understand his emotional ties to the open ocean.

Unfortunately, bureaucratic hassels with visas plus the unexpected need to seek publicity in order to promote lecture audiences wore on Bernard. He tried offering seamanship courses on board *Joshua* and though people who joined his classes came away satisfied, many potential customers felt the price was too high for a day on board a boat tied to a dock, even with the seasoned voyager who could share the experience of 70,000 miles at sea. But Bernard would not untie *Joshua* because as he told me in his heavy French accent while we watched the surf break over her scarred and dented hull, "I am a voyager, not a cruiser. When I head to sea it is not to turn around and come back to the same place. It is to cross an ocean, to find new lands."

After a year in California Bernard left his wife and son and headed south toward Mexico with little more money than when he'd arrived, "I took a paying passenger, an actor, Klaus Kinski, so I could have the money to leave. It was good to be away. Good to see a land where things were more normal."

The mañana spirit of Cabo San Lucas was like a soothing balm to nerves frayed by the crowds, fog and cold of Sausalito. Bernard moored *Joshua* stern to the beach, Mediterranean-style only 75 feet from the ripples that played on the golden sands. Other boats came in to anchor close by and eagerly invited Bernard to join their get-togethers. "I should have trusted my instincts and taken *Joshua* out to the open sea early that day when the weather seemed wrong. But I was surrounded so closely by other boats, it would have been most difficult."

Joshua's 55-pound COR anchor on its heavy chain held for the first hour of the gale but by 1900 it was all over. Ten foot high waves began breaking right across the boat and pulled the anchor through sand stirred and loosened by a hurricane only three weeks before. Within minutes

Joshua lay on her side in the surf, waves pounding over her gleaming red hull.

Now, five days later Bernard seemed almost eager to share his sorrow, his pain and his lessons. "It is all my own fault. I didn't think, I was so tired of thinking hard to live in the crazy United States. When I got here, I forgot to think. I hadn't even read the sailing directions."

When I asked the inevitable question, "What now?" Fifty-eight-year-old Bernard shrugged his shoulders and said, "I am too old to try to rebuild *Joshua* even if she is able to float again. Besides, she is too big for me. I wish I had a small simple boat instead of a big simple one. No, I do not know what I will do. All I can think is first I need a small boat so I must go back to France where I am well known."

He watched his Mexican friends sorting through the wreckage and murmured, "I have never seen breakers come up so quickly with the wind. They did not build, they just seemed to happen."

Bernard's depression caught both Larry and I and late into the night we talked of possible ways of salvaging *Joshua.* Early the next morning Bernard announced, "I must save *Joshua* for *Joshua*'s sake. She must float again." Since he did not have access to the $2,000 necessary to rent

FIGURE 28.2

the only large salvage pump available or the steam shovel and tractor that should have been at work digging a new safe marina behind the beach front hotels, he signed the remains of *Joshua* over to Reto Filli, a young Swiss crewman from another boat who'd worked trying to help Bernard during the past five days.

Three days later when we were back home in California trying to force the picture of carnage we'd seen to the back of our minds, Barry Poole, a local ham operator called to tell us, *"Joshua* is afloat. She's sound and sad in the inner harbor."

Joshua will live to face the open sea again with a new owner we hope will love her as Bernard did.

29

Technical Report from Cabo San Lucas

There were a dozen lessons waiting for Lin and me at Cabo San Lucas. We'd heard tales of how 29 sailboats dragged anchors and broke gear then were shoved through the pounding surf by gale force winds, yet when we arrived five days after the fateful night we were unprepared for the emotional impact of seeing hulls shattered into unrecognizable bits, spars twisted like pretzels and people in shock as they watched the last of their dreams being cut up into truck sized chunks by chainsaw crews who worked to clear the wreckage. It took almost a month to get over the sights we'd seen, to shove the stories of disappointment and lost dreams to the back of our minds. Then we remembered a conversation we'd had a week before we flew to Cabo San Lucas.

"That's the big problem with marine business, it's small! Even the biggest manufacturer of marine fittings is tiny compared to suppliers in any other industry," a friend who is a marine surveyor had commented as a dozen sailors sat around the fire in our living room. We'd been complaining about the problems we'd had as we shopped for just the right gear to outfit boats destined for offshore voyaging. "What's four or five thousand steering gears each year compared to a million carbure-tors?* Marine manufacturers can't afford truly sophisticated testing equipment. They can only try to estimate the destructive forces of gales or breaking waves." he continued. "It's not like the auto industry where they can afford to destroy a dozen cars just to see if the brakes work under adverse conditions. So in effect, no matter how marine engineers try to figure theoretical working loads, it's really the sailing customer who does the product testing and the customer usually tries his best to avoid ultimate or even full working loads on his gear. That's why it's hard to get real technical feed back."

"I guess the same can be said about sailors," another of our guests said. "They all have theory's about what they'd do in this or that emergency situation, but rarely get a chance to test their plan of action for flaws."

Cabo San Lucas had been the test to destruction site of 21 of the boats that went ashore that dark stormy night. At least another 20 offshore voyaging boats escaped the pounding surf but tested various gear until it failed. The ten-foot seas generated by the five hour gale ran into the open roadstead and put many sailors' emergency plans to the full test. Some worked, others didn't. Then during the days that fol-lowed, the wreckage-strewn beach became a testing ground for people who had to try to salvage those boats that had reached the shore intact. As we read through the notes we'd made during twenty hours of inter-views on the beach in Cabo San Lucas, then looked through the hun-dreds of photos we'd taken, we realized that this had been an uncon-trolled testing ground, so we'd have to qualify every consideration with the reminder that forces were far from normal; boats took strains that should never have been imposed on them, hulls collided against each other in ten-foot breakers, people had to react under tremendous emo-tional strains. But once these qualifications were made, we could see that there were failures and successes to be counted at Cabo and these are worth sharing because it is rare to have a marine test to destruction ground.

*The Yacht Specialties division of Merriman Co. says during a good year they can count on selling 1,000 steering gears.

BOW ROLLERS

Without a doubt, bow rollers were one of the weakest links in the anchoring systems of not only the boats that hit the beach but also those that escaped to sea or were actually able to ride the gale out at anchor. A few minutes after we arrived on the beach at Cabo we saw a man walking toward town carrying a stainless steel bow roller fabrication that was twisted almost 180 degrees (figure 29.1). He'd brought the roller and trough from his 36-foot ketch ashore hoping that someone in the tiny village could straighten it. This bow roller was a welded fabrication made from ⅛-inch plate and when downward strains went on it from the bucking of the boat it twisted until the roller was upside down. The owner told us it bent soon after the wind reached 40 knots and the waves about four feet. Fortunately he was able to take his boat out to sea without fouling any of the floating lines that snagged so many less fortunate sailors' propellors.

Very few of the three dozen twisted bow roller set-ups we saw had any provision for side loads (figure 29.2), yet this can be one of the biggest strains you put on your anchor rode when you lie to two anchors. In a case like Cabo San Lucas where the wind shifted until it began hitting the anchored boats beam on, this load was even more exaggerated. One of the ways to add side load strength is to have a closing device such as a bolt that threads through the upper lip of the bow roller from the outboard side into the body of the fitting. This transmits any strains through the whole fitting. Even more important, this closure acts as a guard to keep your anchor rode in the roller where it belongs. This was the second biggest weakness we saw on the beach. Only one of the bow rollers on boats laying wrecked in the sand had any provisions to

FIGURE 29.1

FIGURE 29.2

keep their chain from leaping free of the roller. In several cases people told us of losing their ground tackle because nylon rodes got loose and chafed through either on sharp corners away from the roller or on the edges of gear the line ripped loose as the boat plunged and reared in seas that reached ten feet or more. Three sailors who used chain rodes but had no restraining pin over their bow rollers, described their concern about their chain getting loose. "I could have lost my hand if that chain got free while I was trying to handle it," one owner told us.

The final problem with bow rollers were their chafe-prone edges. Several boats were lost when anchor rodes chafed through on metal that felt smooth to the touch but had too small a radius to prevent wear on the line. The only way to prevent this problem is to flare the lips of the fitting or to make a casting with lips that have a large radius wherever the line can touch.

It's not surprising that it's hard to find an off-the-shelf bow roller that can take all of the strains a storm will place on it. Each boat design presents a slightly different problem. Bowsprits, bow pulpits, headstay arrangements get in the way. Bronze castings which can more easily have the well rounded corners you need, have to be almost custom made, so stainless steel fabrications seem to be a more economical answer. Unfortunately for offshore voyagers, these have to be custom made to work well. So once again we are back to the main problem for the marine industry. Proper fittings to serve every type of boat are almost impossible to make in quantity. To get a perfect bow roller you have to spend a lot of money. But as too many people at Cabo found out the hard way, this cost may be small compared to the alternative.

CHAIN VERSUS LINE

The question of what to choose for an anchor rode in the ultimate conditions such as those found at Cabo San Lucas seemed to be answered with a single word by people who survived that fateful night, chain. Over twenty sailboat owners complained that nylon anchor lines chafed through, yet in spite of initial reports to the contrary, not one anchor chain parted. (One power boat did break the chain on their Mexican-owned mooring but we were told this was poorly maintained and undersized. Another boat owner told of losing the shackle that held his anchor to his chain) On the other hand, chain presented special handling problems. On *Wind Dancer,* a Globe 46 ketch, there was no restraint on the bow roller, no way of securing the chain into its cathead on the windlass. At the height of the gale, *Wind Dancer's* chain leapt

FIGURE 29.3

free and pulled the sampsom post right out of the deck. The boat was
a total loss.

The second problem with chain was getting rid of it when owners or
skippers decided it was time to get out to sea. Since the boats were
anchored so close together at the Cape, most skippers who tried to leave
found other boats were over their ground tackle. They then made the
decision to leave their anchor and chain behind and come back to
retrieve it when things were calmer. "You try cutting a damned piece
of 5/16-inch chain with a hacksaw when your boat is bucking like a wild
horse and its raining and dark as hell," one crewman told me when we
were sitting at an outdoor cafe overlooking the wreckage-strewn beach.
When I explained a trick we'd learned from a powerboater he headed
back to his anchored boat saying, "I'll rig that right now."

We rig a heavy length of nylon line as a safety release at the inboard
end of our anchor chain. We secure it to a strong point inside the chain
locker with two round turns and a half hitch so it can be released even
if it is under pressure. When the time comes to get out quickly you can
buoy the end of the chain then cut or untie the nylon saftey release line.

We discussed this with Richard Spindler, editor of *Latitude 38,* a
California yachting magazine, who'd come down to Cabo to rejoin his
boat and accidently found himself in the middle of a very important
yachting story. When we compared notes he said, "Your solution's fine
for getting rid of the chain quickly and it will work as a good snubber
if there's room to let out all your chain. But here there just wasn't
enough room. The lesson all this taught me is I'm going to carry two
or three heavy duty 30-foot nylon line snubbers just in case." The most
successful way of attaching this line to your chain is to use a rolling hitch.
To get the spring effect you need, let out ten feet of chain and ten feet
of nylon line at the same time. Secure the line then let out another ten
feet of chain to hang in a loop. Heavy vessels like *Elias Mann,* described
in the previous chapter, may need several.

ANCHORS

We were particularly interested in trying to find out which type of
anchor held best. After interviewing an almost equal number of owners
who'd lost their boats and who'd been able to ride out the gale or leave,

there seemed to be no indication of a best type of anchor. On the other hand, size did seem to matter. The boats that survived the breakers at anchor carried oversized gear compared to the apparent manufacturers recommendation. The Broenmans on their 34-foot sloop *Kaskelot* had a 35-pound CQR on 240 feet of ⅜-inch chain and survived the night at anchor. The recommended working anchor for their boat is a 25-pound CQR and 5/16-inch chain. The Burkhardts on *Magic Dragon*, a Valiant 40, used a 44-pound Bruce anchor on 200 feet of chain and held. The anchor recommended in the advertising brochure for their boat was a 33-pounder. It was an 85-pound Danforth used in conjunction with a 66-pound Bruce anchor that finally held the 58-foot schooner *White Cloud* as she bucked and fought through the night right next to the surf line where breakers reached 18 feet and swells close to ten feet. The manufacturers in each case seem to advise that one of these anchors is sufficient for storm conditions for a boat of this size. I say "seem to advise" because in the fine print at the bottom of each of these anchor brochures is a note such as this one from the Bruce anchor brochure, "The anchor sizes above assume winds up to 60 mph [miles per hour, not knots] some protection from the sea, fair holding ground and operation at scope adequate to develop full holding power." As we learned in Sweden where *Seraffyn's* 25-pound CQR dragged when we anchored in a 1,200 foot by 1,200 foot harbor with complete protection from the sea but a two foot surge and 90 knots of wind, any sailor who sets off for foreign ports will some day encounter situations far beyond those anchor manufacturers use as a standard.

One of the most frequent explanations we heard at Cabo was summed up by the owner of an Endurance 36. "My anchor started to drag a bit so I turned on the engine to help take some of the strain. Then it started to drag again and almost immediately my propellor caught the slack in our stern anchor line and it was all over." As too many people learned the hard way at Cabo San Lucas, once your anchor starts dragging you have far less chance of getting out to the safety of the open sea.

WINDLASSES

A very worrisome problem with one type of electric anchor windlass was dramatically presented at Cabo. We saw two wrecks on which the same type of windlass had pulled right out of the foredeck leaving a gaping hole. On *Breaking Free,* a force 50 ketch which disintegrated so completely there was no wreckage left, the owners told us the same type of anchor windlass pulled out of the deck and started the chain of events that lead to a disastrous end. A close look at the windlass installations showed that the hole necessary to allow the electric motor to be set below the foredeck means that there is less than ¾ of an inch of deck area left for the windlass mounting holes. This leaves an inherent weakness that could be solved by placing a large metal backing plate under the foredeck to act like a force distributing washer for the whole assembly (figure 29.4).

ENGINES

Not one person we interviewed at Cabo complained about getting their engines to start. Unfortunately, engines were not a solution for a problem that was basically one of seamanship. The crowded conditions meant that maneuvering out under power once the sea built up became a matter more of luck than skill. Stern lines, other people's abandoned floating anchor rodes and dinghy painters fouled at least 20 propellors and rendered engines useless. Yet at the height of the chaos, just when people were losing their boats in the surf, the crew on a Cal 40 named *Amola II* were able to sail out under storm jib and reefed mainsail after

FIGURE 29.4

their propellor became fouled and, according to several reports, this boat was in among those closest to the beach.

Stirred up sand was a second major cause of engine failure. Seven different sailors told us their engines were doing great, helping their ground tackle hold or getting them out toward open water then, "the damn thing overheated and shut down automatically. The saltwater strainer was clogged with sand." It's this emergency, possibly once in a lifetime situation that makes one wonder, "Why isn't there a way to override the automatic shut off?" In the case of *Breaking Free* which managed to get clear of the moored boats and almost out to open water, a manual override on their overheat shutdown switch could have given them valuable minutes to set sails after the warning came. The extra time might have been just enough to save their boat.

RADIOS

Everyone Lin and I spoke with mentioned having either a VHF radio, a ham set up or both. We had a round table discussion five nights after the gale which included the owners of two boats that were wrecked and two that survived the night. The consensus on radio transmitters seemed to be that they were detrimental before the incident, useless during the gale but helpful afterwards. "We didn't make decisions on our own when the wind came in from the southeast," one owner said (he asked to remain anonymous). "Instead we kept talking to each other on the radio, asking, are you going to stay? Do you think this will last? We should have been making *individual decisions* as if we were the only people in the anchorage. I just know that if a dozen boats began leaving right at the beginning of the blow, we all probably would have picked up our gear and got out, but instead we kept thinking the worst was over and said as much on the radio." This "herd instinct" bolstered by radio communications did seem to be a key to much of the problem before the storm reached its height. When Lin asked people, "Would you have stayed if you had been alone in this anchorage?" Every person said, "No, but when so and so didn't think it was serious enough to move, I decided to wait a bit longer."

During the worst of the blow, when boats were being driven ashore every few minutes, Susan Mitchell on *White Cloud* said the calls for assistance were constant. "But who could get out to throw someone a line? We were all in the same game together by that time." The only rescue operation that was successfully completed happened not because of a radio call but because a dragging sailboat collided with a large sportfishing boat and woke the professional skipper who then started his engines, risking his job and vessel, let go of his permanent mooring and got a line on board the sailboat less than 50 feet before it hit the rock breakwater protecting the ferry dock.

After the seas had calmed down, ham radios began to buzz and provided useful communications link. Susan Mitchell offered to relay messages from her schooners ham set up and worked eight or ten hours a day reassuring stateside families, contacting insurance companies, helping people get funds from home. Although it is illegal to transact business over the ham radio, her efforts organized a network of people in San Diego who then used the legal business channels on SSB to provide replacement parts for boats that were damaged.

HULLS

We had a discussion with a marine surveyor who flew in to settle two claims about his general impression of the boats that had actually gone through the surf. "Why did some make it through intact and others break up so completely?" we asked. "In most cases it was simply the quality of the boat's construction," he stated after asking that his name be kept off the record for legal reasons. "Except for the boat that broke up when it pounded against Bernard's steel hull, the well built boats made it through the surf intact, the cheap ones didn't. Take a look at that wreck over there, the laminations are all coming apart. That shouldn't happen, it's called a dry lay up and means the builder was skimping on resin (figures 29.5, 29.6). And that wreck, the hull-to-deck connection was lousy. No bolted flange at all, the deck was just screwed into the edge grain of the plywood they used to strengthen the transom. Can you believe it, nothing, just woodscrews and bonding inside to hide the lousy connection (figure 29.7). That's no way to build a boat, but that's how they do it in some of the cheap yards."

As we walked along the test to destruction grounds his words seemed to be confirmed. The boats that cost the most, either pound for pound

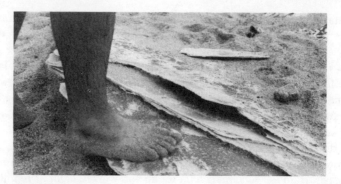

FIGURE 29.5

FIGURE 29.6

or foot for foot, were salvageable. The 28-foot Bristol Channel cutter which weighs 14,000 pounds and sells as a ready-to-sail but not outfitted boat for close to $70,000 lost her bowsprit (figure 29.8) and boomkin but suffered only a minor hull fracture on one bilge. The Olsen 40 which weighs only 10,000 pounds, has a sailaway price of about $135,000. It came through the surf with a slightly bent lead keel but no hull damage. Other survivors such as the Cabot 36 and steel *Joshua* are also considered higher priced boats compared to the shattered 37-footer, one of a quite popular class of boats advertised as perfect cruising boats, which

FIGURE 29.7

weighed 22,500 pounds and cost only $70,000 sailaway or the destroyed 50-footer that weighed 52,000 pounds and cost $125,000 direct from the far east manufacturer.

CREW

One interesting corollation from that fateful night had to do with the number of crew actually on board at the time of the storm. On sailboats over 37 feet, crews of 2 or 3 got into trouble where crews of 4 or 6 were able to handle their gear and get offshore or hold their own at anchor. Among boats driven ashore, one 54-footer had no one on board, another 50-footer had three people on board, the other 20 boats ranging from 26 feet to 46 feet in length had one or two on board. Only two of these boats were under 35 feet, nine of them were over 40 feet in length. Jerry Sieren who lost his 37-footer said it, "A couple just can't hack it on a boat this big in a real emergency. The gear is too heavy, the forces are too big. We're going again, but since we don't want crew we're getting a boat around 32 feet." We think this was one of the most important questions that was raised by the storm at Cabo. In an emergency situation can the smallest member of the working crew (who will probably

FIGURE 29.8

be a woman) handle the ground tackle while the helmsperson either powers or sails clear?

EMERGENCY TACTICS

Once we began looking at the Cabo incident as a testing ground, certain facts became more interesting. *Grace,* an Omega 46, came through the surf almost unharmed in an area of beach where other boats shattered completely. When I interviewed her owner he stressed his feeling that a stern anchor was the secret. When the boat lost its bow anchor it swung quickly until it was held stern to the seas and wind by its stern hook. As the smaller anchor began to drag through the sand, the boat was kept stern on to the seas. "She hit the beach bow on and the strongest part of the boat, the keel, dredged a supporting trough as waves shoved her higher and higher on to the beach. She came to rest gently on her bilge with her decks tilted away from the pounding surf and subsequent high tides."

A power boat delivery skipper friend of ours told of having to beach a sportfishing boat when he lost his engine near a sandy shore. His description of getting the boat through the surf was almost the same as that described by the owner of *Grace* and once again the boat survived with minimal damage. Although we hope we never have to make a decision to beach our boat during a storm, this may be an important point to remember.

Another lesson we learned was that keeping your boat's deck tilted away from the surging sea is vital. One of the main factors that lead to Bernard Moitessier's abandoning his steel hulled *Joshua* was that each day's salvage efforts were ruined by the subsequent high tide which brought as much sand and water back into the hull as three people working with buckets could remove during the low tides. Even though Bernard sealed up the cabin ports, there was no way he could keep the pounding waves from breaking through the temporary hatch boards he installed. Although the way your decks actually end up may seem completely a matter of luck, in fact this is one of the things you might be able to change with a relatively small crew of workers. If your boat should be beached on a sandy shore, the first plan of action would be to lead lines to a masthead halyard then put as much tension as possible on the line either by securing it to a tree on shore or to your largest anchor set high up on the beach. By winching on this line with your halyard or sheet winches you can keep a constant tension and cut out some of the thumping on your hull. I realize some people will be saying, "What poor sailor is going to think of that when his boat is lying in the surf late at night with rain pelting down." I cannot answer from personal experience (thank God) but several years ago when we sailed between Ibiza and Formentera on board *Seraffyn* early one morning after we'd spent a night at anchor while squalls reached 60 knots or more, we were shocked to see a 28-foot cruising sailboat sitting high and dry on a point that had been a lee shore the night before. We hove to and I rowed in to offer assistance. The hapless singlehanded owner explained he'd fallen asleep during a calm while on passage from Malta. He'd left his mainsail set and the squalls hadn't wakened him until his boat sailed itself onto the only patch of sand on Ibiza's southern tip. He'd done as I described except that he lead his anchor line through pounding surf to some rocks high up the beach then attached it to his halyard to hold the boat, decks toward the beach. He then used his bunk cushions as pads for the side of his ten-year-old wooden boat as she rose and fell on the surge. His boat was freed three days later with only scratched topsides and a broken rudder and split boom.

Taking action immediately is important not only because you might prevent further damage to your hull, but also because you must protect your personal gear. The crew on *Grace* never left the scene of their beaching unguarded. They set up a camp right against the tilting decks of their cruising home, roped off a security area and hired Mexican fishermen they knew to stand guard whenever they had to leave. This paid handsomely (see figure 29.8). They lost no gear, nothing was looted from their boat. This was not the case on board several other boats. Even though the Mexican authorities immediately posted guards to protect the unfortunate sailors at Cabo, looting happened, not only on the boats at the far end of the beach away from the guard post but within a few hundred feet of the armed guards in broad daylight. Richard Bower (figure 29.9) who owns *Vagabundo* told us he came from the home he was staying in right after having breakfast and saw an American man dis-assembling *Vagabundo*'s sheet winches. The looter was working calmly away within easy calling of a guard. When the arrest was made the guard explained to Richard, "He was a gringo and looked like he was sup-posed to be doing that job. How was I to know?" Only you can protect your interests in a situation like this and the gear you save could be the difference between going cruising again or abandoning the whole affair.

FIGURE 29.9

SALVAGE TACTICS

One the saddest lessons learned on the beach was that it may not pay to accept offers of assistance until you've planned and done some research yourself. The owners of *Ayorama* an uninsured Endurance 36 that managed to reach the beach with no hull or rigging damage, made the mistake of accepting a local construction crews offer of help for what seemed like a simple job. Just use the bulldozer to shove *Ayorama* into the water at low tide. Then she'd float out at high tide. Even though the crews tried to protect the hull with old tires, the bulldozer exerted so much force that the deck buckled and damage was so extensive that *Ayorama* will probably be declared a total loss. (See following note for a happy ending.)

This was in complete contrast to *Dancing Bear* a Cabot 36 which also survived the surf in fine condition. Her salvage was done under the eagle eyes of Doc Ross an almost legendary Englishman who is resident at Cabo San Lucas and known as a fix-it magician and mechanic. He hired a steam shovel to dig a channel to where *Dancing Bear* was stranded.

FIGURE 29.10

Then she was allowed to settle into the hole until she was upright. the insurance adjuster, David Cookingham, rigged a well-thought-out towing bridle that went completely around her hull just below the waterline. The bridle was held in place by lines secured at various points on deck. By the highest tide of the month, the diesel shovel had dug a channel to within inches of the expected high tide line. A large fishing boat was in place, anchored off the beach, ready to keep a constant pulling strain on *Dancing Bear*'s bridle as water entered the hole around her. She floated but did not clear the beach completely and Doc Ross kept his crew at work most of the night so at the following high tide she could be floated free with no further damage from the salvage operations.

A difficult problem for owners who are stranded far from home with a wrecked boat that does carry insurance is, should we abandon the boat as a write off or should we try to salvage some of the work that we put into it? Insurance payments rarely cover the cost and time you spent outfitting your boat and for Richard and Betty Bower on *Vagabundo* this was a particularly hard choice. They had spent three years finishing a bare hull, putting on wooden decks, a handsome interior, rigging and outfitting the boat. Since they still had a bank mortgage on the boat, the insurance money they'd receive if the boat was written off was not enough to buy another completed boat. Abandoning their boat meant putting cruising four or five years down the road. "Besides, I don't want another boat. I built this one. I don't want someone else's interior, I want this boat," Richard told us as we looked at the two-foot crack on the side of *Vagabundo*'s hull, the broken boomkin and bowsprit, the scarred bulwarks and sand-covered deck. When he asked us what we'd do next our answer echoed that of Lee Washburn a sportfishing skipper with 20 years of experience at the Cape. "See if the other side of your hull has any damage before you make a decision. You need all the facts you can get." Richard could not quite believe it was possible to right his boat on the beach as simply as Lee and I said it would be but agreed to let us try. Lee supervised a crew of volunteer workers who cleaned as much sand as possible away from the hull and dug under the beached side of the boat as far as they could to reduce the suction caused by wet sand. Lee actually walked up the tilting mast to re-rig a halyard to use as a hauling line (see figure 29.6) while I inspected all of the rigging. It was intact expect for the backstay and headstay. We rigged a temporary headstay to the stem head. But since there was no boomkin left we came up with a quick and dirty way of rigging a backstay. We removed the engine exhaust hose, tied a line to the backstay turnbuckle then led it through the lazzerette hatch, out the exhaust hole and back to itself and tightened it. A four-wheel-drive vehicle commandeered by one of the volunteers provided the winching power, but Richard's halyard winches and an anchor led as far as possible out to the side could have done the same. The mast bent less than ten inches as the boat came slowly upright, easily controlled by the 44-foot-long lever of the mast. Volunteers shoveled sand into the hole she left so even if things went wrong she'd only slip back a few inches. Three hours after the idea started becoming an action, *Vagabundo* stood upright, shored by 4 by 4 timbers borrowed from other boat owners who'd been less fortunate. Not only did she look less forelorn but Richard could now see there was only cosmetic damage on the starboard side. Even more important, the next day's high tide and a rising southerly swell could have started filling *Vagabundo* with salt water and sand. Instead it carried sand into the crater around her to hold her even more firmly upright while subsequent salvage plans were put into action.

As we looked back on the lessons that lay along the beach at Cabo San Lucas we couldn't help but remember the most important thing that gale taught us all, a lesson for which there could be no photographs, no drawings. At least twelve owners or skippers chose to leave the anchorage. One left at 1700 soon after the first gusts of wind came from the southeast straight into the open bay. Another left at 2000 when his bow began dripping into the building seas. The rest left their anchors behind sometime during the later hours either because gear broke or other boats dragged past and left room for them to maneuver out to open water. The last boat to leave, the Cal 40, sailed out at midnight. Only one of these boats was lost, *Breaking Free* who's engine failed before the boat cleared the cape, before the crew had time to remove their sailcovers. The escaping boats reported heavy seas and winds that gusted to over 55 knots during the five hours the gale lasted. Not one reported breaking any gear while they waited out the tempest in open water and each one we interviewed said, "I'd go to sea again but next time I'd get underway sooner."

AFTER NOTE ON CABO SAN LUCAS DISASTER

During the year following the Christmas '82 storm, cruising voyagers, including some of those who had been at Cabo San Lucas that frightening night, sailed through two more unusual weather catastrophes. The first hurricane in 60 years roared through the Tahitian islands and over 100 boats were thrown onto the reefs at Maeva Beach and scattered along the rocky shore. Fifty of them had to be declared total losses. Then in Neiafu, the main port in the northern Tongan Island group of Vava'u over two dozen cruising boats suffered extensive damage and several were lost when the worst hurricane in 30 years blew through this coral head studded bay with winds up to 120 knots.

It is now 1986 and the infamous El Niño current, which is blamed for each of those unusual storms, has diminished. The weather throughout the tropics seems more normal, yet the lessons of the 1982–83 cruising season linger. As we spent the last year and a half sailing past the sites of each of these catastrophies, we saw parts of hulls being used to decorate restaurants or still littering shorelines. In each of these three places we saw hulls being slowly restored by new local owners who had purchased the salvage rights for a few hundred dollars. We also met or corresponded with the crews of five of the boats that were driven ashore that night at Cabo.

Bernard Moitessier was on board his new 31-foot steel boat, moored to the quay at Papeete when we sailed in. Donations of money and assistance had arrived from around the world when fans read of the loss of *Joshua*. A California boat builder, Jim Hutton, donated much of his labor and within a year Bernard was afloat again. He has been in Papeete for a year now and is working to write a new book, and enjoying the children of cruising sailors and local Tahitian friends who flock to see him.

Bernard's old ship, *Joshua*, was restored and sailing when we passed through San Diego. Her new owners were planning to take her to sea again within a year or two.

Betty and Richard Bower took eight months to salvage and refinish *Vagabundo* with the help of their insurance settlement. They did rough repairs right on the beach at Cabo, then sailed and powered to La Paz to finish her. they returned by land to Canada to earn new cruising funds and after a year were able to set sail for nine months of voyaging to Australia where they found full-time work.

When we sailed into Moorea, a handsome Canadian yacht came by and called hello. *Meridian Passage* was the new home of Dave and Olive Adams who had lost their boat at Cabo. The insurance helped them return to the sea two years later. But as Olive said to us, "I've never felt as comfortable about cruising after that horrid night in Cabo San Lucas." The two years of cruising they originally planned for are now almost completed and *Meridian Passage* is headed home from New Zealand as soon as the South Pacific cyclone season is over.

Jerry and Gail Stern who lost *Sea Wren* in Cabo, used their insurance to do some land cruising in a camper van, while they looked for a new cruising boat. They got back to sea after two years.

Among the boats that were destroyed that night we only know of one that was uninsured besides Bernard's *Joshua* who has been able to get back to cruising as of this date. At the time we flew to Cabo to write these stories, *Ayorama* had seemed like a total loss. But through sheer determination and hard work, Grant Nichols salvaged and rebuilt her in Baja California over a year-and-a-half period. He then sailed her back to his home in Canada.

30

A Ground Tackle System List

Eight of us sat in a tight circle, almost oblivious to the rest of the party that ebbed and flowed around us. All forty or fifty of the guests in that Newport Beach bayside home were involved in sailing—yacht designers, equipment manufacturers, racing sailors—but interesting as their conversations were, our attention kept being drawn to our kindred souls, the long-distance voyagers who had all ended up in the same place at the same time, all bound away within the next few months for yet another voyage. Together the four couples had voyaged over 300,000 miles on boats ranging from 24 feet on deck to 62 feet. Two major topics held us together as hors d'oeuvres dwindled and the other guests left: the perfect place to cruise, an unanswerable question and, the ideal ground tackle system, one on which all eight of us seemed to agree in principle if not in detail. A week later we got together with two couples who were out fitting their first offshore boats in anticipation of their first long cruise and the same two topics dominated the evening but with one big difference. Whereas the experienced cruisers had talked about their ground tackle as a system, the soon-to-be-cruisers, seemed interested only in anchors and anchor types.

Larry and I sat down later that week to make up a list of what we still needed to finish the last minute outfitting on *Taleisin*. Then we grew more sympathetic towards all new cruisers. Anchors, chain, windlass, bowrollers, cleats, all the gear for the ground tackle system our voyaging experience taught us we needed to carry, came to a total retail cost in excess of $4,000. Even with the most careful shopping, trading and fabricating of some of our own gear, we still spent over $2,000 on our anchor system and added 800 pounds to our new boat's cargo burden. Or, to put it another way, we used five percent of her eventual displacement just for ground tackle. If she had been a lighter, length-to-weight displacement type boat, say a 32-foot boat displacing 12,000 pounds, which is more normal for production type boats, this weight burden would have increased to almost seven percent of the boat's total displacement.

Fortunately for us, we were building our own boat so we could incorporate some parts of this ground tackle system right into the design, parts like the stern roller, the bits and boom gallows that serve as mooring cleats. The person who buys a stock boat, has to add labor costs to their budget as they try to fit rugged offshore ground tackle on a boat that was originally planned for coastal cruising. It is no wonder they look for the lightest, cheapest, simplest way to go. This can be the biggest single mistake potential sailors make. If you drag anchor and lose your boat, insurance money will never replace the boat preparation time or the confidence of family and crew.

The following list shows the gear *Taleisin* carries, gear we feel makes up our anchor system. Remember this is a system for extensive offshore voyaging. The person who is going for a four-month voyage, choosing his seasons carefully, could probably cut this system down 30 percent in weight and eliminate back ups that are much more important when you get far away from sailing centers. I know the spare anchor we carry is not an absolute necessity, but it means the loss of our working anchor would not be quite so problematic. We wouldn't have to resort to using the bulky, hard to winch up, storm anchor until we reached the next marine stores. The starred items are discussed briefly after the list. Other items marked with cc are discussed elsewhere in this book.

TALEISIN'S GROUND TACKLE SYSTEM

		weight	
*Working anchor	35-pound CQR	35	
Stern anchor	12 H Danforth	12	
Spare anchor	20 H Danforth	22	
Storm anchor	Luke 3 piece folding fisherman	65	cc
Dinghy anchor	folding Northhill	5	
Main chain	275 feet of 5/16 inch high test	302	cc
Main bower Line snubber	50 feet 5/8-inch nylon	5	cc
Second bower	30 feet 5/16-inch high test chain	33	
Second bower line	300 feet 5/8-inch nylon	34	
Stern bower	10 feet 1/4-inch B.B.B. chain	8	
Stern bower line	250 feet 1/2-inch nylon	16.5	
Dinghy bower line	60 feet 3/8-inch nylon	2	
*Anchor windlass	Two speed bronze A.B.I.	75	
Chain pipe and splitter		5	
Second bower pipe		3	
2 bow rollers		14	cc
Stern roller		14	cc
Mooring cleat and bits		15	
Bowsprit end pennant block		2	cc
Snubber lines	Two—15 foot 1/2-inch nylon	2	cc
*Boat hook/chain scrubber		3	
*Dinghy and long oars		90	
*Lead line	130 feet marked every five fathoms, 3-pound lead	12	
Line chafing protection hoses		3	
Shackles, swivel for permanent mooring, Spare thimbles and galvanized seizing wire		17	
Total weight		798	

*Although our anchors may appear oversized when you first compare them to the manufacturers' recommendations, once you read all of the fine print, you'll find they are not. Manufacturers of anchors must suggest sizes for the whole range of sailors and fishermen they sell gear to. According to the Danforth company, over 70 percent of their anchors are sold to inland fishermen for use with small open boats. They would therefore be unwise to base their recommendations on the needs of offshore voyaging boats when people like ourselves make up less than two percent of their customer base. They try to cover the cruising sailor by stating that the recommendations are for winds of up to 60 knots with moderate protection from the seas. Offshore voyagers cannot guarantee they will avoid winds over 60 knots, so its necessary to choose working anchors at least one size higher than manufacturers' recommendations.

*Not only does a windlass make it possible for all of the crew to handle the proper size ground tackle, but, used in conjunction with well arranged cleats, it could also prevent future back strain problems and keep you more active all through life. For any chain over ⅜-inch we would recommend the use of a hydraulic anchor windlass with electric as a second choice.

*A hard dinghy with long oars becomes part of your ground tackle system when you must kedge out an anchor, either to increase the anchoring power you need because of an approaching hurricane, to get another anchor set if yours starts to drag, or to set a stern hook in a crowded anchorage. You may not have the time to inflate a rubber dinghy and attach your outboard in this situation. Using the longest oars possible will assist tremendously when you have to row against heavy winds and pull the weight of ground tackle with you.

*Although many people rely on their depth sounder to decide where to anchor, a lead line is still necessary. It serves two purposes. It picks up a sample of the bottom to show you which anchor to use, and it can be taken with you into the dinghy so that you can sound a suspect channel or check all the way around the boat to make sure there is no chance of bumping into rocks or shallow spots should the wind shift.

One of Larry's latest inventions is a chain scrubber that snaps onto a fitting at the opposite end of our boat hook. The scrubber is made from the brushes off two toilet bowel scrubbers. They are wrapped into a spiral that is wound onto the chain. Then we can scrub the chain while it is just at the surface of the water and avoid bringing bottom mud on deck. One person scrubs, one cranks on the windlass. The only improvement would be to have a high power hose to use for this job.

Eric and Susan Hiscock, who have been voyaging for far more years than we, provided the following list of their primary ground tackle for each of three *Wanderers*.

Wanderer III, sloop. LOA 30¼, LWL 26½, beam 8½, displacement 9 tons. Bower anchor 35-pound CQR on 45 fathoms of ⁵⁄₁₆-inch chain. She was fitted with a chain pawl at the stemhead to assist when weighing.

Wanderer IV, Ketch. LOA 49½, LWL 40, beam 12½, displacement 22 tons. The original bower was a 60-pound CQR, but this got badly bent in a storm and we replaced it with a 75-pound CQR on 45 fathoms of ½-inch chain. Handling was by electric windlass with handlever back up.

Wanderer V, sloop. LOA 39½, LWL 33¼, beam 12¼, displacement 11 tons. Bower, 60-pound CQR on 40 fathoms of ⅜-inch chain. Handling by electric windlass with hand-lever back up.

The bower anchors of Wanderers IV and V do not have to be lifted on board as they stow themselves on the bow rollers. Of course the above yachts all carried kedges (CQR's) and nylon rodes and had five fathom ground chains to go with them.

Good advice on anchoring, and choosing ground tackle can be found in each of the Hiscock books including *Cruising under Sail,* 3rd edition which incorporates *Voyaging Under Sail* published by Oxford.

31

Selecting Chain

Whether you anchor with an all-chain rode or with a combination of chain and line, you'll still have to choose, then maintain those links that connect you and your boat to its anchor. Fortunately for yachtsmen, chain is one of the few items we have to buy that is widely used throughout industry. Because of this there are not only rules governing the testing and rating of chain, but sufficient competition so prices are kept relatively modest. In fact, prices for higher quality grades of chain have actually fallen over the last twenty years (if inflation is taken in account). This is because industrial users are demanding stronger, lighter chain to increase safety margins in their plants. Furthermore, industrial users have increased their demand for not only galvanizing, but also re-galvanizing services, so maintaining our chain as we cruise seems easier than when we first outfitted *Seraffyn* in 1968.

We had only two types of chain reasonably available to us back then, BBB and proof coil. Proof coil was sometimes called long link chain. It was tested by stretching it to twice its registered working load then inspecting every twentieth link. It was the standard chain used for moorings in our area. BBB, on the other hand, was a short link chain, i.e., more links per foot, heavier per foot and inspected every link. This made it a better choice for anchor rodes because it was more flexible (more joints per foot) and stronger because there was less room between links to permit distortion and the alloy used to make it was stronger. The more careful inspecting of each link was also important to us. We did

FIGURE 31.1

Specifications

Trade Size, Inches	Material Size, Inches	Inside Length of Link, Inches	Inside Width of Link, Inches	Outside Length of Link, Inches	Outside Width of Link, Inches	Links per Foot	Approx. Wt. per 100 Feet, Pounds	Working Load Limit, Pounds	Trade Size, Inches
3/16	7/32	0.78	0.37	1.21	0.81	15 1/2	43	800	3/16
1/4	9/32	0.85	0.43	1.41	0.99	14	75	1325	1/4
5/16	11/32	1.00	0.50	1.68	1.19	12	114	1950	5/16
3/8	13/32	1.09	0.62	1.90	1.43	11	164	2750	3/8
7/16	15/32	1.21	0.68	2.15	1.62	9 3/4	221	3625	7/16
1/2	17/32	1.34	0.75	2.40	1.81	9	292	4750	1/2
9/16	19/32	1.56	0.78	2.75	1.97	7 3/4	350	5875	9/16
5/8	21/32	1.68	0.87	3.00	2.18	7 1/8	443	7250	5/8
3/4	25/32	1.87	1.00	3.43	2.56	6 3/8	620	10250	3/4
7/8	29/32	2.25	1.25	4.06	3.06	5 3/8	840	12000	7/8
1	1 1/32	2.56	1.37	4.62	3.43	4 3/4	1050	15500	1

BBB CHAIN

Uses
Same general applications as Proof Coil Chain. This type of chain not recommended for overhead lifting purposes or where its failure will cause damage to property or life. For over head lifting Cam-Alloy chain should be used.

Standard Material
Electric Furnace, Open Hearth or Oxygen top blown low carbon steel.

Special Properties
Similar to Proof Coil in general characteristics. Shorter links than those of Proof Coil increase the Working Load Limits. Greater number of links per foot provide added flexibility, permit wider distribution of strain and wear.

hear talk of stronger chain being introduced, but we checked and found prices—if we could get this stronger chain—would be five to eight times higher than we had to pay for BBB. So BBB is what *Seraffyn* used successfully as long as we owned her.

Since *Taleisin* was 20 percent longer, presented 20 percent more frontal area to the wind and weighed 65 percent more than *Seraffyn* we choose a ⅜-inch BBB chain for her. This new chain was too heavy for us to handle, and also put *Taleisin,* who is fine bowed, down by the head. For these reasons we became interested in high-test chain. We were pleased to find this once expensive chain now cost just a bit more than BBB yet offered double the safe working load at a slightly lower weight. That meant we could trade in our 300 feet of ⅜-inch BBB that weighed 492 pounds and had a working load limit of 2,750 for 300 feet of ⁵⁄₁₆-inch high test chain that weighed only 333 pounds yet gave us a safe working load of 3,900 pounds, or more than a 25 percent strength gain with a ⅓ weight savings. We did realize we would be giving up some of the advantage of the shock-absorbing effect of a chains' weight-induced, catenary curve but figured we could counteract this by veering more chain and increasing our scope in heavy wind situations.

We contacted Campbell Chain Company, one of two major chain manufacturers in the U.S., to discuss our decision. They told us all U.S. firms now use a numbered rating system for chain since specifications must be to government standards. Proof coil is now called system 3, high test is system 4, system 7 and 8 chains are also available, with the higher system number indicating greater strength versus the chain weight. (The

THE CAMPBELL SYSTEMS

System 3 Chain:

Excellent general purpose, carbon steel chain, of standard commercial quality, for uses not requiring high strength-to-weight ratios. This electrically welded chain is frequently used to fabricate tow chains, binding or tie-down chains and logging chains. DO NOT USE FOR OVERHEAD LIFTING. Proof tested. Elongation minimum: 15%. Hallmark: P or CP-C3. (Traditionally referred to as proof coil.)

System 4 Chain:

An electrically welded carbon steel chain often used for load binding, towing, logging and many other applications requiring higher strength-to-weight ratios than System 3 chain. Proof* tested. May be heat treated. DO NOT USE FOR OVERHEAD LIFTING. Elongation minimum: 15%. Hallmark: CH-C4. (Traditionally referred to as High Test.)

System 7 Chain:

This chain is made from a high-hardenability, boron-treated steel for higher strength-to-weight ratios than System 4 chain. System 7, specifically developed for use in load binding, towing and binding, will meet stringent Department of Transportation regulations with smaller chain that is lighter in weight and easier to handle. Manufactured, electrically welded, proof tested and heat treated using methods developed by Campbell. DO NOT USE FOR OVERHEAD LIFTING. Elongation minimum: 15%. Hallmark: C7.

System 8 Chain:

This higher strength, alloy steel chain is SPECIFICALLY RECOMMENDED FOR OVERHEAD LIFTING. Heat treated and proof tested, it provides a combination of high working load limits and minimum weight. Elongates in excess of the 15% minimum requirement. Tensile strength of System 8 chain meets or exceeds all existing OSHA, Government, NACM and ASTM specification requirements. Hallmark: C8-CA and CA.

Warning: Do not exceed Working Load Limit.

Chart Courtesy of Campbell Chain Division McGraw-Edison Company

	Size					Dimensions				Mechanical Properties				General Information		
Campbell System Number	Trade Size Inches	mm	Actual Material Diameter Inches	mm	Inside Length Inches	mm	Inside Width Inches	mm	Working Load Limit* Pounds	Kg.	Proof Test (Minimum) Pounds	KN.	Use Index	Approx. Weight Per 100 Feet Pounds	Kg.
3	1/8	4	.156	3.96	.89	22.61	.29	7.33	375	170	750	3.3	17	22	10
3	3/16	5	.218	5.53	.95	24.13	.40	10.16	750	340	1,500	6.7	18	41	19
3	1/4	7	.251	7.14	1.00	25.40	.50	12.70	1,250	567	2,500	11.1	17	72	33
3	5/16	8	.343	8.71	1.10	27.94	.50	12.70	1,900	862	3,800	16.9	18	106	48
3	3/8	10	.406	10.31	1.23	31.24	.62	15.75	2,650	1,200	5,300	23.6	17	155	70
3	7/16	11	.468	11.89	1.37	34.80	.75	19.05	3,500	1,590	7,000	31.1	16	217	98
3	1/2	13	.531	13.49	1.54	39.12	.79	20.07	4,500	2,040	9,000	40.0	17	270	122
3	5/8	16	.655	16.66	1.87	47.50	1.00	25.40	6,900	3,130	13,800	61.4	17	415	188
3	3/4	20	.784	19.84	2.12	53.85	1.12	28.45	9,750	4,420	19,500	86.7	17	577	262
3	7/8	22	.905	23.01	2.34	59.44	1.37	34.80	11,375	5,160	22,750	101.2	14	770	349
4	1/4	7	.281	7.14	.79	20.07	.40	10.16	2,600	1,180	4,300	19.1	33	80	36
4	5/16	8	.343	8.71	1.01	25.65	.48	12.19	3,900	1,770	6,400	28.5	35	111	50
4	3/8	10	.406	10.31	1.15	29.21	.58	14.73	5,400	2,450	8,900	39.6	34	160	73
4	7/16	11	.468	11.89	1.29	32.77	.67	17.02	7,200	3,270	11,900	52.9	33	216	98
4	1/2	13	.531	13.49	1.43	36.32	.76	19.30	9,200	4,170	15,300	68.1	33	280	127
4	5/8	16	.655	16.66	1.79	45.47	.90	22.86	11,500	5,220	19,500	86.7	28	413	187
4	3/4	20	.781	19.84	2.21	56.13	1.10	27.94	16,200	7,350	27,000	120.1	28	580	263
7	1/4	7	.281	7.14	.86	21.84	.45	11.43	3,150	1,430	6,300	28.0	42	75	34
7	5/16	8	.343	8.71	1.01	25.65	.48	11.68	4,700	2,130	9,400	41.8	51	111	50
7	3/8	10	.394	10.00	1.10	27.94	.55	13.97	6,600	2,990	13,200	58.7	44	150	68
7	7/16	11	.468	11.89	1.29	32.77	.67	17.02	8,750	3,970	17,500	77.8	41	212	96
7	1/2	13	.512	13.00	1.55	39.37	.72	18.29	11,300	5,130	22,600	100.5	47	238	108
8	7/32	5	.218	5.53	.69	17.53	.30	7.62	2,500	1,130	5,000	22.2	59	42	19
8	9/32	7	.281	7.14	.86	21.84	.45	11.43	4,100	1,860	8,200	36.5	55	75	34
8	5/16	8	.315	8.00	.94	23.88	.46	11.68	5,100	2,310	10,200	45.4	55	92	42
8	3/8	10	.394	10.00	1.10	27.94	.55	13.97	7,300	3,310	14,600	64.9	49	150	68
8	1/2	13	.512	13.00	1.55	39.37	.72	18.29	13,000	5,900	26,000	115.7	55	238	108
8	5/8	16	.630	16.00	1.84	46.74	.92	23.37	20,300	9,210	40,600	180.6	52	394	179
8	3/4	20	.787	20.00	2.20	55.88	1.09	27.69	29,300	13,290	58,600	260.7	51	572	259
8	7/8	22	.881	22.40	2.45	62.23	1.22	30.99	39,900	18,100	79,800	355.0	53	750	340
8	1	25	1.000	25.40	2.80	71.12	1.40	35.56	52,100	23,630	104,200	463.5	54	965	438
8	1 1/4	32	1.250	31.75	3.50	88.90	1.75	44.45	81,400	36,920	162,800	724.1	53	1,525	692

All English dimensions and English weights are subject to tolerances of plus or minus 4 percent. Use Index provides comparative guide for certain applications. The higher the Use Index number the greater the strength vs. chain weight.

FIGURE 31.2

higher system number also indicates higher price.) Unfortunately BBB does not comply with the same rating system and some companies would like to discontinue this specialty chain. But because it had been the standard for marine use for so many years, and because so many naval users have chain wildcats, (chain gypsy) calibrated for BBB, both Campbell Chain Company executives and those at ACCO (American Chain Company) assured us they would continue to produce BBB for many years. They also assured us that the same windlass wildcat would fit both high test and BBB chain of the same diameter if the recesses for the chain are slightly tapered. (I would still take your wildcat with you when you shop for chain. If this isn't possible, ask the chain supplier to send a one foot sample and check to see that the chain slips easily into the wildcat recesses and settles right to the bottom without jamming.)

Mr. Anderson, director of consumer marketing at Campbell Chain Company, said to consider chain strength as the recommended safe working load, not breaking or ultimate strength. "The only way you can really tell the ultimate breaking strength of a piece of chain is to break it," he wrote. Safe working load is about one quarter of a chain's theoretical breaking strength. Chain testing or proof testing is done by stressing chain to twice it's safe working load, then inspecting each link for signs of cracking or elongation.

There are two ways to decide not only which system of chain to buy, but which size within that system. The first is to look at boats of comparable weight, length and windage, that have successfully anchored in a variety of conditions, then choose comparable chain. Figure 31.3, made up by naval architect Jay Paris compares information from several engineering sources plus input from successful long-term voyagers. The chart gives a good idea of the chain sizes we'd feel fit offshore cruising boats if, as Jay says, you choose the higher value when entering the table (i.e., if your boat is 29-feet long and weighs 17,000 pounds, you look under the 15,000 to 20,000 pound boat figures and conversely if your 38-footer weighs only 12,000 pounds, you use the boat length figures). These chain sizes are for BBB or short link chain.

The second method uses the windage your boat will present to storm winds as the major criteria for selecting chain. The American Boat and Yacht Council recommends that "your chain should have sufficient breaking strength to withstand at least five times the normal horizontal

SAILING YACHT ANCHOR CHAIN SELECTION

Developed using data from Chapman, Uffa Fox, Herreshoff, Eric Hiscock, James Ogg, Jay Paris and Don Street.

Remember the relationship between boat length and weight is only approximate. Enter the table with whichever charactoristic gives the largest chain diameter.

Chain recommendations for short link or BBB chain.

Boat length feet	Boat weight pounds	Chain diameter inches
25–30	5,000–10,000	1/4
30–35	10,000–15,000	5/16
35–40	15,000–20,000	3/8
40–45	20,000–30,000	7/16
45–50	30,000–50,000	1/2
50–60	50,000	9/16

Chart by Jay E. Paris Jr., naval architect and engineer. Brunswick, Maine
FIGURE 31.3

load placed on it by the vessel under the condition for which the rode was selected." To get this horizontal load figure, you must know the windage presented by your yacht when she lies at anchor. The simplest way to compute this is to multiply bow height times maximum beam then add 2/3 to account for spars, rigging and deck gear. If your boat has a doghouse or dodger that is higher than the bow as viewed from the waterline, add its frontal area. Double the figure you get to account for the affects of yawing when your boat might present most of its beam to the wind. Use this square footage to compare the forces wind will exert on your boat using the following table, then multiply the highest wind force you might reasonably expect to meet times five and you will have the theoretical breaking strain of the size of chain you need for your boat.

Of course all of these computations assume the chain has a minimum of five-to-one scope and that there is moderate protection from the seas, i.e., no more than a half-a-mile fetch from the protecting shores. Ideally, we would all like to be lying to two anchor rodes in storm conditions. But it is best to figure your main bower (be it chain or a combination of line and chain) to take the strains of winds up to 70 or 75 knots

COMPUTING CHAIN STRENGTH NEEDED FOR TALEISIN, USING WINDAGE METHOD

Maximum beam—10′9″
Maximum freeboard at bow—4″
    10′9″ multiplied by 4 equals   43 square feet
    ⅔ added to account for spars and
        deck equipment   28 square feet
    windage presented head to wind   71 square feet of frontal
                                            surface

	Head to wind i.e. 70 sq. ft.	*Yawing maximum* 140 sq. ft.
At 60 knots	894 lbs. pressure	1788 lbs.
at 80 knots	1,561	3,122
at 100 knots	2,268	4,536

Recommended chain size should be able to take a direct load of five times maximum expected pressure without this figure exceeding the ultimate breaking strain of the chain. At 60 knots we would need chain with an ultimate breaking point of 8940, but at 100 knots the chain would have to have an ultimate breaking point of 22,680. Since we have never encountered sustained winds in excess of 80 knots while at anchor, we have chosen high test 5/16 inch chain with a theoretical breaking strain of 15,600. (Maximum horizontal pull at 80 knots 3,122 multiplied by a five to one safety factor equals, 15,610.)

To compute the theoretical ultimate breaking strain for any given chain, multiply the safe recommended working load by four.

FIGURE 31.4

because squalls of this force are not unknown during otherwise fine weather in the tropics.

    Once the chain strengths are considered, costs and the ability of your boat and your crew to handle the weight of the chain come next, so if it is fine ended, extra heavy chain could depress the boats bow and cause it to hobby horse. The owner of one 62-foot, light-weight boat computed his windage and figured he needed a chain with an ultimate breaking strength of 35,000 pounds to feel comfortable at anchor. To get this with BBB chain he had to have ¾-inch chain at 620 pounds per hundred feet or 1,860 pounds for 300 feet. If he used system 4 chain he could carry ½ inch at 280 pounds per 100 feet or 840 for 300. He went one step further since weight savings meant more for him than

Dynamic pressure in pounds per square foot exerted by wind on a frontal surface

Frontal surface in square feet	*30-knot wind*	*60 knot*	*80 knot*	*100 knot*
1	3 lbs.	12.6	22.3	32.4
50	150	630	1115	1600
100	300	1260	2230	3240
150	450	1890	3345	4860
200	600	2520	4460	6480

Dynamic pressure in kilograms per square meter

Frontal surface in square meters	*30-knot wind*	*60 knot*	*80 knot*	*100 knot*
1	15 kilos	60	107 107	155
5	75	300	535	755
10	150	600	1070	1550
15	225	900	1605	2325
20	300	1200	2140	3100

According to Alain Gree, who discusses these frontal pressures in detail in his book *Anchoring and Mooring,* published by Adlard Coles Ltd., the above chart gives a 30 percent higher reading than necessary. His reasoning is that the figures are for flat frontal surfaces where many of the surfaces of a boat are round or tapered. We know he would probably be correct if these figures were for everyday sailing boats and decks were cleared of all extraneous gear. But to allow for deck storage, dog houses, rigging gear, spreaders etc., I would prefer using these figures.

These tables are computed for a relative humidity of 60 percent and barometric pressure of 1013 mb. High barometric pressure increases air density, high temperature and humidity lower it. For a given wind speed, wind resistance will be marginally greater on a cold, dry day than on a warm humid one.

FIGURE 31.5

cash savings and opted for the much more costly, but stronger system 7 chain where he got his ultimate breaking strain of five times safe working load using 7/16-inch chain at 212 pounds per 100 feet for a total of 636 pounds of chain in his box. He saved 1,200 pounds this way, but paid not only in initial cost but in eventual replacement costs.

One persistent comment we heard whenever we mentioned using higher strength-to-weight ratio chain was, "You'll be sorry when you want to get it regalvanized; your high-test chain will lose its heat treating, it won't be as strong." This began to worry us when we saw the first sign of wear on *Taleisin's* high-test chain. So we wrote again to Campbell Chain Co. and to quote from J.B. Anderson's letter of October 24th 1985,

Two items reduce the strength of chain in the hot galvanizing process, i.e.,

1. Lubricity of zinc affects the ultimate strength by an amount less than 5 percent of the breaking strength of the chain. This could possibly affect your chain, but the effect will be minimal.
2. Excess heat in the hot galvanizing process could affect the heat treatment qualities of the chain if it happens to be a heat treated high alloy chain. Your system 4 is not, and the heat of the galvanizing will have no effect.

The only loss of strength relative to the hot galvanizing of high-test chain would be that that is generated through the lubricity, and that ranges from negligible to less than 5 percent and for the most part is a factor that shows up only under laboratory conditions.

All that I have said above is also true of BBB chain, as both BBB and high test are made of relatively low carbon steel. The additional strength of the high test is due to the fact that it is a higher carbon steel than the BBB. BBB is normally made of 1008 steel and high test is made of 1026 steel, or a higher carbon content. Yes, these factors would apply to any U.S.-made chain no matter what the brand.

That means since our high test system 4 chain is not heat treated, we can continue to regalvanize it as often as necessary. Our friend who chose the system 7 chain cannot. His chain is, as the chart on page 348 shows, heat treated as one of the ways to gain greater strength for less weight. He spoke with the chain manufacturer who assured him it was safe to regalvanize his chain two or three times at high quality galvanizing plants where regalvanizing temperatures were kept as low as practical. After that the chain would begin to lose an appreciable portion of its heat-treated strength.

It is best to have your chain regalvanized as soon as a large number of links have signs of definite rust showing where link rubs against link. If you wait much longer, not only do you risk losing chain strength

through metal loss, it will cost you more to have the chain replated.*
At this early stage, the galvanizers can clean old zinc, minor rust, synthetic markers or paint off the chain by dipping it in an acid bath. If
there is actual scale build up the chain must be cleaned by shot blasting
or burning. Both of these methods cost extra. Shot blasting is more
expensive but the only choice you have with system 7 chain. Burning,
if done with proper controls, is not supposed to harm system 4, 3 or BBB
and costs less than shot blasting.

Choose a galvanizer who is used to working with chain and has either
a centrifuge or shaking device to assure that as the chain is lifted from
the molten zinc alloy coating tank, excess metal is shaken off and links
are not stuck together. If this coating is too lumpy, if links are stuck,
the galvanizing may break away from the chain when the links are
separated. Excess lumps may cause your chain to jam in the wildcat.
They will also snag and rip hands or lines that get near the chain.

We usually find we need our chain regalvanized every third year of
offshore cruising. If we are secured in marinas or on moorings the
frequency drops, if we are anchoring in rocky or coral-strewn areas, the
frequency increases. We've had good regalvanizing done in Malaysia,
England, the U.S. and New Zealand. The prices have been reasonably
consistent. This year it cost us 71 cents a kilo (U.S.) or 32 cents a pound
to regalvanize 300 pounds of chain in New Zealand. Look for industrial
or mining centers to find galvanizing firms. Singapore, Malta, Australia,
almost all western European countries have been mentioned by cruising
friends as good places to get galvanizing done.

To prolong the life of your chain and its galvanizing, end for end your
chain each year. Make sure your chain locker drains well so the chain
does not sit in a pool of water month after month. Make sure your chain
roller runs free so the galvanizing is not dragged off as it runs out. (To
further reduce wear of the galvanizing against the roller we now use
delrin (nylon) instead of bronze for the roller. The delrin might need
replacing after five years use, but could save us far more than the trouble
and money by protecting the galvanizing.) Touch up any links that have
the galvanizing worn off against rocks by using metal primer or red lead
paint to protect the exposed metal.

*Theoretically, because of its higher carbon content, system 4 chain should rust more
quickly once the galvanizing has rubbed off. But according to chain distributors here in
New Zealand, no tests have verified any appreciable difference.

After five or six years of extensive use, it would pay to have your chain re-tested. We watched the tester in Malta check ours by hooking 30 foot lengths to a test machine, then applying pressure up to the proof load or two times recommended working load. Since he saw no elongation of the links he certified the chain as safe.

You should inspect your chain for elongation whenever you suspect it has been subjected to intense strains. Look for signs like cracked or peeling galvanizing and cracks near the welds. If the chain seems to slip and jump in your cathead after a storm, suspect elongation. At the first sign of elongation replace the chain.

Buy only brand-name chain. You will be depending on it as your first line of insurance as you cruise. If you are not buying from a dealer, where you can find the brand on the barrel, or are buying secondhand, you will find the chain manufacturers code stamped on the links approximately every foot. Since all manufacturers in the U.S. use the same specifications, shop price and ease of delivery rather than brand name. Overseas, contact the chain manufacturer for his strength and systems ratings.* Then refer to working load ratings for all computations. Properly purchased and maintained chain will last the life of your boat.

*The British and Australian equivalent to BBB chain is called short link proof coil. The system 4 chain equivalent is grade P which may or may not be heat treated. Check this before you buy any particular length of grade P chain.

32

Stern Anchor
Systems

San Diego has a place for every cruising sailor, from the opulent guest
docks at the San Diego Yacht Club to the free anchorages of Coronado.
That's probably why this 15-mile-long bay seems to be filled with voyagers bound to and from Mexico and the South Pacific. A casual glance
at their ground tackle shows that these people are prepared for both of
these cruising areas, areas which are famous for their lack of docks or
moorings, their preponderance of coral-studded roadsteads and deep
anchorages, areas that will challenge every sailor's anchoring skills and
gear to the maximum.

When *Taleisin*'s sea trials took us to San Diego, I went for a row in
the dinghy and became intrigued by the variety of solutions sailors had
used to solve stern anchor problems. I decided to photograph the stern
anchor systems of yachts that had apparently returned from "down
south" in the spring of 1984.

The stern anchor set-ups ranged from the one on the ULDB sloop
returning from the Manzanillo race, which carried the minimum ground
tackle allowed under the IOR rules, to the other extreme, a Cal 46 just
back from French Polynesia which had all chain, a large roller and
anchor windlass on both bow and stern. Somewhere in between these

two extremes lies a safe, practical convenient stern anchor system for any sailor who plans to anchor overnight on a regular basis.

The basic criteria for a stern anchor system is that it should have about 250 feet of nylon line which is easy to flake into your dinghy when it becomes necessary to row out a second anchor in a crowded harbor. You also need a lightweight anchor such as a Danforth, which is a good choice for your stern system as it has a high holding power-to-weight ratio, and usually stows easily in chocks or on a roller fairlead. The roller fairlead should be a direct line with a sheet winch to control and retrieve your stern hook, and the fairlead should be designed to eliminate chafe and be capable of taking strong sideloads. Finally, a stowage system for your stern anchor rode should allow the anchor to be shackled and wired, ready to run out the fairlead any time you need it.

Good seamanship is nine-tenths preparation and one-tenth application, and it's experienced sailors who learn that a stern anchor set-up is necessary for those times when you have to kedge off in an accidental grounding, or stop your yacht from swinging and fouling its bow rode on an underwater obstruction. This same system will allow you to anchor bow to the dock in small harbors like you'll find in Europe and the Mediterranean, so you keep your rudder and self-steering gear away from the potentially dangerous quay. A stern hook will hold your bow up comfortably to a swell in a rolly roadstead anchorage, and finally, a good stern fairlead will minimize chafe if you have to tow another vessel.

Figure 32.1 shows the minimum set up for local cruising. The anchor chain and line are probably stowed in the lazzaret under sails, fenders

FIGURE 32.1

FIGURE 32.2

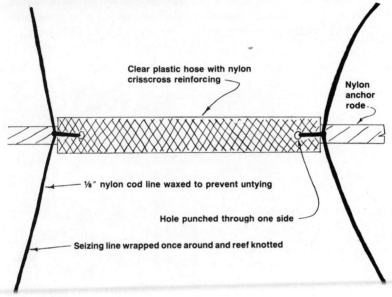

Clear plastic hose with nylon
crisscross reinforcing

Nylon
anchor
rode

⅛" nylon cod line waxed to prevent untying

Hole punched through one side

Seizing line wrapped once around and reef knotted

FIGURE 32.3

and mooring lines. This chock has sharp corners and would chafe the
anchor rode. I would radius the inside corners with a file until they
approximated the curve of your little finger. For nylon anchor rodes you
would still need chafing protection. I like an unsplit plastic hose with
nylon criss-cross reinforcing. This hose stays permanently on the anchor
rode and can be slid down to the chock and secured with waxed three-
strand nylon cod line (figure 32.2).

Figure 32.3. This closed chock is less convenient to use than the one
in photo 1. In order to get the rode through it, you have to feed the bitter
end through the chock or unshackle your anchor from its chain then

reconnect it. But on the other hand, the rode can't jump out of the chock in rough conditions.

Figure 32.4. This set-up is more convenient. The chain leads out of a ventilator, over the stern roller and the anchor is in chocks on the stern rail. If the eyesplice and thimble run through the vent without fouling, this should be quick to use. The rope and chain should be flaked down below decks in a figure eight to prevent fouling. The one flaw in this system is that the fairlead is bolted only to the ¾-inch thick taffrail.

Figure 32.5 shows the same roller with a spacer and bolts through the deck, a much stronger arrangement. This is a neatly flared roller set-up with no dangerous sharp corners. A line or sail gasket could be tied

FIGURE 32.4

FIGURE 32.5

FIGURE 32.6

through the open body of this roller set-up to encapsulate the rode in rough conditions.

Figure 32.6. The lips on this roller are not as high as those in photo 4. Any side load on the anchor line could cause the line to jump out of the roller.

Figure 32.7. This is the same stern roller set-up as seen in photo 6.

FIGURE 32.7

FIGURE 32.8

FIGURE 32.9

High cockpit coamings spoil a direct lead to either cleat or sheet winch.

Figure 32.8. This is a more modern set-up with efficient side rollers. I see two possible problems here. The anchor line could jump out and the vertical roller pins seem to be unsupported. A metal strap from bolt top to bolt top could solve these problems.

Figure 32.9. There is no metal side cheeks or retaining pin on this

FIGURE 32.10

FIGURE 32.11

FIGURE 32.12

deep-throated roller which is mounted on a stern platform. This is unsatisfactory except in the best of anchoring conditions. Furthermore, it seems as if the roller has jammed on its shaft and caused the chafe that is visible on the plastic roller. Note the temporary lashing holding the roller to the windvane support. This was obviously added to counteract side loads.

Figure 32.10. This bronze roller chock on a Cal 46 is super stout. Apparently the windlass is set up for both chain and rope on the gypsy.

Figure 32.11. The addition of two holes drilled into the vertical cheeks of this fairlead with a removable rode retaining bolt would make this system 100 percent. Many modern boats with cut-away underbodies, like this Cal 46, lie more comfortably anchored stern to the wind. That is why the stern anchor tackle is as husky as its bow tackle. A stern roller and gear two-third the size and strength of the bow gear should be adequate for vessels that lay-to happily by the bow.

Figure 32.12. The roller on this afterdeck is made useless by the fixed chock aft of it. If you removed the chock and positioned the roller over the rail, this set-up would work fine.

Figure 32.13 shows a good roller set-up, ready to go. Note the high retaining ears and retaining pin on the roller.

Figures 32.14 and 32.15 show two views of a full-on stern anchor system. The welded retaining loop over the roller is an inconvenience when you want to remove the anchor or rode.

Figure 32.16. Here's a unique solution on a double ender. The owner has used the hawsehole to support the U channel and roller.

Figure 32.17. This is a novel method for storing a stern anchor rode. The line should be covered as nylon deteriorates in the sun.

Figure 32.18. This portable anchor system on wheels lightened my morning row. Note the tripline/float and Irish pennant. The development of a portable stern fairlead or roller would make this system super convenient to use on a flushdecked yacht.

Figure 32.19. Lin suggested that I build *Taleisin*'s stern fairlead into the boomkin end. This roller is supported by the backstay and boomkin stays vertically. The boomkin itself takes the side loads.

Figure 32.20. The anchor pulls up easily but needs to be helped off the roller fitting when we let it go.

Figure 32.21. *Taleisin*'s unpatented yacht brake. The anchor line is figure eighted into the cockpit coaming box. Note that the line leads fair from winch to roller. The aft end of the coaming box has a notch so the line can be left connected and ready to use. The bitter end has a round turn and two half hitches around the bronze sheet winch supports inside the coaming. We normally don't shackle chain to our stern rode when we are using it as a kedge. It's easier and cleaner to handle that way. But when we are planning to leave the anchor down for more than one night

FIGURE 32.13

FIGURE 32.14

FIGURE 32.15

FIGURE 32.16

FIGURE 32.17

FIGURE 32.18

we shackle 30 feet of chain onto the anchor to reduce the chance of chafe.

Chafe was a factor we also considered when we decided on the material for our stern roller. Metal rollers fitted so they allow for at least ⅛-inch end play and ⅟₃₂-inch play on their shaft, are very reliable. But they tend to hammer the galvanizing off your chain as it clatters out. The edges of the metal roller also tend to chafe nylon lines. On *Taleisin* I am trying some loosely fitted delrin (nylon and teflon) rollers. Delrin tends to swell when it gets wet, so I have allowed for ⅛-inch end play and ⅟₁₆-inch slack on the roller pin. After three years of cruising, the roller seems fine.

Figure 32.22. Although this is a photo of a bow anchor set-up, it has an important story to tell since it shows what can happen if a rode jumps out of the fairlead. When this happens in storm conditions, it is very difficult to work the chain back into the fairlead without injuring your

FIGURE 32.19

FIGURE 32.20

hands. If it is a nylon stern anchor rode that jumps out of the fairlead, chafe is the main problem. The sharp corners of your toe rail hardware or stern pulpit can cause it to part in what seems like seconds.

Stern anchors have many uses but one potential danger. This danger was dramatized when 28 yachts were smashed through the surf at Cabo San Lucas, Baja California (December 1982). About half of the yachts we saw on that sandy beach had nylon lines wrapped around their propellors. A number of their skippers told us a similar story, "My bow

FIGURE 32.21

FIGURE 32.22

anchor started to drag so I started the engine to take the strain. Bang, the slackened stern line wrapped in the prop and stopped the motor dead. We didn't have a chance after that."

One way to remind yourself of this potential screw-up (pun intended) is to loop your excess nylon stern rode in a clove hitch around your gear shift lever. Then in the panic of dragging your anchor, you will be reminded to take in and hold some tension on your stern line, so the slack can't get into your propellor and make your engine useless.

33

Your Anchor Light —A Friendly Beacon for Other Sailors

We had been at sea for two and a half days when the light on Cape Lazzaro finally came clear. We'd ended up ten miles further out to sea than we'd needed to be because we'd kept steering offshore to counteract the current that usually swings in toward Baja California's curving, lagoon-edged shoreline. So it was after midnight when I woke Larry to say my bearings on the lighthouse plus the setting moon reflecting on the surf at the foot of the peninsula that protects Bahia Santa Maria, made me feel certain we could now reach in towards shelter. "With any luck we could be in by 0230 and sleep together tonight," I said as he dressed and checked the chart. Larry came on deck, confirmed my bearings and together we dropped the whisker pole, let the lapper across and began the reach into blessedly calmer water.

There is always a feeling, call it doubt, call it caution, when you sail behind a point of land at night and your only navigation beacon is blocked from view. For ten minutes we reached along with no lights to guide us, hearing the crash of surf to windward, discussing how we'd time our tacks across the four-mile-wide bay, then start sounding towards the calm anchorage we'd visited several times before. Then we saw one of the friendliest sights I know. First one, then another small white light seemed to leap into view until we could see five anchor lights marking our goal, five guiding lights that made the dark seem less menacing and a night together in the bunk much closer. Yet after we'd tacked towards those beacons, we had a bit of a start. As we prepared to drop sail and get our anchor over, a sweep with our high-powered flash light just caught the glimmer of another yacht only a hundred yards ahead. This boat had no anchor light, nothing to warn us of its existence. I was startled and a little put out. But as we settled back on our anchor, Larry reminded me that the lone, lightless boat could have run out of battery power or kerosene. "Besides, the other anchor lights helped us get in almost an hour ahead of your estimate."

As we continued cruising further south and west on *Taleisin,* boats at anchor with no lights became more the rule than the exception. So that by the time we sailed into Taihoe Bay on Nuku' Hiva in the Marquesas islands at midnight, we weren't surprised to find nine cruising boats from four different countries laying at anchor with no lights at all.

The international collision regulations (Col-Regs) state that any vessel between 7 and 50 meters in length must show an anchor light in the forward part of the ship at a height that will leave the light visible from all directions. The light must be visible for two miles in fine conditions. Vessels over fifty meters need a second anchor light near the stern. Boats under 7 meters, anchored outside normally navigable waters and outside narrow channels are exempt. The American inland water rules are only slightly different. Under these rules the anchor light can be anywhere on the vessel as long as it is visible all around. Inland rules also state the only time an anchor light is not necessary is when you are inside a specially designated anchorage. This is where we think some confusion comes in. To find out what constitutes a specially designated anchorage we had to search through the chart symbols section of Chapmans where we learned that it is only when you anchor or moor in an area enclosed by solid red lines on the chart and labeled, "Special anchorage" that you are exempt from showing a white light from sun down to sun rise. These "special" areas are usually found well inside busy harbors or near marinas. Rarely are the getaway coves we cruising sailors prefer marked as special anchorages. In foriegn countris we've rarely found exempt anchorages.

The two-mile visibility required by Col-Regs is easy to obtain. When translated to candle power, the figure used to measure the brightness of a white light, one candle power, the light cast by one wax candle with a normal wick, will show for one mile on a dark clear night. It takes 5½ candle power to show for the regulation two miles. A dioptic lense anchor light, a 5-watt bulb or a ½-inch wide kerosene burning wick will give you the required range.

Hanging your anchor light in the forward part of the ship as the international collision regulations suggest is important in crowded anchorages. Since the majority of vessels anchor by the bow, the position of anchor lights can help an incoming skipper gauge whether boats are

FIGURE 33.1   Setting the anchor light as we lie in Papeete harbor, waiting to be assigned a spot on the quay.

lying to the wind, to the tide, or between bow and stern anchors. It can also help him steer clear of your anchor rode as he maneuvers.

Although under the American inland water rules, an all-around masthead light would be acceptable as an anchor light, experience has taught us to agree with that dean of prudent voyagers, Eric Hiscock who writes in *Cruising Under Sail*, "At close quarters a masthead light often goes unnoticed or is misleading and I do not recommend it." On *Taleisin's* maiden ocean voyage we had to beat into Cat Harbor on Catalina Island at midnight on New Year's day with almost 45 knots of wind against us. There were over a hundred boats at anchor, all showing lights. But as we began maneuvering between them we found we almost missed seeing several of the larger dark-hulled boats whose masthead lights blended with the stars, 60 feet or more above us.

Another fallacy is that your cabin lights will show well enough so that an anchor light only becomes necessary when you go to bed. Unfortunately, cabin lights can rarely be seen except when a vessel is laying beam on to you. From forward, the incoming skipper sees no light, from aft he sees nothing unless the companionway on the anchored boat is open.

Although most sailors show anchor lights for the courtesy and convenience they offer other sailors, the legal reasons for showing a light may someday prove even more important. If someone showing legal running lights hits your vessel while it lies at anchor without a proper light, not only are they free of responsibility for any damage they cause, but you are totally responsible for any damage to their boat. Such a case occurred in Mexican waters in the early 1980s. An anchored American yacht was hit by a local fishing boat. The American complained to the local authorities and found not only was he at fault, but in turn the fishing boat owner had put a lien on the yacht for collision damages. Carried only a theoretical step further, your insurance company could use your lack of anchor light as reason to refuse your claims in a collision.

Not all authorities take a completely literal attitude towards the anchor light regulations, but even so, failure to show one could drastically shorten your cruise. A young sailor we first met in California told us this story when we met him a year later in Papeete. He had been anchored near a dozen other yachts (none of whom were showing anchor lights) in the main bay on Huahine in French Polynesia during mid-1984 when a local 240-foot freighter hit and dismasted him. He asked the shipping company to accept some responsibility for the replacement of his spar since he had no insurance to cover him. He was impressed with the French sense of justice when after nine months the courts suggested a settlement amounting to one-third of his costs. The courts reasoning seemed to have been that the ship's captain knew this was a popular anchorage and should have been using a search light to avoid possible collisions. But the sailors who didn't show a light was considered to be two-thirds responsible, and the two thirds of the cost he paid destroyed his cruising funds and sent him back to California a year sooner than he'd planned.

Although it is obvious here in French Polynesia that few port officials fine unlit boats, there are places where this is not the case. England, Spain and Portugal have regulations that incoming yachtsmen are supposed to read, which mention these fines.

But the threat of fines, the concern over legalities seems like less important reasons for showing an anchor light than the sheer convenience this small beacon offers. Soon after we arrived in the Marquesas we rowed ashore late in the afternoon to have dinner in Taihoe Bay's only restaurant. Halfway through dinner a wind packed, rain squall raked across the bay. Like all sailors, the concern of a dragging anchor is never far back in our minds. So as the squall cleared we tried to locate *Taleisin*, just to be sure. The golden glow of her kerosene light pin-pointed her, exactly where we'd left her, a quarter mile out from shore. We relaxed and enjoyed another cup of tea, another hour of pleasant companionship.

That same golden glow has served as a beacon when it is time to row home late at night. There were four couples on shore barbecuing fish we'd speared that day near Isla Partida in Baja California. We'd eaten our fill, the bonfire had died down and as we packed to row the half mile to our boats, all of us were shocked at how dark the starless night had become. Two of us had lit anchor lights. The other two couples followed us home then rowed in the direction they estimated was right to find two invisible boats we all knew were within 200 yards of us.

We found another use for our oil anchor light when we had to leave our previous cruising boat, *Seraffyn*, at various times to go on deliveries. As a form of preventative insurance, we'd hire a local watchman and set our own mooring. The watchman was paid to light the lamp each evening and put it out each morning. Every time we returned from one of these deliveries, people told us *Seraffyn* had never looked abandoned

FIGURE 33.2 Our perko brand anchor
light secured to the staysail stay.

because of that lamp. Other yachtsmen could also assure us our watchman had been doing his job because they saw the lamp burning. Potential thieves were possibly discouraged by the obvious light and caretaker.

An anchor light can help your neighbors, especially during a squall or rough weather. By taking bearings on your light they can see if they are dragging anchor, if they are swinging too close to you or maybe they can even warn you that your anchor is dragging before it is an embarrassment or worse. Your light could also help them leave if the weather deteriorated during the night. We were in this type of situation recently. We'd seen two boats come in and anchor to the east of us just before dark in the semicircular roadstead at Bahia San Gabriel. The owners didn't set anchor lights but this seemed of little importance at the time since approaching boats would see not only our light but those on *Gilpie* and *Wild Spirit,* two boats anchored slightly to the west of us. Six hours later we saw this situation in a totally different context. A line of thunder storms began marching across the mountains on the mainland, forty miles to the west of us. The low rumble of thunder and the humid air woke us, and although no wind was blowing through our anchorage, we reefed the mainsail, prepared the staysail and shortened up on our chain just in case one of those squalls turned San Gabriel into an unprotected lee shore. Then we sat down to wait and realized that in the dark, cloud-covered night, we couldn't locate those two boats that we knew were within 200 yards to the southeast of us. That meant if we did have to beat out in a heavy squall, we'd have to bear off on the port tack toward the boats with the anchor lights to guide us or risk a collision with the two unlit boats.

The choice of what type of lamp to use as an anchor light definitely depends on your cruising style and battery capacity. For the person who only needs an anchor light for a once a month overnight cruise, a masthead light or electric anchor lamp will probably suffice. But for longer term cruising, these lamps use too much battery power and few voyagers are willing to run their engines each day in port or rig a wind generator just to power an anchor light. So most cruisers will have to resort to either a kerosene anchor light or a solar powered unit.

We used a kerosene anchor light for eleven years on *Seraffyn* and for the past year and a half on *Taleisin*. Since all of our lighting is kerosene powered, we have a gravity feed tank for filling the lamp so we don't have to chase after a funnel and oil can. We use a Perko brand, small-sized anchor lamp to which we have added an internal chimney. Without this chimney the lamp will go out in winds above force six; with it,

FIGURE 33.3 The anchor light opened up to show the internal lens we added. To make this addition, we took the chimney holding fringe from a Perko Junior cabin lamp and attached it to the anchor lamp burner. Then we used standard cabin lamp chimneys.

we watched the lamp glow through force ten gusting eleven. Several European anchor lamps come complete with these internal chimneys. Since a half-inch-high flame on a half-inch-wide wick provides all the light you need to be seen for the regulation distance, we've found the two-thirds-cup capacity oil font gives up to 28 hours of continuous burning or two plus nights a fill. That's over a month of anchor light burning for a gallon of kerosene. We use a short lanyard to secure the lamp about seven feet up our staysail stay with a rolling hitch. That gets it above both the furled mainsail and the tropical sun cover to give all around visibility.

Some more electrically clever cruising sailors are using unipack solar-powered lights just like those on many of the channel buoys we saw in Mexico. A small solar panel is connected directly to a lamp and really sophisticated electrical whizzes add a light sensing devise to automatically turn the lamp on at sunset, off at sunrise.

FIGURE 33.4 For daytime use in crowded or commercial harbors, we have an inflatable black ball to hang from the forestay. This serves as an indicator that the boat is not underway. It provides the same legal protection that the anchor lamp does at night. (See *Chapmans Seamanship*, page 65.)

Although the cold facts of arranging for and using an anchor light may sound a bit boring or even annoying, in reality, we've found this ritual seems to add a special aura to the end of each voyage, the end of each day. The anchor is set and holding, the sails furled and running lights shut down. Then Larry lights and hangs the lamp that seems to announce all's well and we sit down to a cocktail and toast the beginning of another secure, peaceful night together.

Appendix

We finished writing *The Self-Sufficient Sailor* in late 1981. During the five years since then, we've noted a few changes we'd have liked to make, a few bits of information we've wished we could add to update the book and keep it more current. Unfortunately, our publisher has reminded us, it is very costly to re-edit an existing book. "Furthermore," he said, "people who already have that book won't know there are updates." So we have decided to put these revisions at the back of this book in the hope that they will reach most of the people who might benefit from them.

CHAPTER ONE
HITCHHIKING ACROSS OCEANS

Crew positions seem to be even more readily available now than when we first wrote this chapter. On page 19 we list where to look for berths and when. We'd like to add some other ports where you might have a good chance to find crewing positions. They include San Diego and other Southern California ports in September and October for boats headed toward Mexico, February for boats headed to the South Pacific.

La Paz, Baja California from January to March for boats heading towards the South Pacific. New Zealand, March or April, boats headed toward all areas of the South Pacific and Australia. Miami, New York, South Coast of England, September or October for boats heading to the Caribbean. Honolulu, August, boats are delivered back to the U.S. mainland.

Charter companies in remote areas like Raiatea, French Polynesia and Tonga often asked us if we knew of good crew or cooks we could recommend. They offer only $40 to $50 a day plus room and board, but you can gain invaluable experience working with these charter boats and you would be right on the route of many cruising boats, so could probably pick up a good berth for further voyaging.

CHAPTER 13

OAR POWER

Page 105. Sculling a dinghy, so you can move easily between moored boats or through tight marinas is essentially the same as sculling your bigger yacht, but far easier. Because the top of your dinghy transom is closer to the water, you can use a short oar. We have sewn a protective leather band ten inches long on one of our 7 foot 6 inch dinghy oars, half way between the rowlock shoulder and the oar blade to protect the oar shaft from the wear of sculling. Our dinghy transom has a notch cut in it, about ¾ of an inch wider than the oar shaft and as deep. The dip serves not only as a sculling lock but as a fairlead for setting out ground tackle. Since we use captive oar locks, we just let the lock dangle against the oar blade when we scull the dinghy. We find we do not need the hold down lanyard for dinghy sculling since there is far less pressure exerted on the oar.

An afterword on this chapter is that for *Taleisin* at 29 feet 9 inches length on deck and a cruising displacement of 17,900 pounds, our 15-foot 9-inch oar works well. Lin can propell us at approximately 1½ knots in calm conditions.

CHAPTER 14
ELECTRICITY—THERE ARE OTHER WAYS

Page 118. One good source of information on hydraulic starters is the American Bosch Company, Springfield, Mass. 01107 U.S.A. Ask for information on their Hydrotor Fluid Power cranking systems.

CHAPTER 17
TOOLS AND SPARES FOR OFFSHORE VOYAGERS

Page 142. The telephone number for Mr. Z's Rigging Vises is (818) 340-4001.

Page 144. If we were working in countries with 220/240-volt electrical power, using 220/240-volt tools, we would also carry a throw-out switch transformer to protect outselves while working near the water. These transformers, which shut the electricity off immediately if there is an overload or grounding cost about $50 U.S. for sizes sufficient to handle drills and sanders. They are about the size of a twenty-five-pound package of sugar and probably could have saved the lives of the two sailors we describe in the caption on page 143.

CHAPTER 19
THE SELF-SUFFICIENT SAILOR'S EMERGENCY ABANDON SHIP KIT

In addition to the items listed we now carry two solar blankets plus aspirins in our emergency kit. The solar blankets are not only for protection from cold and heat, but can serve as water catchments and reflectors to flash signals toward any ships passing during daylight hours. The aspirins can effectively alleviate the discomfort of sunburn.

We have also (as explained earlier in this new book) switched to a more reliable solar distillation unit. We now carry energy bars, instead of canned meats.

Two other additions to our kit include an Add-A-Buoy which is a buoyancy chamber that straps around the outside of our hard dinghy as described in the chapter on dinghies, plus an Australian-made EPIRB with replaceable ten year, shelf-life lithium batteries. There are several reasons we decided to carry this emergency radio beacon. After investigating the vastly improved rescue systems covering the Epirb broadcast frequency now, compared to 1965–1979 when we voyaged on *Seraffyn*, we began to feel there would be a chance that someone with assistance capabilities might be listening. There are still large areas of the southern hemisphere and Indian Ocean where your EPIRB would not be effective. This is because these areas do not have regularly scheduled commercial airline flights, nor do the present communications satellites cover them with EPIRB frequency pick-ups. The modern EPIRB units are far more compact, more water resistant and affordable now. (The one we bought in 1984 cost only $119 compared to $389 we would have had to pay in 1975, and that is actual dollars, not including the effects of inflation.) Furthermore, we can carry a set of replacement batteries for this unit which means we could broadcast our emergency signal for up to 14 days if necessary. Are we more likely to call for help instead of trying to save our ship because we have the EPIRB? With our skepticism we'd probably figure the radio wasn't working when we needed it. But, we can't really answer that question without a trial we hope never comes. We do know it makes relatives and friends happier so it is worth the cost and space. But we strongly feel the EPIRB is an addition to, not a substitute for, a well thought out emergency kit and careful preparations before you sail, plus vigilance when you are underway.

We made one final change in the emergency kit we carry on *Taleisin*. When I (Lin) tried to lift *Seraffyn*'s kit I often worried about its weight, especially when I thought of handling it on a rolling deck in an emergency situation. *Taleisin*'s kit weighed 14 pounds more. So we divided them into two kits, one in a red, water resistant pack, the other in a blue one. In the red pack we put items we'd need to survive for one to three days if we had to abandon ship in coastal areas. This includes the EPIRB, solar blankets, signal equipment and Add-A-Buoy. The red bag is kept easily available just inside the lazzarette hatch even when we are only gunkholing or doing local races. The second bag has longer term offshore survival gear like the solar stills and food supplies. Both bags are light and easy to handle and as soon as we head offshore on a passage, both bags are stored inside the dinghy ready to go overboard with it if we should have to abandon ship.

CHAPTER 22
OIL LAMPS AT SEA

The caption under the drawing on page 189 was inadvertently omitted by the editors. It should have read, "The drawing on the left shows a Perko type cabin lamp with its wick turned up for trimming. This wick is properly trimmed to alleviate smoking and give the best possible light. The drawing on the right shows our Perko type running light fount, modified to have an internal chimney which cuts out excessive drafts. As you can see, the lamp fringe is the same as for the cabin lamp. I bought spare cabin burners, sawed the fringe off and soldered them to the wider wicked navigation lamp burners.

CHAPTER 24
PLUMBING IDEAS

Page 204. The sit down, tub type shower described here has worked wonderfully on *Taleisin.* Ours is under the companionway where an engine might be on other boats. The pump up sprayer (a plastic three gallon insecticide sprayer with a demand type shower head in place of the spray head) is right next to the tub, concealed in a locker. During two and a half years of voyaging on *Taleisin,* we haven't felt like looking for showers on shore once. It has always been easier to shower on board.

CHAPTER 29
SOME SIMPLE MAINTENANCE TIPS

Page 240—This photo shows our updated varnish and paint touch-up kit. Since we have room in one of our cockpit lockers for this small, tupperware container, we keep the touchup jars plus a few pieces of 100 grit and 150 grit sandpaper and a small rag in the box. Then when one or the other of us has a few minutes to spare, we can look around for touchup spots and take care of them before they start to peel or the wood beneath turns gray.

CHAPTER 31
THE TRUTH ABOUT WINDVANES

Page 246. On *Taleisin* we put 23 percent of the trim tab area forward of the pintle centerline. This seems to work fine.

CHAPTER 35
WINTER PROJECTS FOR A COOL SUMMER

Page 266. Andy, an American sailmaker cruising on his large ketch *Jakaranda,* added a fine water collection system to our sun awning with only about two hours work. He sewed four fabric udders to the cover, three inches in from the edges at the middle of each section. We lash lengths of hose to each udder and lead them to various watertanks. During a 20-minute squall we have sometimes collected 60 or 70 gallons of water with his system. When we do not need to collect rain water, the udders can be rolled up and kept out of the way with tiny straps Andy has placed right next to the collection holes.

CHAPTER 37
CRUISING, GUNS, PIRATES, AND THIEVES.

Our views remain unchanged about carrying guns. The customs officials we have met here in the South Pacific say one of every five non-American yachtsmen may carry sporting weapons on board, while four out of every five American yachtsmen carry defensive weapons. One official told us, "If you want a really formidable close-range weapon, your flare pistol will legally serve the purpose, especially if it is one of the Italian made models that look just like defense weapons."

A defense and protection specialist with the Royal Canadian Mounted Police gave us another suggestion. "Keep a can of Mace (tear gas) near your bunk. Then if you hear a burglar inside your boat you can immobilize him without endangering yourself or possibly killing another human being. In a scuffle in close confines, like on a boat, you are just as likely to get hurt by your own gun as the thief is. Worse yet, you could accidentally kill some friend who is playing a practical joke if you have a gun. The mace would turn the joke without having permanent effects."

CHAPTER 38
SAILING THROUGH THE RED SEA

Page 287. No longer must you deny you have been to Israel in order to pass through the Suez canal. Furthermore, clearance procedures have been simplified for canal clearance. Port facilities have improved on the Mediterreanean side of the canal. The weather and navigation problems are still the same according to reports of friends we correspond with. The Brothers Light, an important beacon near the top end of the Red Sea, is frequently off since the United Nations no longer is fully responsible for its care. Political situations in the area are constantly changing with a revolution in Southern Yemen making Aden off limits and Djibouti okay this year. The Sudan is in the throes of a revolution but this is not affecting its ports according to 1985 reports. Once again, check for safe ports with sources near the Red Sea when you actually get ready to make the passage.

CHAPTER 39
BUSINESS AND THE LONG-TERM CRUISER

In 1986 telephone communications are still difficult in many parts of the world. Overseas calls can be difficult from the Tonga Islands except at the capital, Nuku'alofa. Communications between Western Samoa and the U.S. were of such poor quality, it was hard to understand parts of the conversation when I tried to call and wish my folks happy anniversary. We did find an international telephone calling card was far more helpful than we had expected. Although we did not have a telephone number in the United States as we cruised, the General Telephone company of California issued us the credit card once they checked our previous record with paying telephone bills while we built *Taleisin.* We found that card accepted for all calls we wished to make to the United States. The cost for calls billed through the card were half of what they would have been had we paid for them in French Polynesia. Furthermore, we could place the calls from any telephone and did not have to wait until we could find a telephone office open. This was especially helpful because of the time differences which meant most of our calls had to be made after working hours to reach family at home.

We had one unexpected surprise when our bank, a major U.S. one, refused to telex funds we had in a checking account in spite of my telephoning direct and also sending a telegram. They would only send funds once they had a written release with our signatures. So it still pays to plan your fund refueling stops well ahead. We did find an American Express card backed by a checking account back home let us buy up to $4,000 worth of traveler's checks at a time with only a 20-minute delay anywhere there was an American Express office. (With a gold card you can get up to $4,000 every 21 days, with a regular card only $2,000.) But to carry this card costs $65 a year which we decided was a bit high for the two times a year we might benefit from its use. We did find you can also get cash, up to the credit limit you hold with Visa or Mastercard in most countries at banks with International Banking Service departments. You will have to pay interest on these funds from the day you request them until you pay your bill. But if you send a check to your card company a week or ten days before you require the funds, there will be no interest charges, only a $2 transaction charge.

As for mail drops, we would warn against port captains offices if you can find any other address. Port captains will not forward mail. Anyone who wants can shuffle through your mail (and usually does). Worse yet, some well meaning cruising people pick up your mail intending to drop it off on your boat on the way home. If you are not there it may never get to you. Someone picked up our mail from the port captains office in La Paz, Mexico, and put it in the saddle bag of our bicycles which were locked near the dinghy launching area. They didn't know that we had loaned the bikes to a friend. The mail reached us two weeks later after we'd missed a date of some importance. That is why we've come to prefer using American Express Offices. They will accept your mail if you have an American Express Card or carry American Express Travelers' checks. For a $4.00 fee they will also forward it. If you do not carry a card, they will still hold and forward your mail, but there will be a charge of $4.00 for the service. To get American Express office addresses, ask for a brochure of their international offices.

For voyagers bound to the Northern Tongan islands of Vava'u, Robyn Coleman, Port of Refuge, Neiafu, Vava'u, Kingdom of Tonga, is a dependable address. Write Robyn a note saying when you plan to arrive and she'll set your mail aside for you. For New Zealand-bound voyagers we recommend writing a note to Margaret, the postmistress at Opua, Bay of Islands, stating your approximate arrival date. She will then hold mail for you and forward it within New Zealand.

Once again we have found having our mail forwarded in one package at one time works best. Our forwarder (my sister-in-law, Elaine) numbers our mail packs if there are more than one; one of three, two of three, three of three, so we know how many packages to look for. She wraps the contents in a plastic bag and puts four fiberglass reinforced strips of tape around the mailing envelope so that even the roughest handling will not let letters fall out of the damaged envelope.

Air mail packets throughout the South Pacific have reached us within 14 days. Surface packages take approximately ten weeks. The only exception to this rule was in American Samoa. Because of restricted flight space, we had a 21-day wait for an air mail package.

Index